15 SPORTS MYTHS
AND WHY THEY'RE WRONG

15 SPORTS MYTHS AND WHY THEY'RE WRONG

Rodney Fort and Jason Winfree

STANFORD ECONOMICS AND FINANCE

An Imprint of Stanford University Press

Stanford, California

Stanford University Press
Stanford, California

Library of Congress Cataloging-in-Publication Data

Fort, Rodney D., author.
   15 sports myths and why they're wrong / Rodney Fort and Jason Winfree.
      pages cm
   Includes bibliographical references and index.
   ISBN 978-0-8047-7436-9 (cloth : alk. paper)
   1. Sports—Economic aspects—United States. 2. Professional sports—Economic aspects—United States. 3. College sports—Economic aspects—United States. I. Winfree, Jason (Jason A.), author. II. Title. III. Title: Fifteen sports myths and why they're wrong.
GV716.F665 2013
338.47796—dc23

                                                            2013014691

Printed in the United States of America on acid-free, archival-quality paper

Typeset at Stanford University Press in Helvetica and 10.5/15 Minion

Special discounts for bulk quantities of titles in the Stanford Economics and Finance imprint are available to corporations, professional associations, and other organizations. For details and discount information, contact the special sales department of Stanford University Press. Tel: (650) 736-1782, Fax: (650) 736-1784

ACKNOWLEDGMENTS

We gratefully acknowledge the support of everybody who put up with us during the writing of this book. You know who you are, but we especially single out our wives, Leslie Fort and Nikki Winfree.

We always see further standing on the shoulders of giants. Fort especially thanks Roger Noll and James Quirk for their good-natured and tireless mentorship through the years.

The book is much better than it could ever have been, thanks to our reviewers, Raymond Sauer, John Siegfried, and Dennis Coates. They all kept us on both the economic straight and narrow and provided food for thought in honing our analysis.

Finally, although she shuns this recognition, our ideas would never have met the printed page without the cheerful and expert hand of our editor at Stanford University Press, Margo Beth Fleming. Thanks Margo, you're the tops.

Rodney Fort
Jason Winfree

CONTENTS

15 SPORTS MYTHS
AND WHY THEY'RE WRONG

INTRODUCTION

Let us begin with a confession: We are both sports fans and economists and, as a result, our worldview is curiously schizophrenic. Sports are an emotion-laden pastime by nature. Like all fans, we enjoy the old "thrill of victory and agony of defeat." We "root, root, root for the home team," hate the "damn Yankees," and "just wait until next year" with the best of them. But as economists, we put aside these emotions and assume that cool rationality rules the world. (Even as economists, we know that this is not entirely true. But, this lens has proven useful to in our professional lives.) Our eyes are open. We see that reason can get us only so far as we seek to understand how the sports industry works. As the old Sioux grandfather, played by Chief Dan George, in the movie *Little Big Man* said, "Well, sometimes the magic works. Sometimes it doesn't." But when it doesn't, the failure of rationality can still point us in the direction of better explanations.

We wrote this book because the economists in us began to see that many preconceived and deeply emotional notions in sports are simply not true. And upon further consideration, we began to see that these "misunderstandings" actually hinder the games we love. When we realized that these wives' tales were not only plain wrong but also a drag on sports fans, players, and the industry alike, we had to do something. Also of a sudden, we found ourselves in a new role—that of myth busters. Myth busters typically approach their targets by pointing out how a belief, previously held dear, is simply incorrect. However, in our opinion, this approach doesn't go far enough. We also try to explain how these beliefs exemplify some ideology (that college sports leach off of universities), or serve the interest of specific people and institutions (a team owner or franchise, for instance). Going to this next level leads to penetrating insights about a myth. And then, we can use economic analysis to examine the motives behind these ideals and institutions.

Since 2007 we've been paring down a list of the most egregious myths in sports—by our account—to present to you with a systematic examination of the worst offenders. As you join us on a tour of the juiciest misconceptions, you'll discover incorrect, but popular, beliefs and will come to see them for what they are: tall tales. But the buck doesn't stop there. This exercise begs for more, and our aim is not only to tell you who is served by each myth but also to provide an explanation of how that party is served by its perpetuation.

In *The Power of Myth*, Joseph Campbell emphasizes how myths invite us all to the table: they provide a common underpinning, a force that works to unleash the mystical part of ourselves. But modern folks tend to go overboard, forgetting that myths are also fabrications that belie the facts. And therein lies a real danger of relying on myths when they do us (or our beloved sports) harm. Bluntly, some people gain power over others by wielding mighty myths. The world is tough and unfair, yes. But we don't have to take all the licks.

We needn't accept college and professional sports myths as they are, time and again, foisted on sports fans and taxpayers. And we hope to show you a handful of instances in which you can plainly see that the emperor has no clothes. But first, a question worth asking is, What do these myths have in common? Sports myths substitute intuitive appeal for a rigorous and more informed explanation of the issue or process at hand. In the "hot" and intense context of the game, few stop long enough to cease watching the plays and apply this kind of thinking. But, of course, careful thought and the application of analytical techniques typically bust myths. Second, as we have suggested, sports myths can serve the interests of those perpetrating the myth at the expense of those who, once enlightened, would abandon the myth and all of its associated baggage. So every one of these myths has a champion—and that person, group, or goliath fans its fire for their benefits. It is not so easy to break free from these myths until we stop to consider them critically. Many, in fact, are passed down over generations. But it is our hope that the end is near for some sports myths, thanks to this book.

We see the collections of misconceptions that follow as breaking down in a few ways. In all but a few chapters of our book, (1) each myth and the source of its power are identified; (2) each myth is busted by applying the scrutiny of economic thinking; and (3) those whose self-interests are served by the myth are identified, indicating who gains by the power of these myths. In the rest of the chapters, where we think the power of the myth has yet to manifest itself, we present the myth and the misunderstanding behind it, clear it up with economics, and suggest why dispelling it is important. We chose the myths purposefully to satisfy these aims. We also believe that these are the most important myths and that more productive discourse about sport policy will be facilitated by their busting.

The first section of the book contains seven college sports myths. The primary beneficiaries of these myths are university administrators, including directors of intercollegiate athletic departments, and the denizens of the National Collegiate Athletic Association (NCAA). Most of the college myths gain their traction because nobody stops to look for just a minute at the relationship between university administrators and the directors of their intercollegiate athletic departments. Partly, this is because they are fans rather than analysts. Partly, this is because universities are quite different from other organizations; most are more used to thinking about sports based on profits, and that is not the goal of athletic departments. Indeed, one of the most often heard charges leveled against college sport is that it doesn't "show a profit," or that the vast majority of athletic departments operate "at a loss." This is simply wrong-headed from the outset, since college sports are *not* about profits. They *are* about the objectives of those in charge of universities—namely, top-level administrators like the board of regents and the university president. Starting from that perspective is at least grounded in the truth of the matter and, we think, the reader will see just how powerful the truth can be.

In the second section of the book, we cover eight professional sports myths. The primary beneficiaries of these are reporters, franchise owners, and, ultimately (though a bit indirectly), players. Exposing the myths also exposes the self-interested justifications that actually explain their perpetration. Similarly to the college case, many of these myths prevail because the objectives of owners or league may not be fully understood. In the pro case, we see that all roads lead back to profits, the profit motive, and really basic economic principles for our observations. In addition, most fans and observers don't have the time or incentive to analyze the data to see what actually does lead to higher profits.

There are plenty of other myths out there, but our fifteen have staying power and pose a real threat if they are not dispelled. These are not the myths du jour, this season's news, but rather misconceptions that haunt the world of sports year in and year out—and that are presented as such. If you read the myths that follow from front to back, you are sure to notice some themes that repeat. We don't mean to nag, but we do want you to see the patterns in these classic pitfalls. Those perennial thorns hold power, and we'd be remiss if we didn't underscore them for you. Alternatively, we invite you to read these myths one by one. They are presented in a straightforward and serialized fashion—knowing that you might pick up and put down this book during March Madness, spring training, football season, the World Series, and the bowl games—hoping to spread the word about the misconceptions that we share with fellow fans.

As Mark Twain said, "It ain't what you don't know that gets you into trouble. It's what you know for sure that just ain't so." As fans, economists, and myth busters, we want the truth. We think you deserve it. And we hope that you find our approach to seeking it as insightful and valuable as we have.

COLLEGE MYTHS

1 REVENUE SPORTS PAY FOR NONREVENUE SPORTS

INTRODUCTION

It is an old adage that without the top men's revenue programs—football and basketball—there would be no athletic department. The idea is that the athletic director (AD) spends any excess of revenues over costs in these sports on all of the other programs. Ipso facto, as football and men's basketball revenue goes, so goes the economic fate of the athletic department. In some cases, the courts have determined that the original implementation of Title IX (enacted in 1972) acted to exclude football from the equation on just these grounds (e.g., *Blair v. Washington State University*, Washington State Supreme Court, 1987). Indeed, as far back as 1974, Texas senator John Tower proposed an amendment that would exempt "revenue generating" sports from Title IX; nobody was fooled that "revenue generating" meant anything besides football and men's basketball. In 1995 the College Football Association (the major conferences minus the Big Ten and Pac 10) argued for the exclusion of football from Title IX in part because it funded other sports. The myth is being used at this writing to bolster the argument against the death penalty for Penn State football—it funds all of the other sports (Scranton Times-Tribune.com, 2012).

In this chapter we first document the number of athletic departments in which revenues from football and men's basketball exceed the costs of running just those two sports. Then, for those departments for which the rest of the sports have operating deficits (indeed, many do not!), we show the number of athletic departments that can cover that deficit with their football and men's basketball operating surplus. Finally, we examine the extent to which any surpluses also cover the remaining costs of running the athletic department.

We need to be clear immediately on an important element in our calculations. The data available on college sports revenues and expenses (we cover the source in detail in a subsequent section) are not submitted according to any rigorously monitored accounting protocols. This does not mean that the data in any way misrepresent revenues and expenses, but they do pose interpretative problems. One of the issues is that the revenue reports are divided into two categories. "Generated" revenues can be attributed to the usual sources—attendance and attendance related revenue for each of the sports, TV contracts by sport, and contributions that are earmarked by sport. "Nonallocated" revenues are not tied directly to any particular sport—direct institutional support, student fees, and general giving. The problem clearly is that some ADs take a portion of nonallocated revenues and allocate them in the data reports while others do not.

And therein lies the interpretative problem. Suppose those ADs that allocated some of their nonallocated revenues to football and men's basketball in their reports had *not* done so. Then we would identify fewer programs in our first step that would have any surplus from these two sports to cover the rest of the sports, let alone any of the other athletic department spending. We take some comfort in our results, since this means that we are overstating the ability of football and men's basketball to provide spillover value to the rest of the department. At the same time, however, we wish there were a consistent accounting protocol, consistently audited, that did not have this problem in the first place.

Here is what is true in the most recent data available (2010–11). About 85 percent of Football Bowl Subdivision (FBS, previously I-A) athletic departments were able to cover any excess of spending over revenue in the rest of men's sports and women's sports with football and men's basketball net operating revenues. The result drops precipitately to about 34 percent for the Football Championship Subdivision (FCS, previously I-AA). Since the myth is that they *all do so*, myth dispelled. But stopping here lets the myth off the hook too easily because these results are about only *allocated* revenue and cost by sport. There are other expenses that are not allocated to any one sport, including salaries, recruiting, event management, and annual facilities costs. All are required to make play happen at its current level for any program. Adding these in, the myth is busted squarely and truly. Only 6 of 118 reporting FBS programs earned enough from football and men's basketball to cover their entire athletic department budget. In order of smallest to largest surplus, they are Syracuse, Michigan State, Notre Dame, Alabama, Penn State, and Georgia. Only one FCS program out of 124 reporting earned this same bragging right—Southern University and A&M. The fact that all reporting FBS and FCS departments at least break even means that they must rely on revenues that are not allocated by sport in order to do so. (And remember that this lack of ability for football and men's basketball to cover other sports and athletic department spending is actually overstated as a result of the data reporting issue noted above.)

So, by and large, the observed facts reveal that revenue sports nearly never cover the costs of making the rest of the sports happen. This myth feeds on the intuition of the misinformed. It is quite easy to believe that football and basketball generate giant revenues and that other sports do not. Thus, if there are to be these "other" sports, the money must come from somewhere. Where else than from football and basketball? And it is especially mythical if the idea is extended to an all-encompassing policy such as Title IX.

We feel almost sheepish busting this particular myth, but we feel compelled for two reasons. First, even though others have pointed the way, they have been nearly completely ignored. Second, nobody (including the earlier pathfinders on the subject) puts substance behind the myth busting by asking a simple question. Why in the wide world of sports would anyone ever expect it to be true in the first place? The breadth and scope of the elements of the athletic department are chosen much like the individual elements of a firm's product line. Successful products are never expected to cover unsuccessful ones; the idea is that all products are expected to be successful. And so it is with sports offerings in athletic departments, but the yardstick is not net revenue. What is missed in the confusion of this myth is that different sports have different purposes for university administrators. Some men's and women's sports will generate operating revenues greater than expenses (just as the medical school might). Some will not (the majority of departments on campus, we dare say), but these sports serve other purposes than generating positive net operating revenues. Some generate other types of values for university administrators—most notably, Title IX compliance for some women's sports. We will get into more detail on the relationship between university administrators and their athletic departments in subsequent chapters. Here, it is sufficient to bring the evidence together and demonstrate the power of just a little data when it comes to busting myths.

This myth is destructive in a number of ways. First, it grants football especially, and men's basketball secondarily, special status that they deserve at literally a handful of the very top programs in the FBS, and at only one program in the FCS. Feeding on the uninformed (and misinformed by those foisting the myth), the myth deflects proper attention to be paid to all aspects of the athletic department when it comes to the implementation of public policy. Surely Title IX or the impacts of the National Collegiate Athletic Association (NCAA) death penalty, generally, cannot be judged by the size of football revenues at a school like Penn State, when nearly no other programs in all of big-time college sports look like that. Second, it confuses people interested in discovering just where it is that university support actually gets spent. Under the myth, it doesn't go to men's major revenue sports because they are generating a positive spillover to the rest of the department. Truth be known, in nearly all FCS and in a large number of FBS departments, university support also goes to football and men's basketball. If policy is to be effectively implemented, and if proper accounting of spending in the athletic department is to occur, this myth must be discarded.

This myth begins to show the pervasive way that the operation of athletic departments is done with purpose—namely, the purpose of university administrators and athletic directors. This type of myth distracts the scrutiny of critics from full attention to the actual allocation of revenue sources. Since athletic directors thrive with full control of that spending, this distraction is clearly in their interest.

A QUICK LITERATURE REVIEW

As we have said, we feel almost sheepish writing this chapter, since others have made the same point. However, by drawing all of the past works together and augmenting with our own, perhaps we will cause the myth to wither under unified scrutiny. The earliest "general consumption" notice we found came from the Women's Sport Foundation's executive director, Donna Lopiano, in a 2002 "Q&A" (Women's Sports Foundation, 2002). Under item 10, Does Title IX Enforcement Hurt Football Programs?, we find the following:

> Among NCAA football programs in all competitive divisions, 81% spend more than they bring in and contribute nothing to other sport budgets. Even among Division I-A football programs, more than a third are running deficits in excess of $1 million per year.

We do not buy the "deficits" characterization, addressed explicitly in Chapter 3, but the point is clear—leftover revenue from football and men's basketball is the exception rather than the rule.

Turning to academic treatments, University of Notre Dame business professor Richard Sheehan (2000) found that a $1 "profit" increase raises spending in other men's sports by $0.10 and in women's sports by $0.20. At Penn State, with net revenues of $15.5 million, that's $3 million for women's sports. At Tulane, losing $3.3 million, that's a decrease in women's spending of $600,000.

While their aim was to study college football and Title IX, Temple University economists Michael Leeds, Yelena Suris, and Jennifer Durkin (2004) found out along the way that only a few of the most profitable football programs provide any actual subsidy at all to women's sports. Almost all other athletic departments, including some with highly profitable football programs, actually drain money from women's sports. They conclude the following:

> Schools with unprofitable football programs have no surplus to provide and reduce the funds available for women's sports. A profitable football program, however, is no guarantee that women's sports will receive ade-

quate funding. Only a few of the most profitable football programs provide a positive net subsidy to women's athletics. Almost all other schools, some of them with highly profitable football programs, actually drain funding from women's athletic programs. Indeed, some of the nation's most prestigious and successful football programs have the most harmful impact drain on women's athletics.

POUNDING THE (LAST?) NAILS IN THE COFFIN

While examples can't prove anything, if they are chosen carefully they can be enlightening. A quotation from the Book of John is well known: "Then you will know the truth, and the truth will set you free." From the secular standpoint, it helps to know where the truth comes from—data sources matter, since they are important for knowing data limitations. For college sports revenues and expenses, there is only one original source. Member institutions respond to an NCAA survey of revenues and expenses. While some surveys were collected prior, the data have been collected under the requirements of the Equity in Athletics Disclosure Act (1996, henceforth EADA) pretty much on an annual basis. In turn, the data are publicly available in four versions.

The NCAA produces and freely distributes its own revenues and expenses report from this survey, most recently from Transylvania State University accounting professor Daniel Fulks (2011). While useful, the NCAA reports provide data at a very aggregate level (representative programs such as the median and largest). Another less condensed (but condensed nonetheless) version of the same survey results goes to the U.S. Department of Education, Office of Post-Secondary Education (OPE) as one of the assessments for Title IX compliance. The OPE data, available freely at their webpage (Office of Post-Secondary Education, 2012), are available by athletic department, for all sports offered, by men's and women's sports, and also at the aggregate individual program level.

The two other versions of the NCAA survey were obtained under the Freedom of Information Act (FOIA) and compiled at two news sources. The IndyStar.com (2012) version contains *all of the data* that went through the NCAA but only for the 2004–05 school year. This is by far the most detailed report, including all of the important elements of revenues and expenses for football, men's basketball, women's basketball, "other" sports, and a non–program specific category for all reporting individual athletic departments. The USAToday.com (2012) version covers a longer period, the 2005–06 through 2010–11 school years, but only for individual *program totals* without any breakout by sport. Both of these versions are valuable despite their limitations, because (1) the reporters went to great lengths through FOIA to make any data of this detail available, and (2) they offer insights that neither the NCAA reports nor the data available at OPE can provide.

To begin our examples, we chose the two major universities in the state of Washington, where we both grew up and spent part of our academic careers. For the purpose of untangling revenue and expense data by sport, and by men's and women's spending, for the most recent period possible (2010–11 school year), only the OPE version will do (we did verify some of our calculations with the USAToday.com version). At Washington State University, the smaller program in the eastern part of the state, athletic department spending totaled $40.6 million. Football operating revenue exceeded operating costs by $3.5 million, and the figure was $1.3 million for men's basketball. Operating costs exceeded operating revenue by $1.8 million on all other men's sports. The WSU athletic department spent $4.0 million more on women's sports in total than those sports were able to generate in operating revenue. Thus the top earning men's sports, football and basketball, fell short of covering the net operating losses on the rest of the men's sports and the women's sports by about $1 million. While this result clearly violates the myth, the final assessment cannot stop here. No sports would occur on just the spending on operations. What of the rest of the spending in the WSU athletic department required to make sports happen?

In addition to sports *operations*, another $16.8 million, or 41.1 percent of the $40.6 million budget, was spent on the rest of the athletic department (salaries, recruiting, event management, and facilities). When we add this "other spending" to the picture, and surely we must, since the athletic department cannot function without it, football and men's basketball at WSU fall even further behind in terms of funding all of the "other programs"! The amount to be covered is the $1 million net shortfall in sports operations *plus* the $16.8 million spent on the rest of the department, or $17.8 million. So, while football and men's basketball helped defray part of the cost of sports *operations*, they did not cover all of it and they surely, then, could not cover any of the rest of athletic department expenses. For the year, the WSU AD reported to the NCAA (subsequently, to OPE) that the Cougars broke even with other revenues that were not allocated by sport. The IndyStar.com version for 2010–11 shows that the rest of the revenue needed to cover all spending came from student fees, institutional support, and contributions.

Things were quite different for the Cougars' hated rival to the west, the University of Washington. Similar calculations for the bigger-budget University of Washington ($67.9 million) for the same budget year, 2010–11, show that football generated $18.1 million in excess of its operating costs and basketball $4.8 million over its costs. The other men's sports spent $4.5 million more than they brought in, and women's sports spent $6.8 million more than they brought in. So, unlike the case at Washington State, the $22.9 operating surplus from football and men's basketball easily covered operating losses for the rest of Husky men's sports and women's sports. Indeed, another $11.5 million remained to go toward all of the remaining "other spending" at UW.

Interestingly, the story is the same for both the Cougars and the Huskies on this other spending. With total department spending at $67.9 million, other spending in the UW athletic department was $23.0 million. So the UW football and men's basketball programs covered half of this other spending, with another $11.5 million to be covered from other sources such as direct university support, contributions, or any past generated reserves (the IndyStar.com data show that no student fees went toward Husky athletics in 2010–11). Unlike the Cougars, which reported just breaking even, the Huskies generated $70.2 million in total department revenues for a department surplus of $2.3 million.

Now, of course, one example doesn't make a case (and indeed WSU men's revenue sports have occasionally more than covered sports operations but never covered the other costs of sports). However, the Cougar/Husky comparison actually sets the stage for the most general type of outcome (the

Cougars) and the exception that proves that rule (the Huskies). Bringing in the rest of the data makes the compelling case, both for the FBS over time and for a cross-section of all of the FBS programs for the 2010–11 season.

On the former, according to the NCAA's own revenues and expenses reports, the same story has typically been true (at the average of reported revenues and expenses) across the FBS. The average net operating revenue for men's sports did not cover the women's sports deficit at all but for a few departments. So those making the argument that encroachment on football might actually kill the golden goose simply have not done their homework. By and large at the top of the college sports ladder, there is no golden goose in the first place, since football and men's basketball typically do not cover spending in excess of revenues for the rest of men's sports and women's sports.

For the cross-section examination, returning to the OPE version of the data for 2010–11 should startle anybody that might believe in the "revenue sports pay for nonrevenue sports" myth. Some 118 of the FBS athletic departments were reported on. Interestingly, and quite counter even to the essence of the myth, *46 FBS programs do not even need any cross-subsidy from football and men's basketball!* The rest of men's sports added to women's sports show operating revenues in excess of operating costs. The net positive here is over $1 million at three programs—East Carolina ($3.5 million), Florida Atlantic ($2.6 million), and Tulane ($1.4 million). For these FBS programs, the myth is simply a moot point. Moving on, five more programs defy the myth because their combination of football and men's basketball do not generate any excess of operating revenues over costs (Tulane also suffers this result, but they are already out of consideration because they didn't need a cross-subsidy in the first place). The five are Wake Forest, Connecticut, Kansas, Hawaii, and Northern Illinois.

That leaves 67 of 118 reporting programs, or just over half (56.8 percent) in which there is even a chance to support the myth, and that support dwindles to nearly nothing as follows. Whittled down to just those programs that actually do generate an operating surplus from football and men's basketball combined, and just those programs where the rest of men's sports and women's sports run an operating deficit, only 54 programs cover the deficit

TABLE 1.1. *FBS Sports Operating Surpluses and Deficits, 2004–05 and 2010–11*

School	2004–05	School	2010–11
	Top 10 (Surplus)		
Texas	$38,229,408	Texas	$64,154,694
Georgia	$26,376,802	Penn State	$44,014,352
Michigan	$25,001,741	Georgia	$41,166,104
LSU	$23,217,828	Alabama	$36,997,859
Alabama	$19,539,829	LSU	$36,045,694
Texas A&M	$17,208,452	Tennessee	$31,003,408
Ohio State	$16,337,934	Michigan	$28,467,300
Florida	$15,588,826	Florida	$26,960,802
North Carolina	$14,249,313	Arkansas	$25,422,535
Arizona	$13,358,792	Nebraska	$22,353,923
	Bottom 10 (Deficit)		
Florida Atlantic	−$7,820,788	California	−$3,616,057
Buffalo	−$8,035,519	Central Florida	−$4,162,678
Ball State	−$8,165,733	USC	−$6,190,173
Central Florida	−$8,307,228	Oregon	−$6,342,021
San Jose State	−$8,506,686	Hawaii	−$7,331,488
Kent State	−$8,830,290	Northern Illinois	−$8,270,048
Virginia	−$9,486,071	Wake Forest	−$11,731,870
Houston	−$9,833,371	Connecticut	−$13,355,492
UCLA	−$9,861,769	Kansas	−$15,227,776
Georgia Tech	−$10,049,810	Virginia	−$16,842,027

Source: Calculated from IndyStar.com (2012) and Office of Post-Secondary Education (2012).

on the rest of men's sports and women's sports (the top and bottom 10 are in Table 1.1). But as with the Cougar/Husky comparison, to stop here lets the myth off too easily—all of the other spending by the athletic department is required to make sports happen. Two more programs fall off here, since they covered the deficit in the rest of men's sports and women's sports exactly with nothing left over for other costs (Florida International and Arizona State). And the coup de grace for the myth: of the 52 remaining programs, 6 generate enough from football and men's basketball to cover the deficit from the rest of men's sports and women's sports *and* the other costs of their athletic department. They are Georgia (by $7.6 million), Penn State (by $7.5 million), Alabama (by $2.7 million), Notre Dame (by $2.2 million), Michigan State (by $1.2 million), and Syracuse (by $47,397).

It should come as no surprise that the so-called automatic qualifier (AQ) conferences—the ACC, Big 12, Big East, Big Ten, Pac-12, and SEC, with their guaranteed access to the Bowl Championship Series (BCS) bowl system until its upcoming replacement by a playoff system in 2014—dominate the list. Of the 52 programs that at least contribute something to all of the other costs in their athletic departments, 44 are in AQ conferences and 8 are not. It is also the case that we have to go quite far down the list even to find the first school outside the AQ conferences—namely, UNLV (in the MWC with a surplus of about $5.1 million, ranked 31st).

If we impart just a little foresight to the ADs at FBS programs, we can think about the relationships between positive net revenues in football and men's basketball combined, and the size of net deficits that are run up in the rest of the men's sports and women's sports. The correlation between the two for those departments where the former covers the latter is about −0.73. The correlation drops to −0.56 for the other 14 programs where a cross-subsidy was needed and there was a net operating surplus from football and men's basketball but nothing left to send on to the other costs of the athletic department. So across the FBS, as the surplus from the major men's revenue sports rises, the surplus in the rest of the sports gets smaller (gets more negative in the case where it *is* negative); ADs appear to count on the former to cover the latter, and especially where there is any net to send on to the other costs of the athletic department.

Now, don't cry for the rest, since not a single FBS program reported losing money in total for the year 2010–11. So all were able to generate so-called nonallocated revenues from a variety of sources to cover the rest of their spending. But the important take-away cannot be ignored: that FBS revenue sports pay for nonrevenue sports is as mythical as the unicorn. In the first place, about half even need such a cross-subsidy. Further, only 5.1 percent generated enough net positive operating revenue to cover all of the rest of the sports and the other spending by their athletic department.

At the 124 reporting FCS programs, things are much, much worse for the myth. First, by our calculations, 95 programs needed no cross-subsidy in the first place; fully 76.6 percent of programs either covered the operating costs of the rest of men's and women's sports or ran a surplus. Some 14 more failed to run any operating surplus on football and men's basketball

TABLE 1.2. *FCS Sports Operating Surpluses and Deficits, 2004–05 and 2010–11*

School	2004–05	School	2010–11
	Top 10 (Surplus)		
Montana	$1,259,016	Southern U.	$2,714,406
Maine	$531,757	Dayton	$2,617,025
Eastern Kentucky	$489,670	Penn	$1,713,527
SUNY-Binghamton	$326,429	Villanova	$1,672,370
The Citadel	$323,132	North Dakota	$1,529,005
Norfolk State	$272,291	Norfolk State	$1,475,916
N. Carolina-Greensboro	$238,053	E. Washington	$1,209,978
Cleveland State	$212,293	Georgia State	$1,206,739
Jacksonville State	$55,701	Richmond	$1,194,788
Wisconsin-Milwaukee	$18,453	Morgan State	$1,043,361
	Bottom 10 (Deficit)		
Virginia Commonwealth	−$4,837,891	Montana	−$831,017
Texas St.-San Marcos	−$5,066,051	Maine	−$996,962
Charleston	−$5,092,710	N. Colorado	−$1,277,810
Towson State	−$5,211,766	Eastern Illinois	−$1,458,824
Albany	−$5,433,305	Idaho State	−$2,219,628
Cal. St.-Northridge	−$5,474,297	Northern Iowa	−$2,311,082
Sacramento State	−$5,582,203	Wm. & Mary	−$6,727,317
California Poly	−$5,764,781	Stony Brook	−$7,367,563
Massachusetts	−$11,186,236	Towson	−$9,402,604

Source: Calculated from IndyStar.com (2012) and Office of Post-Secondary Education (2012).

and also cannot support the myth. That leaves 15 programs, or just 12.1 percent of FCS programs, even capable of lending any support to the myth (again, we report the top and bottom ten on this dimension in Table 1.2). Three schools did not cover their deficit on the rest of men's sports and women's sports (Yale, South Dakota, and Montana), and 1 more covered it exactly (Tennessee State). So that left 11 programs that covered the rest of men's sports and women's sports and had the potential to cover any of the rest of the spending that was not sport specific in their athletic departments. Alas for the myth, *not a single one of them did so*. Again, as with their FBS counterparts, spare your tears for the FCS, since all of the reporting departments generated enough nonallocated revenue at least to break even for 2010–11.

Let's go ahead and impart the same foresight to the ADs at FCS programs that we did for FBS programs and think about the relationships between positive net revenues in football and men's basketball combined, and the size of net deficits that are run up in the rest of the men's sports and women's sports. The correlation between the two for those 11 departments where the former covers the latter is about −0.96, much larger than the −0.73 we saw in the FBS. In the other 4 programs where a cross-subsidy is in order and there is an operating surplus on football and men's basketball but nothing to send on to the other costs of the athletic department, the correlation is −0.99, essentially a literal dollar for dollar result. ADs at these few FCS programs appear to count on the former to cover the latter to a larger extent than their FBS counterparts.

The upshot of all of this, being unduly generous to the myth (in our opinion), is that 54 of 118 FBS programs and 12 of 124 FCS programs covered any reported operating deficit from the rest of men's sports and women's sports with operating surpluses from football and men's basketball. Treating the myth correctly (in our opinion), 6 FBS programs and no FCS programs generated operating surpluses on football and men's basketball to cover deficits on the rest of men's sports and women's sports and the rest of the costs of running their athletic departments. That's one, very busted myth.

Lest the reader think that the 2010–11 year is an anomaly, a quick check is available without any further laborious calculations on our part from the IndyStar.com version of the data (remember, 2004–05 only). Some 91 FBS programs are reported by this source, and 5 of these did not run any operating deficit on the rest of men's sports and women's sports (Akron, Miami [Ohio], Central Michigan, Rutgers, and Western Kentucky), leaving 85. Of that 85, there were 56 that ran an operating surplus on football and men's basketball, but only 39 of them actually did cover their deficit on the rest of men's sports and women's sports (refer to Table 1.1 for the top and bottom 10). Finally, 4 were able to cover the other spending in their athletic departments—Arkansas (by $12.6 million), Ohio State (by $12.0 million), Georgia (by $10.7 million), and Michigan State (by $7.9 million). Recall that Georgia and Michigan State also did so in the 2010–11 data.

For the FCS, the IndyStar.com version of the data reports 75 programs. Of these, 11 did not run any operating deficit on the rest of men's sports and women's sports, leaving 64. There were 10 of the 64 that ran an operating surplus on football and men's basketball, but only 2 of these actually did cover their deficit on the rest of men's sports and women's sports (Montana and the Citadel; refer to Table 1.2 for the top and bottom 10). The Grizzlies were unable to cover the other spending in their athletic department (by $1.4 million), but the Bulldogs did manage to do so (by $280,728). Recall that no program was able to do so in the 2010–11 data. These comparisons for the FBS and FCS for 2004–05 overwhelmingly verify that the results for 2010–11 are no fluke. The claim that revenue sports pay for nonrevenue sports is simply a myth.

CONCLUSIONS—MORE THAN ENOUGH TO GO AROUND, BUT NOT JUST FROM FOOTBALL AND MEN'S BASKETBALL

This one is like shooting fish in a barrel. The data are simply too clear to everybody who has cared to look. Even at the FBS level, barely a majority of athletic departments can cover women's basketball and other sports (men's and women's) with football and men's basketball net revenues. And only 5.1 percent of the FBS programs can cover the other costs (salaries, facilities, recruiting, and game management) with this same net revenue source. The story is even more binding at the FCS level.

The myth is clearly self-serving to those most interested in a continued and even growing focus of athletic department revenues on men's revenue sports. It is also self-serving to those opposed to the implementation of federal policy such as Title IX and those against the death penalty for Penn State's football program. While we undo myths surrounding Title IX in a later chapter, the two examples are important in this chapter. As the idea goes, athletic departments just break even (more so at FCS schools), and you can't take the money from men's revenue sports without reducing the ability of the AD to cover costs of all the other sports. So even if one supports its noble intent, Title IX is an unworkable policy financially. However, the truth of the matter is that at just under the majority of FBS programs and at nearly all FCS programs, the other men's sports and women's sports don't need any help. And among those programs where the other men's and women's sports do not cover their own operating costs, those men's major revenue sports, football and basketball, simply don't cover all of the other costs of making sports happen in the first place.

As noted in the introduction, the same logic is being used in the Penn State case. And it is true that Penn State has been one of those miraculous few programs in which football and men's basketball can pay for the entire athletic program. But the logic works for only a handful of programs, such as Penn State, so it cannot be supported in any general context. Furthermore, even though Penn State is unique in that football and men's basketball could pay for the other sports, we should think about what would actually happen if there were no football at Penn State. Surely a portion of the money spent by students, donors, and fans would then be spent on other sports at Penn State. The absence of football might be the best thing for women's sports and other men's sports.

In addition, the myth leads people to believe that university support is spent on women's basketball and other sports that can't quite be covered by football and men's basketball net revenues. But the truth of the matter is that nearly the entire FCS and a goodly portion of the FBS football and men's basketball programs also receive university support. The myth interferes with proper forensic accounting on where university support goes inside the athletic department.

So if we want to implement federal policy effectively, or treat programs that misbehave in any coherent fashion, or effectively monitor spending in the athletic department, then this myth simply must go away. But it has staying power, clearly, since everything done on the question to date appears to have simply been ignored. We can only hope that bringing it all together here will weaken the ability of that myth to survive.

2 AN ARMS RACE DRIVES COLLEGE SPORTS SPENDING

Overall, spending on athletics appears to have created a so-called "arms race"
between competing athletic programs and institutions.
  —Knight Commission on Intercollegiate Athletics (2010)

INTRODUCTION

It is now accepted wisdom that college sports programs are constantly
trying to one-up each other and, since they are all competing for the same
prize, this can only happen in a wasteful way. As the Knight Commission
on Intercollegiate Athletics suggests, all spend more, but nobody can gain
more. However, sports business analytics reveal that the "arms race" claim
completely misses the mark on what actually goes on with college sports
spending. So here we are again: a claim that has no basis in fact but serves
the best interests of obvious participants in the process—the type of classic
myth that really needs busting.

People may differ on just what makes this "arms race" in college sports
spending happen. At the more generalist end of the spectrum is some sort
of "keeping up with the Joneses" idea for conference members; Florida did
it, so Georgia must as well. The University of Michigan reluctantly *has to*
put luxury boxes in its Big House (Michigan Stadium) so that it can generate a modern revenue stream—or risk being left in the dust. At the specific,
academic end of the spectrum (covered in detail below) are a set of circumstances whereby all acting in their own interest leads to collective ruin. In
between is just some vague reference to the observation that spending in
college sports is growing much faster than any other area of spending on
campus.

While its description varies, few who spout the myth differ on its consequences. Some have a vague notion that the world would be better off with

less spending in college sports. Others see college spending irrationally spi-raling out of control, eventually ruining college sports and posing no small threat to the university system in the United States. The power of this myth comes from reports on the growth of spending in college sports. This growth often exceeds that of spending on other areas at the university, and yet ath-letic departments appear to struggle to break even. This last claim is based on the fact that the NCAA's own data show that most departments rely on "insti-tutional support" from the university at large as a part of their revenue.

A basic grasp of the relationship between university administrators, abbreviated in this chapter as "UAs," and their athletic directors, abbrevi-ated with the more familiar "ADs," along with straightforward economic analysis, busts this myth. First, none of the characteristics of an arms race actually describe the spending in college sports. This alone, in our opin-ion, should have led to skepticism of the arms race myth from the outset. Second, simple observation of university processes informs us that there is a completely sane and rational explanation for the spending behavior of college athletic departments—competition over revenues that have been growing at very high rates over time. In the university budget setting gov-erning college sports, it ends up that increases in spending simply equal the increase in revenues. Third, this straightforward explanation fits the actual data on college sports revenues and spending.

But we do have to be a bit careful here. If adherence to the arms race myth leads to a policy prescription where all of the participants just sit down and figure out how to cut spending, the Federal Trade Commission may be interested. After all, most companies would love to get together with their competition and limit all of their investments, but that would surely draw antitrust scrutiny.

The myth distracts our attention from the actual self-interested choices made by ADs and their UA overseers. Critics blame some inappropriate logic and then scold the people in charge of college sports for failing to do battle against the arms race. Those who hate college sports have a trumped up justification for their attacks: "social waste." University presidents re-spond by blaming "the unstoppable juggernaut of college sports" for the arms race that must tragically follow. The light of analytical insight suggests otherwise—if there is anything to fix, it is the incentives facing UAs that set the spending rules for college ADs.

The destructive part of the myth is that it is used as an argument against pay for play (only things that are true belong in that discussion), to justify unresponsiveness to the demands of Title IX (gender equity), and to keep some college athletes "down on the farm" (so-called nonrevenue sports). The policy prescription if it is an arms race is to cut spending, and that, invariably, has an impact on participation and the value that boosters place on the endeavor in the first place. Let's go ahead and paint the current arms race picture and then put it under the scrutiny that it can't stand. At the end of the chapter, we'll return to the damage done by perpetuation of this myth.

THE ARMS RACE

The earliest "arms race" reference that we could find for college sports is by the famed University of California, Berkeley, sociologist Harry Edwards (1984, p. 7) in reference to an "athletic arms race" over the recruiting and development of college athletes. By now, the belief in the arms race is pervasive. A simple Internet search reveals:

Un-named college president quoted in Stafford (2010): "The problem is it is such big money. It's an arms race that is self-perpetuating."

Women's Sports Foundation (2008): "If necessary, the NCAA must legislate across the board expenditure limits and insist on a cessation of the arms race . . ."

Policy analyst Lindsey Luebchow (2010): "The commercialization of college sports has fueled an arms race among colleges, resulting in intense competition for recruits and coaches, which in turn has led to excessive spending on salaries and facilities."

Knight Commission on Intercollegiate Athletics (2009): "In the qualitative research respondents voiced broad concerns regarding the sustainability of all athletics programs in the face of what a number of presidents described in the qualitative interviews as an 'arms race' that is driving up costs for athletics programs and creating tensions that cannot be clearly measured in other areas."

On the academic front, Duke University economist Charles Clotfelter (2011) joins the arms race legion, citing as evidence escalation in facilities, coaches' salaries, and the aforementioned growth in athletic spending at a higher rate than at the university at large—or, in his words (p. 123): "This certainly looks like an arms race in spending on athletics." The only dissenting voice along the way was a highly qualified one in an NCAA report by analysts Robert Litan, Jonathan Orszag, and Peter Orszag (2003; see their "Hypothesis 10"). Interestingly, two of these earlier dissenting analysts later softened their position, first in the case of collegiate athletic capital spending (Orszag and Orszag, 2005a, 2005b) and then for spending in general (Jonathan Orszag and his coauthor Mark Israel, 2009).

There is only one actual study, by Cornell University economist Robert Frank (2004) commissioned by the Knight Commission, that actually sets down the known theory of an arms race and concludes that there is one through empirical assessment of college sports spending. The theory is easily described. In a noncooperative game with naive participants, a fixed prize, and a setting in which coming in second is catastrophic, the result is overbidding relative to the size of the prize. With two extensions, the commission suggests that the logic applies to collegiate sports spending. The extensions are (1) UAs with naive estimates of the probability of winning the race, and (2) rising costs of competition in collegiate athletics over time. According to the report, from the perspective of athletic department profit and loss, spending across athletic departments would exceed the expected gain. The overbidding is wasteful spending, since, from society's perspective, the same prize could be had with less spending, and some of the money could go to other, valuable activities.

The report also offers data consistent with the model. Budget allocations from the university to the athletic department are typically referred to as "institutional support." The report labels them "subsidies" and observes the following from NCAA revenue and expense data (used by us later as well): Without the subsidy, athletic department spending exceeds generated revenue. Recognizing claims that perhaps this spending yields value elsewhere to the university, the report concludes: If there is any relationship at all between spending and on-field success, student applications, or general giving to the university, then it is a small one. In other words, athletic departments are trapped in an arms race, typically operate in the red, and offer little else of value to the university. Given this, all athletic departments could simultaneously reduce and cap spending and achieve exactly the same outcome. Since the same outcomes can be had with fewer resources, society would be better off if spending on collegiate sports were restricted.

ARMS RACE? WHAT ARMS RACE?

In his autobiography *The Words*, Jean-Paul Sartre writes one of his most famous lines: "I confused things with their names; that is belief." An analytical approach should start not from belief, but from an actual identification of the thing under analysis. If one names it an "arms race" and then searches for ways that actual operation of college sports spending fits the bill, then the result is a belief rather than an analysis. For us, this means moving on to the abounding cooperative behavior we observe in college sports cited in the last section. For non-FBS championships—e.g., FCS football and Division I basketball—we can add the design of championships through the NCAA. Cooperation of this nature is required in order to define conference play and championships.

But cooperation through conferences and the NCAA also happens in ways that are not required in order to make play happen. In addition to facilitating control of conference membership and negotiating TV contracts, the NCAA is used by its membership to reduce economically competitive urges that cannot be controlled by membership in conferences. The NCAA controls applications to advance to upper levels of play, centralizes the marketing of many sports properties (videos, image use in video games), and most widely known, acts as the compliance arm of collegiate sports. On this last point, the NCAA oversees adherence to the amateur requirement, recruiting restrictions, required letters of intent, the one-year sit out rule, and all rules of practice. Given this extensive structure of cooperation, and the willingness to cooperate in so many ways, it simply strains reality to suppose that UAs and ADs operate in a noncooperative atmosphere.

We need to be very clear here, by the way. All of this cooperation to make more money from play happens *off the field*. Once the prize is established by this cooperative behavior, things take a decidedly noncooperative turn—in the plans of the separate athletic departments and the results on the field, competition to obtain the money dominates all. When it comes to recruiting players, hiring coaches, spending on facilities in order to attract high-quality players and coaches, and, ultimately, who beats whom on the playing field, competition rules the day.

Turning to the assumption that participants are naive, nobody has closely analyzed whether or not this is true of UAs and ADs. But assuming naivete on the part of UAs and ADs does not fit the facts. All administrators and ADs "come up through the ranks"; they must satisfy relentless selection mechanisms. The result should be participants keenly aware of their environment and well trained for the job at hand. UAs are seasoned academicians and long-time observers of the collegiate sports scene. ADs are astute students of business, many are lawyers, and all cut their teeth on the collegiate sports scene. While nothing stops even highly qualified people from erring, the idea that they are naive is, quite simply, far fetched.

The WOPR (War Operation Plan Response) computer in the movie *WarGames* laid out plainly what anybody who has thought at all about arms races knows. Referring to the worst arms race of all, nuclear escalation, WOPR stated: "Strange game . . . the only winning move is not to play." The only way to win an arms race is never to enter in the first place, and surely that could not be lost on heavily selected, non-naive UAs and ADs. Assuming that UAs and ADs somehow ignore the lessons to be learned from the history of college sport finance is not the same thing as demonstrating that they do.

In addition, the prize in college sports is anything but fixed. Since we get to the data later in some detail, suffice to say here that *adjusted for inflation,* the annual growth rate in revenues at the median of athletic department revenues reported to the NCAA is about 4.6 percent. If you think this is extraordinary compared with the typical 2.5 to 3.0 percent real annual growth rate in the economy at large, get this. Again adjusted for inflation, the annual growth rate in revenues for the largest reports to the NCAA is 5.5 percent! At the top of the heap, college sports revenues have grown right around twice the typical growth rate in the economy adjusted for inflation. This seems to us not a fixed prize at all. This also puts to rest any ideas that the arms race can be found in capital spending or coaches' salaries. Chasing ever-growing revenue returns often results in rising input prices for the firms doing the chasing.

Finally, we come to the conclusion that coming in second somehow is catastrophic. Remember, "tragic" in the arms race context means that all bidders pay, *but only one earns any return*. It is said that the United States won the arms race against the country formerly known as the Soviet Union because only one world power could remain after the escalation in arms spending through the Reagan administration. While it is true that there is only one conference champion, and only one subsequent national champion, there are plenty of other winners. All of the rest of the ADs generate revenues and kudos for their competitive performances. Life is still pretty good for coaches and ADs at FBS institutions that seldom see postseason play.

Put another way, coming in second does not lead athletic departments to close up shop; there is no college sports equivalent of the demise of the Soviet Union. Indeed, no FBS athletic department has ever dropped any of its major sports. Instead, demand to enter is keen from sea to shining

TABLE 2.1. *Second through Fourth Place BCS Finishes, 1998–99 to 2011–12*

Year	2nd Place Team	3rd Place	4th Place
1998–99	Florida State	Kansas State	Ohio State
1999–00	Virginia Tech	Nebraska	Alabama
2000–01	Florida State	Miami (FL)	Washington
2001–02	Nebraska	Colorado	Oregon
2002–03	Ohio State	Georgia	USC
2003–04	LSU	USC	Michigan
2004–05	Oklahoma	Auburn	Texas
2005–06	Texas	Penn State	Ohio State
2006–07	Florida	Michigan	LSU
2007–08	LSU	Virginia Tech	Oklahoma
2008–09	Florida	Texas	Alabama
2009–10	Texas	Cincinnati	TCU
2010–11	Oregon	TCU	Stanford
2011–12	LSU	Stanford	Oklahoma State

Source: Compiled from BCS.org.

sea—from the University of Idaho to the universities of Central or Southern Florida. Football has been dropped at Football Championship Series (FCS) universities (recently, Northeastern and Hofstra). However, as we cover in detail below, in each instance that appears to have been a rational response by UAs to changing marginal values of all of the departments within their operations.

Table 2.1 is a list of "also ran" finishers in the final standings over the period that the BCS has designed the championship system. They all seem to be doing quite well, thank you. Indeed, these are precisely the athletic departments that would be enjoying the incredible "top of the heap" growth rates in revenues cited in the last paragraph: Ohio State, Texas, and USC. Again, this crucial underpinning of the arms race belief simply does not hold any water.

SO WHAT IS REALLY GOING ON?

It is all well and good to knock the pins out from under one explanation but much more satisfying if there is a replacement explanation. While there will be variations, a generally descriptive "model" of UAs and ADs is based on the following elements of the observed nature of their environment. First, ADs operate in their university structure, their conference structure, and as representatives of their university members at the NCAA. In this setting, the relevant actors are ADs, UAs, conference commissioners, NCAA administrators, athletes, and collegiate sports consumers.

Expanding the view of the relationship between UAs and their ADs puts the focus on actual organizations rather than forcing the square peg of college sports outcomes into the round hole of the arms race explanation. Rather than assuming noncooperative, naive actors, all we need for this alternative model is for all actors to pursue their own self-interest. As all of us do, the relevant actors in college sports care about income and upward mobility that, in turn, enhances their future welfare. In the context of their environment, enhanced welfare depends upon the performance of their respective organizations. In this context, the crux of the issue comes straight to the fore: There can be areas of conflict between the goals of UAs and the self-interested pursuits of ADs. The welfare of UAs depends on the performance of all their charges, including ADs, along well-known dimensions—research, teaching, and service.

This operational environment suggests a setting that is well known to economists—namely, UAs are "principals" to their university "agents." The agents are academic leaders and nonacademic leaders such as ADs. The president of the university (most typically, but with some exceptions) controls the AD's employment and pay, subject to market forces and the costs of monitoring. Along this well-known line of reasoning, UAs have every incentive to create and manage institutional designs that harness the self-interested behavior of ADs to the enhancement of UA welfare. UAs have clearly chosen to do this by organizing the university into units that facilitate the comparative advantages of each department along the lines of research, teaching, and service, as well as to facilitate monitoring of outcomes.

Given the similarity of the UA monitoring problem across its agent-departments, it is no wonder that all units at the university, including the athletic department, are similarly structured (at a few universities, athletic departments are separate entities reporting directly to the board of regents, but this is still oversight). All of the assistant coaches in a given sport are specialists in different areas, just like individual faculty on the academic side (e.g., in football, strength and conditioning, position coaches, offensive and defensive coordinators). These specialists are organized under the head coach similar to an academic department and its chair. The collection of sports is organized into the larger unit, the athletic department. To keep the analogy truly complete, we could refer to this as the "school of athletics," since, at the top of the athletic department, the AD is the equivalent of an academic dean in terms of oversight and authority. The AD has associate ADs to handle the day-to-day operations of the department, freeing the AD to see to fund-raising and external relations for the athletic department, just as academic deans have associate deans. The AD answers to the president (rather than the provost on the academic side) and up the ladder to the regents and governor (as do academic deans).

That some doubt the power that UAs have over ADs defies the reality of the situation. If ADs do not contribute to UA goals, or if the athletic department becomes costly to the university in embarrassing ways, UAs have a variety of recourses. For one, budget allocations to the athletic department can simply be reduced. This power is clear under the current economic malaise. Michael Cross, AD at Bradley University, covers responses by ADs to the recession at his UltimateSportsInsider.com. ADs are conforming as directed. But there are other, more dramatic actions familiar to all who follow collegiate sports that can be taken by UAs—episodes of unsatisfactory performance followed by AD firings or forced resignations are well known.

Perhaps the most dramatic recourse is simply closing down programs altogether by UAs. For example, in the Colonial Athletic Association, UAs at Northeastern University (the Huskies) cut its football program in November of 2009, and UAs at Hofstra University (the Flying Dutchmen) followed suit the next month. At Northeastern, the official stance was, "The decision is consistent with the university's strategic approach to prioritize programs and invest in signature strengths" (ESPN.com News Services, 2009a). It didn't help that the team had just completed its sixth consecutive losing season. At Hofstra, UAs state flatly that football was eliminated because of a general lack of interest among students and alumni, and a desire to spend the money to greater advantage on academic programs (ESPN.com News Services, 2009b). No public mention can be found in either case that this had anything to do with finally being driven over the edge in an arms race. Instead, a simple assessment of the value of investment in football versus investment in other portions of the university led to the reallocation of funds away from football.

The ultimate result of this principal-agent structure is money and political support that is useful to UAs pursuing their goals. This basic model is portrayed in Figure 2.1. Values from all areas of the university flow out, under the three major headings of research, teaching, and service. Money and political support come back to UAs. In turn, hierarchically, through academic deans and the AD, UAs allocate rewards back to departments. Agents including ADs are rewarded when they contribute to UA goals and punished when they don't.

The principal-agent view here puts an entirely different spin on the budget allocation to the athletic department than is commonly offered among

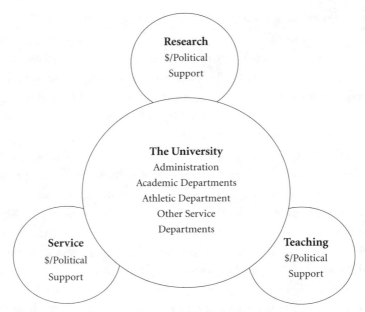

FIG. 2.1. University Principal-Agent Schematic.

observers of the collegiate sports scene. Budget allocations to athletic de-partments are commonly referred to as *institutional support* and typically as *subsidies* in the same breath. Indeed, in the NCAA's own commissioned survey results (the same data referred to in Chapter 1; Fulks, 2011), institu-tional support is tabulated separately from so-called generated revenues. From the principal-agent point of view, two things are clear.

First, all revenues to the athletic department are "generated," some at the gate, some related to attendance (parking and concessions), some from TV, some from booster contributions (alumni and others), and still others in terms of the budget allocation from the university. It is rational for UAs to allocate these rewards to the highest possible return among all depart-ments including the athletic department. Second, there is no difference in the purpose of budget allocations to the academic side and the allocation to the athletic department. All "agents" compete on the basis of their rela-tive success in the eyes of their UA principals. Athletic departments receive their share, as do all departments, through a competitive budgeting process at the university level. If the allocation to the athletic department is a "subsidy," then so is the allocation to any other unit on campus. We prefer to simply "call 'em as we see 'em." These are all budget allocations.

Now, not all departments are equally adept at each of the research, teaching, and service areas, and an effective organizational structure would take this into account. Among academic departments, some are more about teaching and others are more about research. Compared with academic departments, the mix is different still for the athletic department. Although arguably there can be a research mission, there clearly are teaching and service performed by the athletic department. The teaching mission is not typically recognized, but, as in any of the fine arts on the academic side, athletes often become teachers of their sport, and a very few become participants in their sport at the professional level. Completing the comparison, some academic departments—music, dance, and other fine arts—also have a service-entertainment contribution. Indeed, much of this entertainment can be enjoyed on providers like the Big Ten Network! But it is here that athletic departments truly shine. Members of the athletic department, from the AD through the associate ADs, on down to coaches and assistants, and finally the athletes themselves, provide entertainment services enjoyed by millions. Some of their games appear on the Big Ten Network as well, but also on ABC/ESPN, CBS, NBC, and FOX.

So, just like their academic department counterparts, ADs manage their athletic departments to generate resources used to achieve UA goals. These results, however, typically are not direct dollar amounts from the athletic department to the university. After all, there is no tuition equivalent, and UAs do not choose to charge overhead on the revenues generated by the athletic department. Instead, the values created by ADs are collected in other areas by UAs (we provide detail on these in what follows):

- Greater giving by alumni and other boosters to the general university fund.
- A larger and better set of student applicants.
- Favorable general budget treatment by legislators.
- Better faculty and administrators.

- Value added to athletes, many of whom would not be at the university without athletics.

One final observation on the principal-agent problem helps round out the implications of this general descriptive theory. In the same way that UAs are flexible in terms of the relative advantages of their agents along research, teaching, and service lines, they also will allow other types of flexibility. Another place where flexibility is required concerns the uncertainty of athletic outcomes relative to academic results. For athletic departments there can be little disagreement on success (wins and losses). The relationship between output quality and price is also clear in the athletic department. Turning to predictability, however, the scales tip toward academics, since it is all about talent coming to fruition. Very few academic candidates fail. On the other hand, which bowl game the football team achieves (if any), or making it to March Madness in basketball, are much tougher predictions to make.

For all of these reasons, UAs find that athletic departments are most valuable if ADs are allowed budgetary discretion not allowed to academic deans. Deans determine the needs of their departments, put them together in a budget request, and turn it over to UAs. Typically, deans spend their allocation, and if spending is lower or revenues are greater than anticipated, UAs retain control over any balances and are likely to look for reduced budget requests the next time around.

ADs also determine the needs of their department and set their budgets (originally), but, unlike their academic counterparts, if their department spending is unexpectedly low or revenues unexpectedly high, ADs can revise their budgets. Unexpected surpluses can be reallocated to ongoing expenditures, new and ongoing facilities projects, and salary adjustments. Thus, because their output is more difficult to predict, in their own self-interest, UAs allow ADs to spend departmental surpluses as they see fit. Thus, it should be expected that athletic spending would always rise to meet revenues. On the other hand, there is no reason to tolerate budget deficits, so that, if they occur, they should be short-lived.

The upshot of our analysis is a set of descriptions and implications that separate the principal-agent descriptive model from the arms race explanation. The following from the last section are consistent with actual process observation but not with the arms race explanation:

1. There need be no presumption that ADs are involved in a non-cooperative game.
2. There need be no presumption that UAs and ADs are naive.
3. There need be no presumption that ADs act completely independently.

From this section, the principal-agent model suggests two things that are also inconsistent with the arms race explanation:

4. The value of the AD's efforts will be found in places other than the athletic department bottom line.
5. It should be expected that athletic spending will always rise to meet revenues.

We've already spent all the time necessary on items 1 through 3. In the next section we show that 4 and 5 hold as well. All of this is consistent with the principal-agent explanation but rejects the arms race logic.

ATHLETIC DEPARTMENT VALUES, REVENUES, AND SPENDING

Earlier we noted that the Knight Commission report read the literature on nonrevenue "other values" itemized in the last section and found them "small at best." In this section we show that other researchers disagree with the report's assessment, and some others are finding more values than this assessment imagined. Furthermore, we take to task the idea that these values are "small at best." "Small" is only meaningful relative to the size of investment by UAs in the first place!

For example, Western Kentucky University economist Brian Goff's thorough survey (2004) and extension offers some general conclusions. Major achievements (significant postseason appearances) appear to spark general giving. But marginal increases in winning during the season don't. Major athletic achievements also appear to spark increased student interest, even at colleges that already have high academic reputations. But the quality of the pool is better only at very select institutions.

University of Alberta economist Brad Humphreys and his coauthor, Florida State University sport management professor Michael Mondello, found (2007) that giving increased with success but only for "restricted" giving that included, but was not limited to, giving to the athletic department. University of North Carolina, Charlotte, economist Irvin Tucker (2004, 2005) added that football success (but not basketball success) increased the percentage of alumni that give to the general university fund, increased the SAT scores of entering freshmen, and enhanced graduation rates. Tucker and his University of North Carolina, Charlotte, coauthor, economist L. Ted Amato, later (2006) refined this to a statement that affiliation in a BCS conference carried all the weight rather than success of the athletic program. Rutgers University sociologist D. Randall Smith argued (2008) that econometric issues on this type of "advertising effect" are not settled. Finally, according to the aforementioned Brad Humphreys (2006), institutions fielding FBS football programs received 8 percent larger annual state appropriations than those without such programs. He goes on to suggest that this helps explain why the number of institutions fielding FBS college football programs increased by 10 percent from 1998 to 2002.

This leads us to our final observation about the inapplicability of arms race logic to college sports spending. The principal-agent explanation tells us that ADs should spend all of their budgets, including allocations from UAs, so that revenues equal expenses. Put another way, the correlation between revenues (*all revenues*, including the budget allocation by the UAs) and spending would be unity. There would be no reason to expect any budget deficits other than for the usual reasons of mistakes and uncertainty because these would be in nobody's best interest. Turning to the same data on revenues and expenses employed by Robert Frank, but under this alternative principal-agent implication, reveals the major data problem for the arms race belief—spending has grown immensely, but it is pretty much equal to the growth in revenues.

The NCAA data (Fulks, 2011) were discussed thoroughly in Chapter 1. The data are presented in two forms in the original documents, the average (later, median) report and the largest report. So, in any given year, neither of these reported aggregates matches up to the same athletic department; the average revenue reported does not necessarily come from the same athletic department that reports the average expenditure, for example. But the NCAA finds this type of characterization of "average" and "large" programs useful, so it is carried along here.

Simply combining the revenue and expense data for the FBS into Figure 2.2 presents an aggregate picture of collegiate sport revenues and expenses that is unmistakable (the data are adjusted for inflation). One way to see this is by using what is called a "correlation coefficient." Essentially, for two series of data that move together, a correlation of zero means that they don't do so at all, and a correlation coefficient of 1.0 means that they move in perfect lock step. The correlation at the average reports of revenues and expenses is 0.99. Essentially, "average" athletic departments collect ever-growing revenues and, under their UA-imposed budget model, spend them all. For the largest reported values, the correlation between revenues and expenses is 0.96. Unlike their "average" counterparts, the "largest" athletic departments don't spend quite everything they bring in (revenues always exceed spending, especially from 1999 to 2005).

In passing, it is easy to see why some might view with alarm the increase in spending. Adjusted for inflation, the annual growth rate in spending at the average and largest reports, respectively are 4.6 percent and 5.8 percent, quite large relative to the typical real growth rate in the economy (2.5 to 3.0 percent). However, worries about some form of collapse are clearly misplaced. For one thing, while these increases in costs are high, they are not unprecedented. Professional sports teams and other university departments sometimes face cost increases that are quite a bit higher. But more to the point, the real annual growth rate in the average report of revenues matches the growth in expenses, since they are correlated at essentially unity. For the largest reported values, revenues are always at least as large as expenditures, and their real annual growth rate in revenues is essentially the same (5.5 percent).

This is consistent with the descriptive principal-agent model, not the arms race, and apparent if one looks at any athletic department annual revenue and expense sheet just prior to, during, and after an important post-

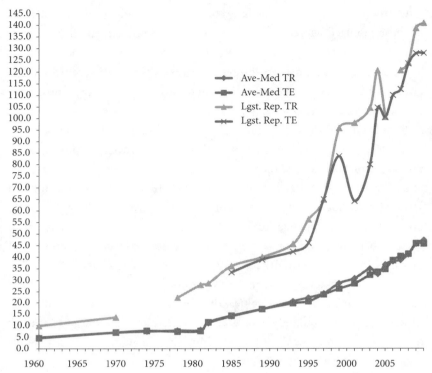

FIG. 2.2. FBS Operating Revenues and Expenses ($2009). Calculated from the NCAA revenues and expenses data, most recently Fulks (2011). Largest Reported Total Revenue omits 2006 because the report that year is just not believable ($260.7 million $2009). Repeated inquiries to Prof. Fulks have yet to yield any response. Upon inquiry, the NCAA responded that a particularly large gift to that program was responsible. But gifts are not operations, so we simply omit any further discussion of this anomaly.

season appearance (major bowl games including the BCS or March Madness). In general, the sharing of postseason revenues already is built into an AD's spending plan. They all know the amounts that will come to the conference and how much will be shared back to their own individual athletic departments. But there will be unexpected additional regular-season TV revenues, contributions, royalties (on merchandise), and merchandise sales revenues during the successful year. And all are spent that same year. Spending always rises to the revenue occasion.

CONCLUSIONS—WHAT HAPPENS IF WE BELIEVE THE MYTH; AND IF WE DON'T?

The arms race in college sports spending, commonly believed and often foisted, is a myth. The theoretical setting for such an arms race is not to be found in the relationship between university administrators and their athletic directors. Further, the actual revenue and spending data support a principal-agent interpretation of college sports spending and reject an arms race explanation. So what can we take away from the fact that, rather than critics, the arms race logic has nothing but supporters?

It is easiest to see if we focus on how a principal-agent view changes the focus from spending caps to institutional design. The focus switches to (1) the effectiveness of the oversight mechanisms from the perspective of the university administrators, and (2) whether university administrators are, indeed, satisfying the needs of their own principals (board of regents and, for public universities, the governor). There are two groups likely to wish that this focus did not occur.

First are the critics of universities and college sports in particular. The "runaway spending" interpretation fits their value judgments to a tee and requires no alteration in any of the usual fiscal conservatism that goes along with them. Indeed, the prescription is to cut spending on sports. This appeals directly to any who wish public spending to go down and to critics of college sports who wish it would just go away altogether.

The second group that might not wish the myth busted is university administrators themselves. From their perspective, this process may be working just fine. The lesson from other areas, especially political science, is that these types of mechanisms afford principals chances to credit-claim and blame-shift. On this dimension, blame shifting could be the explanation for findings that university presidents feel powerless to change collegiate sports (Knight Commission on Intercollegiate Athletics, 2009). If the current designs are not working, then the principal-agent explanation suggests reform targets: (1) improve the effectiveness of the current design—increase the value of monitoring, lower the costs of monitoring, or both; and (2) devise an alternative institutional design. But these alterations would be in direct conflict with the welfare of current university administrators.

The true tragedy of this myth is not really in the spending outcome but in the misguided prescriptions that follow from the myth. Proposed policy implications from an unsupported arms race belief suggest both reducing and capping athletic department spending. These types of spending revisions are highly likely to affect all college sports constituencies and, especially, participation opportunities for collegiate athletes and the value of that participation.

Perhaps this all speaks to the underlying issue concerning the place of college sports in the university setting. Collegiate sports satisfy students who wanted them in the first place, historically, and are enjoyed by many others, alumni and nonalumni boosters, who support them in other ways. Whether this is appropriate or not seems a fitting point of discussion at universities. A parallel is the original opposition to business schools. Business schools were not always welcome and came under scathing attack in the 1950s under a Ford Foundation Report by economists Robert A. Gordon of the University of California, Berkeley, and James Howell of Stanford University (1959). This report even ventured to ask the question, "Does Business Education Belong in the Colleges?" The tone of the Carnegie Foundation Report by Dartmouth economist Frank Pierson (1959) was more conciliatory but just as critical. Harvard University business professor Rakesh Khurana (2007) provided a retrospective on just how these works shaped business education.

As with this early example of academic introspection, essential to an informed discussion is an explanation of collegiate sports outcomes that actually fits the facts. Allowing free rein to those charging ahead on the back of the arms race explanation will ultimately prove destructive. Advocates of play for pay for college athletes will always be stymied by this myth. Champions of Title IX gender equity goals will be similarly repelled by it. Finally, so-called nonrevenue sports will always be fighting an uphill battle in their pursuit of university support because this powerful myth is so firmly entrenched.

3 ATHLETIC DEPARTMENTS ARE A DRAG ON THE UNIVERSITY BUDGET

A newly released NCAA report shows that just 14 of the 120 Football Bowl Subdivision schools made money from campus athletics in the 2009 fiscal year, down from 25 the year before.
    —Associated Press (2010)

Twenty-two elite athletics departments made money in 2010, up from 14 the previous year . . . . At the 98 other programs in the NCAA's Football Bowl Subdivision (formerly Division I-A), the median deficit in 2010 was $11.6 million, barely changing from the previous year, while no programs in the Football Championship Subdivision (formerly Division I-AA) or at Division I programs without football operated in the black. At those programs, losses continue to grow each year.
    —Libby Sander, *Chronicle of Higher Education* (2011)

INTRODUCTION

Using the NCAA's own data, those hostile to college sports foist a myth on casual observers—athletic departments struggle to break even. Article after article echoes the AP quotation above—without institutional support (direct and indirect payments from the university to the athletic department), nearly all of the athletic departments would run in the red. Quoting then interim NCAA president Jim Isch, the AP article in the epigram notes, "The top end . . . still does not have to rely on institutional subsidies. But those that do are falling further behind." Even those who grant that there are values created by college sports wonder why universities should foot the bill. Indeed, for those who insist that university administrators have no control over athletics, it seems the tail wags the dog—athletic directors spend what they like and then tell their university administrators, helpless pawns of boosters, to make up the difference.

We hope Mark Twain was wrong when he said, "The more you explain it, the more I don't understand it." For explain it we will. Dispelling this particular myth takes advantage of the important groundwork on the relationship between athletic directors and their university administrators laid out in Chapter 2. University administrators invest significantly in all departments under their control. In turn, these administrators expect a return along the dimensions that matter for their pursuits—research, teaching, and service. Business schools contribute on all these dimensions, and so do the athletic departments. Thus athletic departments are not a "drag" on the university budget. Instead, they are just another investment center that yields a return that matters to university administrators.

We bust the myth as follows. In the next section, we show the logic that generates the idea that the athletic departments lose money. With nothing up their sleeves, presto! Proponents simply label the investment in the athletic department by university administrators as somehow different than "generated" revenues and call it a "subsidy." From this accounting fiction, athletic departments lose money if generated revenues are less than spending. This is simply accounting sleight of hand that ignores the lesson from Chapter 2 that the investment in the athletic department has a payoff that matters to university administrators. So the issue is the level of return on the investment that universities make, and we turn to that in the subsequent section We show that, first, the size of these allocations to the athletic department is next to nothing compared with the university budget and how it allocates money to other areas. In addition, for both FBS schools in auto-bid BCS conferences and for the rest of the FBS schools, the values seem clearly worth it to university administrators. Rather than losing money, athletic departments pay back at a handsome rate of return on the university investment. The returns are both directly measurable monetary returns, labeled student aid in the athletic department budget, and of the "other values across the university" variety covered in Chapter 2.

Stanford University economist Roger Noll (1999) uses Division II and Division III as a case in point. At these lower levels, since clearly TV revenues do not matter at all and crowds are typically quite small, just why do university administrators still devote something like 3 percent to 5 percent of tuition revenues to college sports? The investment at this level is in accord with the demand by students to be athletes and by the rest of the smaller student bodies to enjoy the activities of their classmates. Clearly, this cannot be a drain on these smaller university budgets but are best portrayed as a modest investment in another aspect of college life demanded by their students.

This myth represents a curious dichotomy of self-serving behavior. On the one hand, the myth is used to suggest that the money spent on athletics has a higher use elsewhere. That is wrong for two reasons. First, as we will show, the money that goes to athletics is actually quite small compared with both the university budget and the budget allocations to many other units on campus. If the athletic department allocation went across the rest of the university, each unit would receive a truly small amount. Second, the same argument is not trotted out against units at the university that receive even larger allocations—say, engineering or the medical school. Besides, if university administrators were to announce that they would no longer invest in athletics, it isn't at all clear that the sources of these funds, students through tuition and fees and legislatures through education budget appropriations, would be willing to have the funds go to some other university spending area.

On the other hand of the curious dichotomy, these purveyors of their own self-interest also ignore in athletics what they claim for their own academic unit. The value of heavily subsidized departments—e.g., English—is to be found in the whole student that graduates from the university. As we show in Chapter 2, the value of the athletic department is not found only in the department's own bottom line, any more than the value of the English department is found in its own bottom line. The returns from all units on campus must be looked at from a holistic standpoint. This requires, by the way, that at the heart of the myth must lie a belief that somehow athletics are just different from academics when it comes to legitimacy on campus. We do not take that argument on here, but do note its proper place in our concluding remarks.

The myth proves destructive as follows. College sports end up under attack for something they have never been, except at a very few universities—namely, economically self-sustaining. Since it is easily swallowed by the layperson, the argument gets made that the rightful place of athletics on campus is tenuous, at best, and certainly not deserving of scarce university budget dollars. That allocation must be cut, at least, and jerked entirely at best. We couldn't agree more that what goes on at the university should be examined and discussed at every turn. But such a discussion would be better off in the bright sunshine rather than the murky shrouds of a distracting myth.

The tragedy that follows is twofold. Rather than allocating budget resources to their greatest advantage, including athletics, university administrators will be faced with restricted alternatives and reallocate their budget inefficiently relative to their end objectives of research, teaching, and service. Then, entirely forgotten in the attack, student athletes will have fewer chances to participate, and those students that enjoy sports will have fewer chances for enjoyment as well. In this money-losing department argument, student enjoyment is often lost in the shuffle as the focus turns to "boosters" and their various evils.

THE MONEY LOSING ATHLETIC DEPARTMENT

Here is how the data are misconstrued to make the case that athletic departments lose money. The first step is to define "generated" revenues separate from institutional support. Generated revenues include ticket sales, NCAA and conference distributions, concessions, contributions allocated by sport, and media rights but *not* institutional support from university administrators, any other direct government support, or student fees. This is completely arbitrary, of course, since the allocation of university budget to athletics or direct government support is no less "earned" than ticket or TV revenue. It simply is earned for other services rendered to the university goals of research, teaching, and service (recall the lessons from Chapter 2). The second step is to practice the worst possible business sense and claim that "generated" revenues and costs would be the same if there were no institutional support. Since "generated" revenues are less than costs, voila, athletic departments are money-losing propositions.

The NCAA survey covered in previous chapters on athletic department revenues and expenses follows exactly these steps and results from its most recent report (Fulks, 2011) are compiled in Table 3.1 (no adjustment for inflation is needed for our purposes). By and large, popular reports like those in the epigraph appear to be quite right if they adhere to the arbitrary definition of *generated* revenues. Based on generated revenues, a distinct minority of FBS programs and nearly no FCS or Division I programs without football have showed an operating surplus over the last seven years (the last column of Table 3.1).

However, the arbitrariness of this definition of "generated" revenue is clear from the reports that the NCAA then turns around and makes to OPE using the same reported data from its members (detailed in Chapter 2). By the OPE version of the data, we calculate that fully 73 of the 118 athletic departments listed for 2010–11 reported that sports operations yielded a net positive amount, from $64.2 million at Texas to $16,910 at Alabama-Birmingham (the average was $10.6 million, and the median $4.9 million across all 73 programs). But this isn't the end of it. Again by our calculation, another 27 reporting FBS programs broke even in sports operations for a nice round 100 out of 118 that showed no operating loss at all (84.7 percent of the total). This arbitrary definition turns the lack of any operating loss for 100 programs into a failure of "generated" revenue to cover expenses for all but 22 of them.

The results in the FBS are not much different. Again by our calculations using the 2010–11 OPE version of the data, 42 of 124 reporting programs showed a net surplus from sports operations, while another 63 broke even (105 of the 124 total, or 84.7 percent). The range of surpluses was from $2.7 million for Southern University to $7,543 at the Citadel (the median was $482,601). Turning to Table 3.1, for the FCS, this arbitrary definition turns the absence of any operating losses into a failure of "generated" revenues to cover expenses *for all 105 of these programs!*

Table 3.1 also makes it clear that, indeed, athletics are big money: more than $100 million for the largest reports by FBS departments. However,

TABLE 3.1. *Revenues and Expenses in College Sports, 2004–10 ($Millions)*

| | Median Report | | | | | Largest Report | | | | | |
Year	Generated Rev.	Institutional Support	Tot. Rev.	Tot. Exp.	Net	Generated Rev.	Institutional Support	Tot. Rev.	Tot. Exp.	Net	# Schools Reporting Generated Rev. > Exp.
FBS											
2010	35.3	13.0	48.3	46.7	1.6	143.5	0.0	143.5	130.4	13.1	22
2009	32.3	13.4	45.7	45.9	−0.2	138.5	0.0	138.5	127.7	10.8	14
2008	30.5	10.6	41.1	41.4	−0.3	118.5	5.3	123.8	123.4	0.4	25
2007	26.1	11.5	37.6	39.2	−1.6	109.4	7.7	117.1	109.2	7.9	25
2006	26.4	9.0	35.4	35.8	−0.4	236.8	4.5	241.4	101.8	139.6	19
2005	24.3	8.5	32.8	31.1	1.7	89.7	0.0	89.7	89.6	0.1	18
2004	22.9	5.4	28.2	29.0	−0.8	103.9	0.0	103.9	90.1	13.8	18
FCS											
2010	3.3	9.9	13.2	13.1	0.1	18.8	21.4	40.2	39.2	1.0	0
2009	2.9	9.2	12.1	12.0	0.1	18.7	23.8	42.6	42.7	−0.1	0
2008	3.0	9.1	12.1	12.1	0.0	17.5	21.2	38.7	40.3	−1.6	0
2007	2.8	7.7	10.5	10.5	0.0	15.2	20.5	35.8	37.4	−1.7	0
2006	2.3	7.3	9.6	9.5	0.2	15.2	18.3	33.5	34.9	−1.4	0
2005	2.2	6.8	9.0	8.7	0.4	14.0	17.1	31.1	32.0	−0.9	1
2004	2.0	5.7	7.8	7.8	0.0	15.4	16.2	31.7	28.2	3.5	0
Division I w/o Football											
2010	2.0	9.1	11.1	11.6	−0.5	14.4	17.7	32.1	32.1	0.0	0
2009	2.1	8.3	10.4	10.5	−0.1	16.8	13.3	30.1	30.1	0.0	0
2008	2.1	8.0	10.1	10.3	−0.3	13.7	15.6	29.2	29.2	0.0	0
2007	1.9	7.3	9.3	9.4	−0.1	13.8	13.3	27.1	27.1	0.0	0
2006	1.8	6.9	8.8	8.9	−0.1	12.5	11.9	24.4	24.4	0.0	0
2005	1.6	6.4	8.0	7.9	0.1	11.0	13.2	24.2	24.2	0.0	0
2004	1.5	5.8	7.3	7.1	0.1	15.4	5.8	21.2	21.2	0.0	1

Source: Calculated from Tables 3.1, 4.1, and 5.1, and 3.5, 4.5, and 5.5 in Fulks (2011).
Notes: Original reports Median Net Revenues, for both Generated and Total categories, but those values are not revenues minus expenses. We use actual differences and calculate them for both the median report and the largest report. The NCAA tells us that the reason for the seemingly large values for the largest FBS report, 2006, is a one-time extraordinary gift to that department.

focusing on the size of athletic department budgets misses the point and falls for the myth—athletics are big money to the athletics department *but not the university at large*. The university is not covering the total athletic budget. Instead, the investment made by the university administrators is institutional support to athletics. As we shall see shortly, these institutional support amounts are a trivial component of university operating budgets. The relevant question is, Do university administrators get a reasonable return on the institutional support investment?

But before we go there, the punch line of the "money losing athletic department" goes like this. In Table 3.1, for the athletic department that makes the median report each year—whether it is FBS, FCS, or D-I without football—*generated* revenues have not covered costs in the last seven years (earlier reports by the NCAA are the same, by the way). Even after institutional support is added, the median FBS and D-I without football departments rarely break even (total revenues were greater than total costs in 2005 and 2010 for the former; 2004 and 2005 for the latter). The FCS departments essentially break even. Thus, for the departments reporting the median budget each year, there is overwhelming support for the money-losing athletic department argument.

Things are much better for the FBS athletic department making the largest report each year. For these athletic departments, generated revenue covers costs for all years except 2008. However, by the last column of Table 3.1, apparently this result is driven by a very few departments in total where this is actually true: 22 such departments for the 2010–11 data but far fewer than that in some years. Interestingly, largest report departments still typically receive institutional support, even though they could typically more than break even without it. Of course, this fits quite nicely with the actual investment value of athletic departments—university administrators at these universities apparently desire a higher level of value-generating activity than generated revenues would support.

However, the table takes a decidedly nasty turn for the largest reports in the FCS and D-I without football. None have generated revenue in excess of costs for any of the years in Table 3.1. Even after adding in institutional support, the largest report FCS departments remained in the red in all years except 2004 and 2010. For D-I without football, of course, budget deficits cannot be positive after support, since there is no point to it. Thus, for the departments reporting the largest budgets, there is support for the "money losing athletic department" only at the FCS level. This fits with the claim that only the truly largest of the big time in college sports see any net return.

Mark Twain keeps occurring to us, and we respond to this idea of the money-losing athletic department in the spirit of this quotation, "It ain't what you don't know that gets you into trouble. It's what you know for sure that just ain't so." From our portrayal in Chapter 2, of course, this depiction of money-losing athletic departments is nonsense. University administrators invest in athletic departments expecting returns along the lines that matter to them—research, teaching, and service. In order to generate the values that athletic departments provide, at the level most preferred by university administrators, investment is on the order of a few million at the median report FBS departments. Less is invested, but the investment is positive nonetheless, at the largest report FBS departments. The question of whether athletic departments break even or not from the perspective of university administrators involves any net return *on institutional support*, not whether athletic department total revenues exceed their total costs. Thus, "big money athletics," where the big money goes to the athletic department, becomes a simple assessment of investment value for university administrators.

But the logic behind the myth of money-losing athletic departments is even worse than just misunderstanding the purpose of university budget allocations. That logic, in its second step, assumes that athletic directors would choose the same scale of operations in the absence of institutional support. This assumes that athletic directors missed the Business 101 class on what to do if revenues decline—every business operator knows that if revenues fall, operations must be curtailed. It is more reasonable to expect that ADs would simply scale back operations if they were told that university budget allocations to their department were to be phased out.

So let's proceed to see what the values and net returns really are for university administrators. Now, a unanimous verdict requires more than space allows here. What we are able to do here is to show the myth for what it is through example and overview—a focus only on the athletic department bottom line, ignoring that the athletic department generates significant returns given the investment by the university. Indeed, as portrayed in Chapter 2, athletic directors, like their academic dean counterparts, are expected to perform along the research, teaching, and service dimensions that matter to university administrators. To the extent that they are needed, university administrators invest in the athletic department as long as the return is there. And it is.

THE VALUES

In 1850, Frederic Bastiat noted the following. Any decision under analysis produces a series of effects. The first, immediate effect is easy to see and relate to the decision that caused it. The rest of the series of effects emerge only later; they are not "seen" but must be "foreseen." From this perspective, Bastiat observed there is only one difference between a bad economist and a good one. The bad economist never gets any further than the immediate first effect. Good economists do their best to foresee the entire series of effects.

We hope that Bastiat is smiling when we observe that the values the athletic department generates for the university at large can be categorized under two headings, directly measurable monetary return calculable from the athletic department expense report, and harder to measure other returns found elsewhere in the university. Under the first heading, all FBS, FCS, and D-I without football athletic departments do, indeed, return money to their university directly. All of these departments pay grants-in-aid (tuition, room and board, and books) to the university for its athletes. The same direct revenues collected for the rest of the student body also are collected for athletes. We make more direct comparisons between institutional support investments by university administrators and these student aid payments by the athletic department, school by school in the next section. Typically, student aid payments pay off handsomely to the university relative to the size of budget allocations to the athletic department.

Also under the directly measurable monetary return heading, a few universities make other direct payments. For example, the Notre Dame athletic department is under explicit contract to return all positive net revenue back to the general scholarship fund. The University of Florida "athletic association," the athletic department organized as a separate corporation overseen by university administrators and the board of regents, contributed $6 million to Florida in 2011. This amount brought the total contributions by the athletic association to the university at large to $60 million since 1990 (Crabbe, 2011). Indeed, Florida AD Jeremy Foley said of the contribution, "It's not our money. It's the university's money. We're part of the university, and we're here to help." Some Big Ten schools use money from the Big Ten network to fund scholarships and facilities. The Ohio State athletic department pledged a five-year, $1mllion payment to the university library (Weiberg and Whiteside, 2007).

Moving on to the harder to measure other returns found elsewhere in the university, in Chapter 2 we demonstrated the list of values created by the athletic department and the state of current assessment of those values. Just as a refresher, the list from Chapter 2 included the following:

- Greater giving by alumni and other boosters to the general university fund.
- A larger and better set of student applicants.
- Favorable general budget treatment by legislators.
- Better faculty and administrators.
- Value added to athletes, many of whom would not be at the university without athletics.

As we documented by the work of others in Chapter 2, these values are relatively small. But the important point from the perspective of making any case against college sports on a pay as you go basis is that these values have repeatedly been found to exist, and they are positive. The rest of the assessment is comparing benefits and costs—small benefits can very well outweigh small costs and generate a handsome rate of return. We now turn to that comparison.

THE NET VALUE OF THE
UNIVERSITY INVESTMENT IN COLLEGE SPORTS

Again we hear from Mark Twain, "Few things are harder to put up with than the annoyance of a good example." We offer a few here to make the point on the value of college sports to its university and then follow up with an overview of what the data show more generally about the net value of university investments in college sports. First, let's look across the so-called automatic qualifier (AQ) FBS conferences—the ACC, Big 12, Big East, Big Ten, Pac 10, and SEC. We use the OPE version of the data described in Chapter 2 to identify the top, median, and bottom athletic departments *based on their most recent football revenues* (2010–11) across FBS departments. The three are Texas ($95.7 million), North Carolina ($26.4 million), and Washington State ($9.4 million). Next, we use the USAToday.com data also described in Chapter 2 in order to get the most recent 2010–11 athletic department level data that also include a category "school funds," which includes direct and indirect institutional support. We also use Internet offerings on the size of university operating budgets for the same year. (Wake Forest and Kansas were both smaller than Washington State, but our search did not locate their university budgets.)

The University of Texas budget was about $2.2 billion for 2010–11. The Longhorn's athletic budget was $133.7 million. There was no institutional support according to USAToday.com (and had not been any all the way back to 2005–06). By the USAToday.com version of the data (containing 100 FBS departments), the athletic department at Texas is just 1 of 15 among the AQ conference programs that reported receiving no institutional support at all. University administrators at these schools still receive student aid payments and other values across the university. The USAToday.com report labels student aid payments as "Scholarships." The amount was $8.9 million for Texas in 2010–11. So, before we even get to the consideration of "other values" across the university, the Texas athletic department made a payment to the university that could cover about 10 percent of the university's total utility bill for that year.

At North Carolina, the 2010–11 budget was $2.4 billion. The athletic department budget was $74.3 million. Institutional support was $1.8 million, a truly trivial 0.08 percent of the university budget. Just on student aid payments of $10.3 million, university administrators realized a 472 percent return on their institutional support investment to the athletic department. This was a few hundred thousand dollars more than Carolina received as capital gifts that year. As with Texas, any other values across the university were all just gravy poured over this already luxurious relative return.

The 2010–11 budget for Washington State was $843.7 million. The athletic department budget was $40.6 million, including $9.9 million in institutional support (1.2 percent of the total university budget). About 73 percent of the institutional support came back to the WSU administration in the form of student aid ($7.2 million). For one perspective, in the tough economy over the last few years, it would take about $10.4 million to generate a 5 percent nominal return on the $9.9 million institutional support investment. The other values across the university would need to be about $3.2 million. This does not seem like much to expect, since it would be found in the overall $843.7 million operating budget (about 0.37 percent of that total).

While examples are informative, an overview of the AQ conference departments lends more depth to our conclusions. We point out that the reason for the seemingly low number of 100 programs in the USAToday.com data is that private universities are not required to supply data under FOIA, and a few others are exempted under state law (e.g., Pennsylvania). Since everything we could cross-reference between the USAToday.com data and the OPE data checked out, we are confident in the following observations. There were 54 AQ conference athletic department reports.

The 15 programs that received no institutional support were:

Auburn	LSU	Purdue
Florida State	Nebraska	South Carolina
Georgia	Ohio State	Tennessee
Iowa	Oklahoma	Texas
Kentucky	Penn State	Virginia

The Texas athletic department was actually below the median value of around $9.4 million in scholarships at Oklahoma, and 12 of these 15 programs generated a larger dollar return than Texas. Since there was no institutional support investment for these departments, we can only note the amounts. In the entire group of 15 schools listed just above, the values ran from $8.5 million at South Carolina to $15.1 million at Ohio State. We know of entire academic departments that don't cost this much money to run.

The vast majority of the AQ conference athletic programs, 33 out of the 54, were like North Carolina, receiving institutional support but more than paying it back in terms of just student aid payments to the university. What seems like a hefty percentage return for North Carolina ends up to be well above the median, but 10 AQ conference departments provided even higher percentage returns, just on student aid payment back to the university. The clear outlier was Texas A&M, where $6.9 million in student aid payments compared with just under $10,000 in institutional support; yes, that really is just over a 69,000 percent return! The median was 254.6 percent. Only 8 of these 32 departments returned less than 100 percent—from 7.9 percent at California to 97.6 percent at Maryland. Compared with a reasonable 5 percent return during hard times, all of these programs performed quite well.

That leaves just 6 AQ conference athletic programs that were more like Washington State, meeting some share of the institutional support investment with its student aid payment but needing other values across the university in order to provide a reasonable return. The amounts needed to get to a 5 percent return ranged from $831,913 at Arizona State to $10.9 million at Rutgers, with a median of just over $7.0 million. Without looking up all of these university budgets, we can't say anything definitive, but we suspect that at most a handful of the total number of AQ conference ADs have a bit of explaining to do to their university administrators.

The clear picture is that the top of the FBS heap varies in the way we would expect. University administrators with the most successful athletic departments put next to nothing into their athletic programs, relative to either their university budget or allocations to other departments on campus. In turn, those programs generate extraordinary return to university administrators on their institutional support investment. The bottom of the heap programs generate a lower return, but even very small amounts of "other values," relative to their university operating budgets, generate reasonable returns overall.

But what happens for the rest of the FBS without automatic-bids to the BCS—that is, programs in C-USA, the MAC, Mountain West, Sun Belt, and WAC? As before, we identify the top, median, and bottom of these non-AQ departments based on their most recent football budgets—South Florida, Florida Atlantic, and Arkansas State. (Actually, TCU and Louisiana-Monroe were at the top and bottom, respectively, but TCU apparently did not have to respond to the USAToday.com FOIA request; we could not find the stand-alone budget for Louisiana-Monroe.) Since the reader is familiar with our approach from the foregoing on the AQ conference athletic departments, we're a bit more succinct for the rest of the non-AQ FBS conference programs. We also omit Air Force, because of its unique funding status, leaving 45 programs for assessment.

The athletic departments at both South Florida (Tampa campus only) and Florida Atlantic paid student aid amounts back to the university that swamped institutional support. USF's operating budget was $488.0 million, its athletic budget was $43.5 million, and institutional support was $1.3 million (0.27 percent of the university operating budget). Student aid payments returned $5.1 million to the university, a cool 392 percent return before we even get to the rest of the benefits across the university. The $3.8 million net was enough to run the entire Student Affairs program. FAU's operating budget was $562.7 million, its athletic budget $16.7 million, and institutional support was $2.6 million (0.46 percent of university operations). Student aid payments back to the university of $3.9 million represented a 50 percent return all by themselves. While the $300,000 or so net return seems small, the relative return on the institutional support investment was large by anybody's standards, even before any other value across the rest of the university. And even in absolute terms, it could have covered the foundation expenses for FAU's College of Science. At both of these programs, the other benefits across the rest of the university are just gravy.

Finally, for Arkansas State (just the main Jonesboro campus), the 2010–11 budget was $158.5 million. The athletic budget was $13.4 million. Institutional support was $4.9 million, about 3.1 percent of the university budget. This was a much higher percentage than at any of the other universities listed above at either equity conferences or for the rest of the FBS. The student aid returned to the university was $4.6 million. Thus Arkansas State, at the bottom of the heap of non-AQ conferences, is similar to Washington State at the bottom of the AQ conference heap—both needed the rest of the values across the university to cover the institutional support investment by university administrators. It would take $5.145 million to generate a 5 percent reasonable target return during a recession on the $4.9 million institutional support investment. About $545,000 in other values across the university would do the trick and, again, on a total university budget of $158.5 million, this does not seem a very tall order.

We can also use the USAToday.com data for an overview of all 45 reporting non-AQ FBS athletic departments. Only one department in this group received no institutional support at all. The Toledo athletic department returned $6.8 million anyway, and all other values across the university only sweetened that return. Some 14 of the 45 that did receive university support returned student aid payments that were larger than this amount received. The outlier was the department at North Texas, returning $3.3 million on institutional support of just $116,893 (yes, that's just over 2,700 percent). The rest of the range was from 5.8 percent at Ball State to 255.7 percent at Akron, with a median of 125.6 percent.

The remaining 30 non-AQ departments all needed returns from the other values created across the university to provide a reasonable return on institutional support invested. To get to a 5 percent return, the amounts needed ranged from $545,000 just described at Arkansas State to $24.2 million at Nevada–Las Vegas, with a median of $3.7 million at Louisiana-Lafayette and Texas–El Paso. The number of ADs we suspect are concerned over their current employment is clearly around twice the number feeling the same at AQ programs.

There are obvious conclusions from the foregoing. First, the budgets of athletic departments are large in absolute terms. However, it is not their total budget that matters in trying to consider whether or not athletic departments are a drag on the university. That determination rests with a comparison of the university investment in athletics to the return. Second, university investments in athletics, relative to operating budgets, are puny yet often yield truly solid *relative* returns. The directly measurable dollar payments to the university by the athletic department, labeled student aid, swamp institutional support at top revenue AQ and non-AQ programs, alike, on down through the median programs. The amount of other values across the university that must be generated by athletic programs toward the bottom of the heap, in order to generate a reasonable (we choose 5 percent) return, appears a cinch for most of these programs. However, a very small number of programs probably are falling short of the expectations of their university administration.

All in all, even if some student aid payments back to the university would have existed without the institutional support, student aid payments plus small other values across the university appear to generate enviable returns. The idea that athletic departments are money-losers, and a drag on the university budget, is simply wrong in all but a very few cases. We suspect that even those few cases cannot persist given the highly competitive nature of athletic department administration.

CONCLUSIONS—THE DESTRUCTIVE POWER OF THE MYTH

We finish with our favorite Mark Twain saying, "All you need is ignorance and confidence and the success is sure." From the AP article in the epigraph, we learn the following:

> In Iowa, the Board of Regents voted unanimously in March to order school presidents at Iowa, Iowa State, and Northern Iowa to come up with plans to scrap—or dramatically decrease—such sports subsidies. Campus leaders are expected to report back to the Iowa regents next month.

Note the use of the words "sports subsidies," indicating that the board of regents appears to have swallowed the myth hook, line, and sinker. This call to reduce the presence of athletics on campus is nothing new. Twenty years ago, one of the primary architects of the money-losing athletic department myth, Indiana University English and American studies professor Murray Sperber (1990, p. 348), said this:

If schools stopped pretending that College Sports Inc. is connected to their educational missions, much of the hypocrisy and corruption now associated with college sports would end. Schools could either cut loose their franchises in College Sports Inc. and have them operate as totally separate businesses employing professional athletes, or they could abolish the franchises and return their intercollegiate athletic programs back into genuine student activities. In either situation, schools would unburden themselves of the current academic fraud perpetuated by College Sports Inc.

Ah, the logic flows so cleanly if one just buys into this particularly destructive myth. But the simple fact of the matter is that college athletic departments are not a drag on university budgets. Turning to the relevant economic comparison, the return on the institutional support investment in athletic departments plus other values across the university, values that matter to university administrators, is solid.

Ultimately, the hostiles believe that passing judgment on allocations to the athletic department involves the opportunity cost of spending the money elsewhere on campus. Could be. However, nearly all could find what they might think is superfluous spending in the university budget if they looked hard enough. Furthermore, it is just as important to wonder if the source of those budget dollars—university supporters including state legislatures—would provide the same size budget if allocations to athletics were reduced or eliminated.

Now, it's completely legitimate to argue that college sports have no place in the academic mission on campus. That is the route the University of Chicago has taken. On the other hand, we should realize that other schools, such as Notre Dame, would be very, very different universities without their athletic departments. And it is certainly true that one size does not fit all when it comes to athletic departments and universities. Trying to find out exactly what the academic mission is on campus has been the essence of many discussions that have taken place over the years on many activities on campus (recall the history of the business school arguments presented in Chapter 2). But foisting off a myth that can only bamboozle the less well informed does not facilitate reasonable debate and discussion of an issue. The actual point of busting this myth is to get all of the cards plainly on the table in any future discussion of the place of college sports on campus.

The costs of this myth are truly heinous given that it is students that benefit from participation and many of their fellow students from the enjoyment of sports on campus. All of these returns matter to more people than boosters, usually portrayed as behind-the-scenes, shifty characters that only come out on Saturday, when they don the complete college sports support regalia. College sports matter to the athletes and other students who enjoy them as well. The distortion of investment returns, leading university administrators away from college athletics, seems to pale in comparison.

4 CONFERENCE REVENUE SHARING LEVELS THE FOOTBALL FIELD AND BASKETBALL COURT

INTRODUCTION

Revenue sharing is one of the most misunderstood devices in all of sports. Since the device reallocates revenues from those programs that make the most to those programs that make less, intuition suggests that revenue sharing will allow those that make less a fighting chance. For example, recipients of redirected revenues can buy more coaching talent or spend more in the pursuit of playing talent (including lavish practice facilities). But intuition clearly fails, since recipients don't always do this. Intuition is so strong here that observers don't turn to the device and wonder why it doesn't seem to change balance. Instead, fingers get pointed at revenue sharing recipients. The conclusion is that failure actually to make more balance happen on the field or court is the fault of those who don't spend the money as the designers of the revenue sharing mechanism apparently intended.

Interestingly, there is a large literature showing that this intuition, itself, is just wrong. Indeed, for North American sports, the conclusion is that there really is no reason to believe that the forms of revenue sharing chosen by pro sports leagues and college conferences was ever intended to level the playing field. Revenue sharing instead reduces compensation to players or other owner investments and then redistributes the proceeds to all teams according to the sharing device. To us, the complete absence from any and all discussions of revenue sharing of findings, so well established, smacks of the presence of a myth.

As with the rest of the myths in this book, the power of this myth rests on something that seems intuitive, that sharing revenues should lead to more equal ability to spend on athletics. After all, if you are in the business of winning, then getting more money should lead you to try to win more; revenue sharing means that you will be able to compete more by obtaining better talent. This has been drilled into sports fans forever with the example of the National Football League. Nearly all revenues are shared, and the NFL is highly touted as the most balanced of all leagues.

It ends up, however, that the NFL has been the most competitively balanced of leagues despite changes in its revenue sharing approach over its history. So leveling the playing field doesn't seem to have anything to do with *changing revenue sharing* in the NFL. In addition, competitive imbalance appears impervious to the *introduction of revenue sharing* where it didn't exist in any other pro league as well (Major League Baseball in 1995, for example). So nothing about introducing or changing revenue sharing seems to have anything to do with leveling the playing field.

College sports, however, are different from professional sports in the way that they share revenue. In modern professional sports (except for hockey), owners all pay the same rate and then take equal shares from the pool. College sports, on the other hand, have a history of very unequal revenue sharing policies. While most of the automatic-qualifier conferences (AQ, for short) share equally, a few do not (e.g., the Big 12). And clearly the proceeds from postseason play are not equally distributed to conferences before that. Potentially, then, one could create a revenue sharing policy that helps balance if it can increase the marginal sharing rate more for larger-revenue athletic departments than smaller-revenue programs. However, if we take a close look at the actual sharing, it seems clear that these policies were never designed to help the smaller-revenue programs in the first place.

In college football and men's basketball, revenue sharing simply does not redistribute the money in any way, shape, or form that looks "equal." There are actually three ways revenues are shared in college sports. First, the Bowl Championship Series (or BCS) shares the revenues from its postseason football games. Second, the NCAA shares revenues out of its championships that occur for all of the other sports except FBS football. Third, both of these revenue streams and all of the rest of the revenues—gate and gate related, and TV for the regular season—then end up being shared among the athletic departments in each conference according to their own, different sharing arrangements. Thus, while some teams in a given conference might share equally, the differences between conferences can be very large indeed.

Spilling the beans right up front, postseason revenue distributions by the NCAA and the BCS are large, but they are *far from equally distributed* among any given division in college sports—FBS, Football Championship Series (FCS), and Division I men's basketball (March Madness). So before the conferences even get around to applying their own sharing rules, whether equal sharing or not, they begin with immensely different amounts of money. In those conferences that share unequally, of course, the chance for "equal spending opportunity" is even less. Given that revenue sharing in college sports isn't actually *equal* revenue sharing, it should come as no surprise, then, that the outcome on the field or court is far from balanced. And the data on competitive balance in football and men's basketball back it up.

The myth, then, is worth busting for the same reason that any myth about college sports is worth busting. This destructive myth deflects attention to some other, off-base explanation for imbalance, such as weak management or lack of innovation by athletic directors and poor coaching in athletic departments that fail to compete. Such misdirection plays right into the hands of those that benefit from the status quo. It is not the revenue sharing mechanisms that are at fault; it is that the mechanisms are flawed on purpose, in favor of some college conferences and teams, if what one cares about is enhancing balance on the field or court in college football or men's basketball.

In addition, this underlying revenue imbalance is a primary force behind the most recent episode of conference realignment in the FBS. Now, conferences have changed membership over time and typically for the same reasons—chasing money. When programs left the original Southern Conference in 1933 to form the SEC, or later in 1953 to form the ACC, it was about rules governing postseason play. But the value on the table now, even for the same level of imbalance, is so much larger that more teams are taking the drastic action of changing conferences in order to pursue it. The modern episode of conference jumping has laid waste to conferences such as the Big East that had managed to become competitive enough to be included in the BCS sharing arrangement. This episode is also leaving in a shambles the so-called non-AQ FBS conferences like the Mountain West and the WAC.

We first lay out everything we know about the current sharing arrangements for the BCS, NCAA, and conferences. We then move on to the straightforward conclusion. None of this revenue sharing occurs in any way that can possibly level the playing field (or court, as the case may be). We can't help but phrase revenue sharing as an incentive design issue with an obvious result that there will be no change in competitive balance to follow. Then we take a look at balance in football and men's basketball. Conclusions round out the chapter.

SHARING, SHARING EVERYWHERE . . .

The BCS

While it will go by the wayside in favor of an FBS playoff starting in the 2014–15 season, the BCS remains the focal point for the football postseason until then. It is essential to distinguish the AQ conferences (the ACC, Big East, Big Ten, Big Twelve, Pac 12, and SEC) from the rest. In addition, the AQ conferences are sometimes erroneously referred to as the "BCS conferences." Actually, all eleven FBS conferences (AQ and non-AQ alike), the three football independents—Army, BYU, and Notre Dame—and some FCS conferences share in the BCS results, so technically all are "BCS conferences" in terms of how that organization distributes the revenues it helps to create.

The BCS has an explicit distribution formula. The publicly available BCS sharing scheme goes like this for the season just played (Bowl Championship Series, 2011):

- The share for an automatic qualifier from one of the five non-AQ conferences (that is, a conference without annual automatic qualification) will be approximately $26.4 million—18 percent of the net revenue. (Those conferences have elected to divide the revenue among themselves according to a formula they have devised.)

- If no team from the non-AQ conferences participates, those conferences would receive approximately $13.2 million—9 percent of the net BCS revenue.
- The net share for the automatic-qualifying team from each AQ conference will be approximately $22.3 million.
- The share for each team selected at-large by one of the bowls will be $6.1 million.
- Notre Dame will receive $6.1 million if it participates in a BCS game; its share will be approximately $1.8 million if it does not—1/66th of the net BCS revenue.
- Each FCS conference will receive $250,000.
- If Army, Navy, or BYU becomes an automatic qualifier or is selected at-large, it will receive $6.1 million; if not selected, each will receive $100,000.

The same BCS source claims that the distribution "formula" is guided by the simple principle that conferences in the BCS bowls receive the largest portion of the revenues. You can see where this is going—non-AQ teams rarely make a BCS game, and most of the money goes to those that make it in the first place. Let's look a bit more closely and see how it will all work out for the most recent BCS season, 2012. Since the actual details had not been released at the time of this writing, we fully realize that the actual amounts may end up a bit more or less than stated above. But we should be pretty close once we get to the overall distribution by percentages among all of the recipients.

For the AQ conferences, the champions each appear in a BCS game (National Championship, Fiesta, Orange, Rose, and Sugar) and would earn their conference $22.3 million, for a total of $133.8 million. In addition, four AQ conferences had second teams participate (Virginia Tech in the ACC, Michigan in the Big Ten, Stanford in the Pac-12, and Alabama in the SEC). At $6.1 million each, that's another $24.4 million. The grand total for the AQ conferences would be $158.2 million.

For the rest, no non-AQ conference team played in any of the five BCS games. So the non-AQ conferences would receive $13.2 million to split among all five. Once the BCS gives the non-AQ schools their share, it is divided with the use of a "complicated distribution method" (Smith, 2010) whereby conferences with teams that played in a BCS game get a bigger share than other conferences. Notre Dame did not play in a BCS game, so it would receive $1.8 million. Only eight Division I conferences participate in the FCS (Big Sky, Colonial, Mid-Eastern, Missouri Valley, Ohio Valley, Patriot, Southern, and Southland). At $250,000 each, that's $2.0 million for them. Army, Navy, and BYU would each get $100,000, since none played in a BCS game either, a total of another $300,000. So, the breakdown will be pretty close to the following:

AQ	$158.2 million	90.1%
Non-AQ	$13.2 million	7.5%
FCS	$2.0 million	1.1%
ND	$1.8 million	1.0%
Rest	$0.3 million	0.2%
Total	$175.5 million	100.0%

Again, while the actual dollar amounts await the final 2012 BCS tally, the percentages will surely be spot on. Only 10 percent of the BCS net proceeds get beyond the AQ conferences. Simple-mindedly, but informatively, each group could choose to distribute evenly among its members (they don't, as we get to directly and note above for the non-AQ conferences). Four of the six AQ conferences received $28.4 million each, and the other two $22.3 million. With ten to twelve teams in each, that's $1.9 million for some programs and up to $2.8 million for others. Notre Dame's $1.8 million is quite close to this (and small wonder, since it receives 1/66th of the total and there are 66 programs in all of the AQ conferences, combined). There are 48 programs in the five non-AQ conferences. Equal shares would be about $275,000 (it can be no coincidence that Army, Navy, and BYU get around $100,000 each for not even appearing). So AQ programs get in the neighborhood of ten times the return from the BCS formula that non-AQ programs do.

We know that things will be just a bit rosier for non-AQ FBS conferences when they do get a team in a BCS game, as they have in the recent past, or for BYU or Notre Dame. But we think the inequality of the BCS distribution result is obvious no matter which way you cut it. More important, from the perspective of sports mythology, the BCS distribution system was designed that way on purpose. The BCS is composed of the FBS conference commissioners and, essentially, ESPN. ESPN knows where the money is, and the conference commissioners know where they want the money to go. The money is almost completely loaded to the AQ FBS conferences. There is no way in the world that the BCS revenue sharing rules, so heavily weighted toward the AQ conferences, can close the gap between the AQ conferences, the non-AQ conferences, and on down to the FCS conferences.

The NCAA (March Madness)

For their 2011–12 budget, the NCAA (ncaa.org, "Finances") anticipated $777 million ($700 million from TV and Marketing Rights Fees, $69.5 million from other championships revenue, and $7.5 million from sales, fees, and services). The major expense items are "Division Specific Expenses" of $597.5 million (Division I Distribution and Championships, and allocations to Divisions II and III). The balance is "Association-Wide Expenses" of $150.9 million (Services to Student Athletes, Membership, Educational Communications, Legal and Insurance, and General and Administrative). Some $28.6 million is left in Reserve. So about 77 percent of NCAA receipts go back to members, and 23 percent stays in with the NCAA in Indianapolis.

But we can look a bit behind the scenes at how the NCAA distribution actually occurs. There are eight categories of distribution (any amounts noted are for 2010–11):

- Academic Enhancement: Each Division I institution gets $66,000 to use for academic support service for student-athletes.
- Basketball Fund: Monies are distributed based on a six-year rolling period. Institutions receive one unit for each appearance, not including the championship game. Each unit is worth $239,664.
- Conference Grants: Each conference receives $261,744, less an agreed-upon amount remitted to the regional officiating advisors program. Funds must be used to improve officiating, enhance conference compliance and enforcement programs, drug abuse educa-

tion, enhancement of opportunities for ethnic minorities, and development of gambling education programs.

- Grant-in-Aid Fund: Each school's share is determined based on the number of grants-in-aid awarded.
- Special Assistance Fund: This fund assists student-athletes with financial needs that arise in conjunction with participation in intercollegiate athletics or enrollment in an academic curriculum, or that recognize academic achievement.
- Sports Sponsorship Fund: Each school's share is determined based on the number of varsity sports sponsored. Points begin with the Division I required fourteenth sport, and $30,091 is distributed for each sport above thirteen.
- Student-Athlete Opportunity Fund: The fund is distributed by conferences based on the formula used for sports sponsorship and grants-in-aid. Money is to be used to meet student-athlete financial needs of an emergency or essential nature for which other financial aid is not available.
- Supplemental Support Fund: This fund supports campus-based initiatives designed to foster student-athlete academic success at eligible, limited-resource institutions.

So, at least on the face of it, only half of these funds in the NCAA distribution are "flat rate" and equal for all conferences. The rest all appear to favor successful participation in March Madness, schools with the largest number of grants-in-aid, and schools with the largest number of varsity sports in excess of the required fourteen. Again, it doesn't seem very likely that this type of differential distribution can close the gap between the already "haves" and "have nots."

Conferences

Conference sharing rules cover regular season gate/concessions and conference TV (including their own conference network TV), the conference football championship game and men's championship basketball tournament, the BCS and NCAA distributions just described, and all other non-

BCS bowl appearances. Three of the six AQ conferences—the ACC, Big Ten, and SEC—have adopted an "All for one, and one for all!" approach to these revenues. Equal sharing occurs net of expenses such as travel and hosting at bowl games (all bowl games, not just BCS games). The Big 12, Big East, and the Pac-12 explicitly do not have full sharing of these revenues, although popular reports are that the Pac-12 is moving in that direction soon.

Revenue sharing has been unequal in the Big 12 since its predecessor, Big 8, had to "dicker" on revenue sharing in its bid to get Texas and (ironically) Texas A&M to join in 1998, to the demise of the Southwest Conference. The Big 8 members had to dicker because the (then) Pac-10 was courting Texas, and the SEC—as it successfully did just last year—was courting A&M. The result clearly bought Texas into the Big 12, and it should come as no surprise that the Longhorns did quite well in the move. There was equal revenue sharing *except for TV revenue.* Half of TV revenue is shared equally, but the other half is distributed according to the number of times an athletic department's football and men's basketball teams were on TV. This especially favors the strongest athletic departments, such as Texas, because nonconference games earn twice as much as conference games from broadcasters. The strongest teams both appear more and have a fully televised slate of nonconference games. Again, intuition suggests that this sharing system cannot do anything to enhance balance.

Most recently, conflict arose in the Big 12 over The Longhorn Network (or TLN), the individual athletic department network of the University of Texas. TLN will generate a fee of $15 million per year from ESPN. ESPN also has promised that another $12 million goes to the remaining Big 12 teams. The resulting contribution to further inequality in the Big 12 should be apparent.

In the Big East, the revenue from the BCS, NCAA, and conference TV contract is dispersed as follows. Each conference member receives one conference dispersal for football and another for men's basketball. For football (basketball), conference TV money is put in the revenue pool along with money from bowl partners (the NCAA) before it is distributed to conference members. Some adjustments are made to the final distribution to each member, based on the number of national television appearances, bowl travel expenses, and the prominence of the bowl game. Since nearly nothing is equally shared, inequality is greater in the Big East than in the Big 12. Again, we stress that it is not revenue sharing, per se, that fails. It is that revenue sharing designs simply are not what many think they are.

Finally, the Pac-12 Conference represents perhaps the most instructive example on unequal sharing, but mainly in impact rather than design, because of the extreme economic differences in member schools, from Washington State to USC. We note at the outset that the new commissioner, Larry Scott, recognizes this issue and is pushing the conference toward more equal revenue sharing. However, at present, the Pac-12 athletic departments share postseason revenues equally, net of expenses, but departs dramatically from this path with the rest of revenues.

First, there is unequal gate revenue sharing. To see the inequality generated here, it is best to start with the gate sharing that occurs for rivalry games—for example, the Civil War between Oregon and Oregon State, or the Apple Cup between Washington and Washington State. Rivalry game gate revenues are split evenly. For a feel of just how these rules drive revenue disparity, the University of Washington received just under $450,000 for its 2008 rivalry game at Washington State University. But at the preceding rivalry game, held at the University of Washington in 2007, WSU received just over $1 million. So at the gate in the Pac-12, larger-revenue hosts enjoy a distinct revenue advantage.

The Pac-12 handles gate sharing for the rest of its games with a "guarantee" system. In recent history, the visitor receives $200,000 (there is a minimum promise of $125,000, but that seldom occurs). It is easy to see that, rather than $1 million when it played the Apple Cup in Seattle, the Washington State Cougars would have received only $250,000 if rivalry game receipts were not shared equally. Thus it is strictly the home team share that dominates gate revenue disparity in the conference.

Turning to TV revenues, first, none of the revenue earned by the participating Pac-12 team is shared with the rest of the conference for *nonconference games*; the participating team keeps its entire share. Second, for conference games, 40.5 percent is shared evenly. But the athletic departments of the teams that actually appear on TV split the remaining 59.5 percent. So, if all twelve teams appear on TV (as is typically the case), but a given team appears n_i of the N total broadcast conference games, that athletic department gets $(n_i/N \times 59.5) + (1/12 \times 40.5)$ as their share. Thus, since better teams appear much more often (have a much higher "n_i"), they get the highest share of conference TV money. The Pac-12 TV sharing system clearly can't do much of anything to enhance competitive balance because revenues are never shared much in the first place.

BUT NOT A DROP TO DRINK

The most reasonable assessment of the devices in the preceding section is as follows. BCS distributions are decidedly lopsided in favor of just six AQ conferences in the FBS—the ACC, Big 12, Big East, Big Ten, Pac-12, and SEC. NCAA distributions are decidedly lopsided in favor of conferences whose teams already make it deep into the March Madness basketball tournament, with large athletic departments in terms of number of grants-in-aid and number of varsity sports. If this sounds like most of the FBS AQ conferences again, BINGO! In this section, we document the extent to which this really is true. In addition, we go ahead and observe the resulting imbalance on the field in football and on the court in men's basketball.

The BCS

The distributions for the 2011 BCS game season are at ncaa.org and shown in Table 4.1. For later comparison, we identify the AQ FBS conferences, the non-AQ FBS conferences, and then the combined category of FCS conferences for football and the "mid-majors" for men's basketball (the rest of Division I).

The inequality revealed by these data is clear. The first jump, from the FCS conferences to the non-AQ FBS conferences, represents a doubling in average value per conference. And the jump to the average value per AQ FBS conference is five times the average value per non-AQ conference. The imbalance is predicted by the BCS sharing rules, and the actual imbalance shown in Table 4.1 is quite large. If there is anything approaching a system that can level the playing field among athletic departments in a conference,

TABLE 4.1. *BCS and NCAA Distributions, 2010–11*

Conference	BCS Distn.	%	NCAA Distn.	%
AQ FBS Conferences				
ACC	$22,515,095	12.4%	$38,724,762	8.1%
Big 10	$28,515,095	15.7%	$42,691,368	8.9%
Big 12	$22,515,095	12.4%	$35,949,380	7.5%
Big East	$22,515,095	12.4%	$44,074,162	9.2%
Pac 10	$28,515,095	15.7%	$33,586,746	7.0%
SEC	$28,515,095	15.7%	$33,671,053	7.0%
AQ FBS Conf. Ave.	$25,515,095		$38,116,245	
AQ FBS Conf. Total	$153,090,570	84.2%	$228,697,471	47.8%
Non-AQ FBS Conferences				
Mountain West	$12,734,033	7.0%	$16,702,798	3.5%
Mid-American	$2,633,683	1.4%	$15,839,969	3.3%
Sun Belt	$1,933,567	1.1%	$12,925,836	2.7%
C-USA	$3,333,800	1.8%	$20,445,493	4.3%
Western Athletic	$4,033,917	2.2%	$11,798,464	2.5%
Non-AQ FBS Ave.	$4,933,800		$15,542,512	
Non-AQ FBS Total	$24,669,000	13.6%	$77,712,560	16.3%
Independents				
UND	$1,702,742	0.9%		
Army	$100,000	0.1%		
Navy	$100,000	0.1%		
Indeps. Total	$1,902,742	1.0%	$1,346,937	0.3%
FCS/Mid-Major Conferences	$2,250,000	1.2%	$170,198,032	35.6%
FCS/Mid-Majors Ave.	$250,000		$8,509,902	
Grand Total	$181,912,312	100.0%	$477,955,000	100.0%

Source: Compiled from data at ncaa.org.
Notes: There were nine FCS conferences listed and twenty Mid-Majors.

or between AQ FBS conferences, non-AQ FBS conferences, or the FCS in any of this postseason distribution data we can't find it, either in form or outcome.

The NCAA (March Madness)

The NCAA distributed a total of $478 million in 2010–11 (data going back five years or so reveal about the same story), and, from Figure 4.1, it's a bit tough to see how any of these distribution rules have either much of anything to do with any education mission on the part of student-athletes, or any sense of leveling either the football field or the basketball court. On any

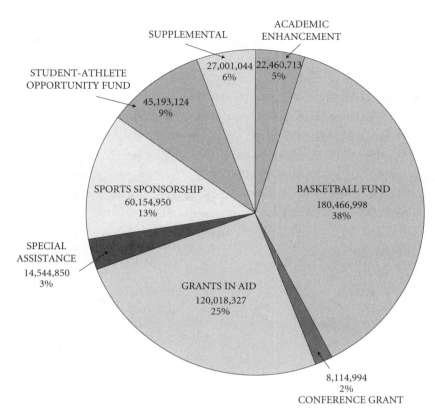

FIG. 4.1. NCAA Distributions by Fund, 2010–11. Created from data at ncaa.org.

educational mission, it's just sheer volume. Being generous according to the definitions in the last section, possibly academically oriented funds—Academic Enhancement, Special Assistance, Student Athlete Opportunity, and Supplemental Support—are only 23 percent of the total. The remaining 77 percent is all about the athletic departments in college sports conferences.

Turning to leveling sporting opportunity, let's look behind the scenes to the conference level. (We couldn't get any deeper because, as the rules state above, much of the distribution to individual programs depends on conference revenue sharing and other rules in the first place.) The data are also in Table 4.1. The inequality in the NCAA distributions is even larger than the inequality in the BCS distributions.

The six AQ FBS conferences received $228.7 million (Range: $33.6 million for the Pac-10 to $44.1 million for the Big East). That's $38.1 million per conference and 48 percent of the total $478 million that the NCAA distributed that year. The rest of the FBS, five conferences, received $77.7 million (Range: $11.8 for the WAC to $20.4 million for C-USA). That's $15.5 million per conference and another 16 percent of the total. So, in total, the FBS conferences received 64 percent of the total distribution. The twenty mid-majors received $170.2 million ($4.6 million for the Atlantic Sun to $15.4 million for the Atlantic 10), a paltry $8.5 million per conference and 36 percent of the total. All in all, the data show practically a doubling of average conference values at each of the three levels, from $8.5 million for the mid-majors, to $15.5 million for the rest of the FBS, to $38.1 million for the AQ FBS conferences.

Again, this type of increase across the AQ FBS conferences, the non-AQ FBS conferences, and the FCS is only slightly less than in the case of the BCS distributions. However, we hasten to add that the NCAA distributions, in total, swamp the BCS distributions. So the doubling from the mid-majors to the non-AQ FBS conferences is a jump from $8.5 million to $15.5 million, while the corresponding BCS doubling was from $250,000 to $4.9 million. And the doubling from the non-AQ FBS to the AQ FBS conferences is a jump from $15.5 million to $38.1 million, while the corresponding BCS jump was from $4.9 million to $25.5 million. Just over twice $15.5 million is a lot more than five times $4.9 million.

Conferences

All distributions by AQ FBS conferences are in Table 4.2, with non-AQ C-USA included for comparison. In order to make more sense of these distributions, we also include the following information on conference television contracts (Hoover, 2011):

- ACC: 12 years, $1.86 billion, ESPN (through 2024).
- Big East: 6 years, $200 million, ABC/ESPN (through 2013).
- Big Ten: 10 years, $1 billion, ABC/ESPN (through 2016); 25 years, +$2.8 billion, Big Ten Network (through 2032).

TABLE 4.2. *Conference Distributions, 2010–11*

Conf./Schools	Distn.	Conf./Schools	Distn.	Conf./Schools	Distn.	Conf./Schools	Distn.
ACC		*Big 12*		*Big East*		*C-USA*	
BC	12.3	Baylor	10.2	Cincinnati	8.8	E. Carolina	4.2
Clemson	12	Colorado	8.3	Connecticut	9.7	Houston	3.9
Duke	11.1	Iowa St.	8.9	Louisville	8	Marshall	3.2
FSU	12	Kansas	12.1	Pittsburgh	8.8	Memphis	3.3
Georgia Tech	13.4	Kansas St.	9.4	Rutgers	8.6	Rice	2.7
NC State	10.9	Missouri	10.4	S. Florida	8.1	SMU	3.8
Maryland	11	Nebraska	9.3	Syracuse	7.5	S. Miss.	3.2
Miami (FL)	12.1	Oklahoma	11.2	W. Virginia	10.4	Tulane	2.6
N. Carolina	12	Oklahoma St.	10.7	Total Distn.	69.9	UAB	3.3
Virginia	11	Texas	12			C. Florida	3.1
Virginia Tech	12	Texas A&M	9.3			UTEP	3.4
Wake	10.8	Texas Tech	9.7			Tulsa	3
Total Distn.	140.6	Total Distn.	121.5			Total Distn.	39.7
TR	158.2	TR	148.9	TR	113.3	TR	50
Diff	17.6	Diff	27.4	Diff	43.4	Diff	10.3
Gini	0.034	Gini	0.064	Gini	0.049	Gini	0.075
FB/MBkB TV	77.6	FB/MBkB TV	72.5	FB/MBkB TV	35.6	FB/MBkB TV	15.8
Big Ten		*Pac-10*		*SEC*			
Illinois	20	Arizona	9.4	Alabama	18.2		
Indiana	20	Arizona St.	8	Arkansas	18.2		
Iowa	20	California	8.9	Auburn	18.4		
Michigan	20	Oregon	10.9	Florida	18.3		
Michigan St.	20.1	Oregon St.	8.9	Georgia	18.2		
Minnesota	20.1	Stanford	9.6	Kentucky	18.3		
Northwestern	20	UCLA	7.8	LSU	18.2		
Ohio St.	20.1	USC	11	Mississippi	18.2		
Penn St.	20	Washington	7.5	Mississippi St.	18.2		
Purdue	20.1	Washington St.	6.5	S. Carolina	18.4		
Wisconsin	20.1	Total Distn.	88.5	Tennessee	18.3		
Total Distn.	220.5			Vanderbilt	18.3		
				Total Distn.	219.2		
TR	232.4	TR	101.6	TR	244.4		
Diff	11.9	Diff	13.1	Diff	25.2		
Gini	0.001	Gini	0.088	Gini	0.002		
FB/MBkB TV	—	FB/MBkB TV	58.2	FB/MBkB TV	153		

Source: Condensed from data in Hoover (2011).

- Big 12: 13 years, $1.17 billion, Fox (through 2025); 8 years, $480 million, ABC/ESPN (through 2016)
- Pac-12: 12 years, $2.7 billion, Fox/ABC/ESPN (through 2024).
- SEC: 15 years, $2.25 billion, ESPN (through 2024); 15 years, $825 million, CBS (through 2024).

These distributions include everything according to conference rules including BCS and NCAA distributions. For example, ACC total revenues were $158.2 million. After conference TV of $77.6 million, that leaves $80.6 million for all other conference distributions—namely, gate and related revenue, plus NCAA and BCS distributions. The sum of NCAA and BCS distributions was $61.2 million that year, leaving $19.4 million for gate and related distributions. The Big Ten results from the same calculation are about twice as much in terms of gate and related revenue distributions, about $41.2 million. The TV contract data give about $120 million that year, $100 million from ESPN and $20 million from its own BTN.

Sharing in the Big Ten is more equal than in any other conference. Literally every entry for every athletic department is identical at $20 million, and the variation is simply appearance allowances (travel and hosting during the postseason). But to drive the point home with a bit more precision, Table 4.2 also shows Gini coefficients for inequality by conference. A Gini coefficient of zero means a completely equal distribution, while a Gini coefficient of one is completely unequal (all of the revenue going to just one athletic department).

The first things to notice is that the Gini coefficients in all of the AQ FBS conferences pale in comparison to our usual notions of "inequality." The most recent Gini coefficient for income in the United States was calculated at about 0.4 for the mid-2000s, and none of the conference revenue Gini coefficients are anywhere near that. Inequality is always a relative thing, and situation-specific to boot, but those that decry massive inequality *within* a given college sports conference are quite clearly overplaying their hand.

The second thing to notice in Table 4.2 is that the Gini coefficients are much lower in the three conferences that share more fully than in the other three. Indeed, the Big Ten (0.001) and SEC (0.002) have essentially achieved complete revenue equality. The remaining three AQ FBS conferences have monstrous inequality compared with the "Three Musketeer" conferences: (then) Pac-10 (0.088) > Big 12 (0.064) > Big East (0.049). The Big East is 44 percent more unequal than the worst of the other three, the ACC (0.034). Note that C-USA, our non-AQ FBS conference example, which does not share revenues equally, manages to look more like the (then) Pac-10 in terms of inequality than it does any other conference.

The upshot of all of this is that the difference in BCS and NCAA revenues across AQ FBS conferences, non-AQ FBS conferences, and on down to the FCS, coincides with quite unequal outcomes in terms of the level of revenues across these conferences. Further, many conferences then also fail to share revenues equally, and additional revenue inequality results. The ADs at schools like USC in the most unequal revenue Pac-12, or Texas in the *next* most unequal revenue Big 12, must hum that old George Gershwin song as they stroll across campus:

Nice work if you can get it
And you can get it—if you try.
Who could ask for anything more?

The Data on Competitive Imbalance in Football and Men's Basketball

Turning to the imbalanced outcomes on the field in football requires nothing more than reference to other works. In their manuscript under preparation, Fort and his longtime colleague, retired California Institute of Technology economist James Quirk, have a chapter on competitive balance in college football. Looking at a variety of balance concepts, they begin by finding that end-of-season conference-schedule winning percentages have always been unbalanced in the FBS. While unbalanced, however, most of the AQ conferences are more balanced than the most balanced pro league, the NFL. In addition, reaching far back into conference history, there were episodes of relatively high balance for some conferences in the past, but typically modern conferences are more so. Turning to another balance concept, the AQ conferences simply own other conferences in terms of nonconference winning percentages. On yet another, conference championship outcomes, the least balance of all is revealed. Championships are dramatically unbalanced in every conference, with two or three teams holding distinct majorities of the results. By the "dynasty" concept of imbalance, winning over consecutive seasons, college football may be the most dynastic of any North American sport. Finally, access to the postseason has been completely dominated by a small number of AQ teams. This was just as true prior to the BCS, when polls determined the mythical "national champion." Since all of this history of imbalance has occurred when some conferences had no sharing, or when some conferences introduced sharing, it appears that redistributing revenues really hasn't had any effect in terms of equal outcomes on the field.

And what do the data show on balance in basketball on the court? First, there is the actual outcome by seeding position in the tournament. Since the playoff grew to sixty-four teams in 1985:

- #1 seed is 112–0 against #16 seed (100%).
- #2 seed is 106–6 against #15 seed (94.6%).
- #3 seed is 96–16 against #14 seed (85.7%).
- #4 seed is 88–24 against #13 seed (78.6%).
- #5 seed is 74–38 against #12 seed (66.1%).
- #6 seed is 74–38 against #11 seed (66.1%).
- #7 seed is 67–45 against #10 seed (59.8%).
- #8 seed is 54–58 against #9 seed (48.2%).

And we all know who the higher seeds are in the tournament. Then there is also the additional evidence on how difficult it is for smaller schools, nearly always seeded low, to advance in the tournament. Again, since 1985:

- No #16 seed has ever defeated a #1 seed.
- A #15 seed has reached the round of 32 six times.
- A #14 seed has reached the Sweet Sixteen twice; not since 1997.
- A #12 seed has reached the Elite Eight once (2002).
- A #11 seed has reached the final four three times.
- A #8 seed has reached the championship game twice (1985, 2011).
- A #8 seed has won the championship once (1985).

Chances for any real advancement by the lowest seeds are truly de minimis. While it is somewhat easier for a mid-major to get competitive in basketball, it just doesn't happen that often. Even giving the Butlers and George Masons their due, the scales weigh almost exclusively in favor of the higher distribution conferences, mostly the FBS.

CONCLUSIONS—IF BALANCE MATTERED TO THOSE IN CHARGE, WE'D SEE MORE BALANCE

Our overriding conclusion is that the sharing of revenues, from the BCS, NCAA, and the rest of conference sharing, is designed in a way that guarantees the continuation of an uneven football field or basketball court. The data show that imbalanced outcomes on the field and court are, indeed, the result. The AQ FBS conferences make out like Casanova.

Interestingly, imbalance appears ameliorated in the SEC and the Big Ten, where things are literally distributed for all intents and purposes completely equally. But this masks that the amounts that they share are heavily imbalanced from the outset by the extreme imbalance in both NCAA and BCS distributions. Nothing about revenue sharing has anything to do with it, and the result is the nearly total imbalance that is actually witnessed on the court and on the football field, less so but still so in the SEC and Big Ten. In addition, looking just at the SEC or Big Ten ignores the widespread imbalance between conferences, especially between the AQ FBS conferences, non-AQ FBS conferences, and the FCS in football, and mid-majors in basketball.

At the outset, we stated why we think this myth was worth busting. The myth deflects attention to off-base explanations for imbalance such as weak management or lack of innovation by athletic directors and poor coaching. Losing potential critics in that morass protects those that currently benefit quite dramatically from the present distribution of college sports revenues.

But we return to what we think is now the most destructive result of this myth. The underlying revenue imbalance is behind the most recent wave of conference realignment, a process that simply cherry-picks in an effort at least to lock up this revenue inequality into the future and, at most, to increase it. Here is the football version of this domino effect wrought by dramatic revenue inequality.

In rapid succession, the Big East lost Miami and Virginia Tech to the bigger money ACC, and Temple went independent for a short time after the 2004 regular season. Boston College also went to the ACC after the 2005 season. In response, worrying about holding on to its BCS status, the Big East added an independent and lesser conference athletic departments to get back to eight teams—independent Connecticut, and previous C-USA members Cincinnati, Louisville, and South Florida.

Army had already left C-USA the season before, and TCU left for the Mountain West in 2005. To get back to ten teams for 2005, C-USA added Central Florida, Marshall, Rice, SMU, UTEP, and Tulsa. All of these schools moved up from FCS status. C-USA had made strides to be competitive, but then was pushed back as the last domino in the chain.

But that wasn't the end of it by a long shot. Syracuse and Pittsburgh are leaving the Big East in 2013 for the bigger money ACC. It also appears, as court proceedings are winding down, that West Virginia is leaving the Big East in 2013 again for the bigger money Big 12. In response, the Big East is hitting lesser conferences to bolster its membership—for 2013, Central Florida, Houston, Memphis, and SMU from C-USA, and Boise State and San Diego State from the Mountain West. Independent Navy will join the Big East in 2015.

With all due respect to fans of their remaining teams, C-USA and the Mountain West have simply been reduced to rubble. C-USA has made no statements about its future and looks to be stuck at eight teams. The Mountain West will add Fresno State, Nevada, and Hawaii from the WAC to get back to eight teams for 2012. Indeed, the Mountain West and Conference-USA recently discussed simply joining forces with what they have left, what would be the first sixteen-team conference.

The WAC, by the way, demonstrates the bottom end of the domino effect. It has become an eight-team conference by moving down a notch to the FCS. University of Texas-Arlington, University of Texas–San Antonio, and Texas State–San Marcos will join the WAC for the 2012 season. From the Big East on down to the FCS, this is all driven by the pursuit of revenues unevenly distributed according to BCS, NCAA, and some conference "revenue sharing."

So, quite bluntly, the type of revenue sharing employed in college sports simply does not do what many people believe that it does—namely, level the playing field or basketball court. But if people think it should, and as they stew and argue over why it hasn't, some programs make moves to lock up the returns to college sports. This chasing of the same revenues is, in the short run, purely wasteful behavior; it could all be redistributed after the fact without any impact on the current power structure of college football and men's basketball. But in the long run it also proves detrimental to long-standing fan interests. As economists, we cannot say outright that this is on net costly to society, since it involves a comparison of lost satisfaction to historic rivalry fans and gained satisfaction for national champion fans. But we can point out that it is true, nonetheless. In the pursuit of ever-growing TV money, fan loyalty to geographic, historical rivalry is sacrificed to nationwide lust for national championships.

5 PAY-FOR-PLAY WILL BANKRUPT COLLEGE ATHLETIC DEPARTMENTS

If indeed we were to pay our student-athletes in those sports [he means high-revenue sports], we probably would eliminate maybe 22 of the other sports that we have at the University of Minnesota because only three of them generate enough money to pay for themselves.

— University of Minnesota Athletic Director Joel Maturi (*Twin Cities Pioneer Press*, www.twincities.com, April 24, 2009)

INTRODUCTION

Frankly, we are agnostic on whether athletes should be paid more than their grant-in-aid along with the rest of the future values they choose to generate with their education and training at their university. We also feel that arguments about how to do it, if ever, put the cart before the horse because they are based on a lack of understanding of college sport finances (Joe Nocera [2011] at the *New York Times* is just the latest in a long ongoing discussion). But we are not so noncommittal on arguments used to defend the current system of player compensation (in addition to what we will show as weak logic in the epigraph, see NCAA counsel Donald Remy's defense [2012] at NCAA.org).

As in the epigraph, the unwavering response to calls for pay-for-play by athletic directors is that they are barely breaking even, so where will the money come from? The answer is that the money is already there, but it takes a book chapter to demonstrate that this is true. The power of this myth comes from the same misunderstanding about the relationship between university administrators and their athletic department apparent in the other myths we have examined about college sports. The power of this

myth also is reinforced by general feelings about the special treatment perceived for athletes. When pressed, opponents of pay-for-play turn to other
"fairness" arguments—for example, won't different athletes be paid different amounts (especially women athletes)?

In the economic actuality of it, if conference presidents and athletic directors are already maximizing revenues (and how can anyone argue that
they are not doing so?), then athletes are already generating the money that
is the source of their current grant-in-aid payment and would be the source
of any increased payment. The trick to busting this myth is to determine
where athletic directors are currently spending this money that is generated
by athletes. The answer is patently obvious.

If players were to be paid something like the amounts that they generate
for their athletic departments, then coaches' salaries, administrator salaries,
and spending on facilities where athletes play and study separately from the
rest of the student body all would fall. And they would fall proportionately
to revenue generated across all athletic departments. Under the current play
for grant-in-aid scheme, the value of inputs to the college sports process
that help recruit players—such as coaches and athletic facilities—are inflated. This is because the recruitment process ultimately generates what
the fans pay to see—namely, talent on the field. Coaches and facilities bring
in the players that generate the revenue. From society's perspective, then,
this leads to inefficient allocation of revenues by the athletic department
director toward coaches' pay, administrator pay, and facilities.

Some argue that all athletic revenue is derived from the brand of the
university, a view we'll discuss later. However, we have never seen anybody
deny that premiere college athletes are worth a great deal to the university.
We have already discussed these values in previous chapters—direct payment of student aid (grants-in-aid) back to the university, plus other values
across the rest of the university, such as improved student admissions and
donations. While these effects might be relatively small considering the size
of total university budgets for some large universities, they can still be in the
millions of dollars.

Furthermore, there is a clear relationship between athletic success and
athletic department revenues. So while the exact number is not always easy

to estimate, superstar athletes in college are at least in the same ballpark with professional athletes in terms of revenue generated. In fact, University of North Texas economists Robert W. Brown and R. Todd Jewell (2004, 2006) find that some of the top college athletes are easily worth millions of dollars in revenue to athletic departments, *over and above the cost of their grants-in-aid.*

So pay-for-play cannot possibly bankrupt college athletic departments. And it surprises us that the self-serving part of the myth, when it is foisted by athletic directors and coaches whose pay is higher than it would otherwise be because of the amateur requirement, is not a featured item in all pay-for-play discussions. Remember, we are talking about coaches and ADs that make millions. Fort documents in his textbook *Sports Economics Third Edition* that Alabama football coach Nick Saban, at $4.2 million, made 35.4 times more than Alabama governor Riley in 2007.

As we stated at the outset, we are agnostic on whether players should be paid more than their grant-in-aid plus the other values that accrue to their education and training. Instead, we hope that this chapter informs the debate over the disposition of revenue generated at universities. If ever there were a sincere, meaningful debate on the disposition of the money generated by college sports, perhaps the outcome would still be that it does not go to the athletes themselves. But wading through the myth that rearranging current athletic department spending would bankrupt those departments might send the money to other worthy causes at the university besides coaches' pay and facilities dedicated to varsity athletes.

Unless Mark Twain was right, previous chapters have helped readers understand the relationship between university administrators and their athletic departments. We use that understanding as our launching pad in what follows. First and foremost, it is quite clear that athletic directors do not have to find some other revenue source in order to cover a pay-for-play alternative. The money is already there. Second, bringing economic logic to bear, it is easy to take on the rest of the arguments against pay-for-play—competitive balance, impacts on women's sports, differential pay, the infinite value of a free education, and an even more exploitative recruitment process.

THE MONEY IS ALREADY THERE

Let's start from an indisputable point made in previous chapters. College athletes generate millions of dollars for their athletic departments and their universities. Nobody will pay to watch administrators administer, or coaches coach. Coaches and administrators do make play more valuable to fans. The best coaches recruit top prospects, which is worth millions to the university. But, again, that is a marginal value over and above the millions that the player will generate. Athletic directors create, promote, and manage events. But there would be no money generated at all without the athletes. Athletic directors collect the value generated from boosters, sponsors, media providers, and the university administration through institutional support. Under current amateur rules, athletes see some of it in the form of a grant-in-aid (tuition, room, board, and books).

Thus, all of the money that can be generated by athletes is, indeed, being generated and collected. So it is quite true that there is no more money to be had if there were a regime change dictating payment to athletes in addition to their grant-in-aid. Glossed over in that observation, however, is that the amateur requirement reduces actual compensation to some college athletes to a level that is below the revenues they generate for the athletic department and the university at large. This is especially true for star players. As a result of the amateur requirement, athletic directors keep a pot of money generated by star athletes. It is this pot of money that represents the most that athletes could possibly be paid, since it is the money they generate in the first place. If pay-for-play were ordered tomorrow across all athletic departments, not one of them would go bankrupt. Athletic directors would simply redistribute this pot back toward the athletes, paying coaches less and spending less on facilities (we get to so-called nonrevenue men's sports and women's sports later).

Currently, that pot of money goes to coaches' salaries, administrator salaries, and separate facilities for varsity athletes (both athletic and academic), in part because those are the things that attract the best recruits. So if pay-for-play became the order of the day, where will the money come from? The answer is that it would simply be redistributed from coaches, administrators, and facilities right back to the athletes. With or without pay-for-play, millions of dollars are generated by players, and somebody is going to collect it. How it is spent currently rests with athletic directors, beholden to their university administrators, under the amateur requirement they enforce upon themselves through membership in the NCAA. It can't go to the players, so ADs redirect it according to their own ambitions, related directly to their programs. If it were otherwise decided that the money couldn't go as ADs now choose to spend it, and it were still collected, then the money generated by athletes would go somewhere else in the athletic department (lagging gender equity comes to mind) or somewhere else in the university at large (perhaps the general scholarship fund).

With just this much under our belt, the myth that pay-for-play will bankrupt college athletic departments is busted. The myth of the "money-losing athletic department" in Chapter 3 is used to lead the casual observer to believe that there is no money available to pay athletes over and above their current grant-in-aid. But the economic truth of it is that a pot of money is already denied to athletes under the amateur requirement and spent elsewhere in the athletic department. Pay-for-play would simply lead to sending that pot of money back to athletes, reducing pay to coaches and administrators, and reducing facilities spending.

Some have argued that in fact the athletes really are not worth very much. The argument goes that college sports fans are very loyal and will spend money regardless of who is on the field—that is, they root for uniforms. The purported evidence that gives credence to this is that some athletic programs show no variation in revenues over time; some programs appear to sell out tickets regardless of whether the team is winning or losing. Football programs at places such as the University of Nebraska or the University of Michigan see little difference in attendance in good years and bad.

We make three points here. The first is simply prima facie; apparently college athletes do have a large value, since colleges put a lot of effort into getting top recruits. If it really didn't matter, they wouldn't. This leads directly to the actual fact of the matter, our second point—anybody can point to a few teams that do sell out regardless of team performance, but they should also admit that these are the exception, and typically good teams that still have winning records. A "bad" year at Nebraska or Michigan is when they have to settle for anything less than a BCS bowl. They are just not as good as fans expect.

Michigan is a perfect case in point. Historical myopia suggests that any bunch in the Maize and Blue will draw; Michigan has the longest streak of attendance exceeding 100,000 per game in college football, even through a rough three years under Rich Rodriguez. But that actually is a recent phenomenon tied to success during the successive tenures of the last three coaches, Bo Schembechler (194-48-5, 0.796; AP ranked 19 of 21 years, 1969–89), Gary Moeller (44-13-3, 0.758; AP ranked 5 of 8 years, 1990–94), and Lloyd Carr (122-40-0, 0.753; AP ranked 12 of 13 years, 1995–2007). Attendance during the immediately preceding Bump Elliot years (51-42-2, 0.547; AP ranked 2 of 10 years, 1959–68), on the heels of the success of Bennie Oosterbaan (63-33-4; AP ranked 7 of 11 years, 1948–58), was actually atrocious.

Fans of FBS teams outside the elite know for a fact that attendance varies dramatically with team fortunes. We can remember sitting in the "crowd" at Washington State Cougar football games both before Dennis Erickson (12-10-1, 0.543, AP ranked 1 of 2 years, 1987–88) and after Mike Price (83-78-0, 0.515; AP ranked 5 of 14 years, 1989–2002), when they quit playing the "guess the crowd size" game. There was no reason to guess, because you could count them. So most schools see a severe drop in revenues when athletic programs are unsuccessful. Even when currently premier programs slip so can their attendance, and even the teams that do continue to sell out will see a drop in merchandise sales and TV appeal. Furthermore, the programs that sell out with bad teams cannot do so indefinitely. Athletic directors at these schools understand that there are very tangible long-run consequences of fielding a bad team. Eventually bad teams lead to a decrease in merchandise sales, television contracts, and attendance.

Finally, if it really is all about the university brand name, and players do not have much value to the university, then the market will determine that they will not be paid much. Of course, there is little to fear from pay-for-play if that is true. It seems unlikely that university officials are so dumb that they would pay athletes exorbitant amounts if in fact the athletes bring in little revenue. After all, if leagues like the National Lacrosse League can pay their players, then sports like college football could pay their players a pittance and be financially viable if it really were the case that college athletes generated little value.

COMPETITIVE BALANCE

A common argument against paying players is that it will ruin competitive balance—the biggest, most successful athletic departments have the most money, and they would simply buy the best players. But this is all relative, since these departments already get almost all of the best players now. So the question is not if the biggest departments will get the best players (they clearly do already), but rather if the bigger departments have an *even easier* time of it under pay-for-play.

Long ago, economist Simon Rottenberg pointed out that the distribution of talent in baseball wouldn't change just because players, rather than owners, receive a larger share of the revenues generated through league play. His discussion was about free agency, but the logic is just as clear for college sports. Currently, grants-in-aid are larger at more expensive, prestigious schools that also happen to have a concentration of the best football programs. Thus, in addition to grooming their talent "for the next level," there is already differential compensation that players consider when choosing those athletic departments where they can make the most of their athletic talent. If the amateur requirement were removed, pay would also rise to higher levels at these departments than at the rest. Why would any of the athletes find it in their best interest to move to another department? Rottenberg's logic (he didn't address college sports) is that they wouldn't. So not much would really change in terms of competitive balance.

Just to be clear, an alteration in the structure of pay certainly does matter to the parties that are being paid; players might rejoice, while coaches and administrators would rail against the decision. But the implication is that competitive balance wouldn't change. Under the current system the larger departments are still spending more to attract athletes by building better facilities and hiring better coaches. The larger departments can typically offer future athletes the ability to play in better conferences, practice in better facilities, and get a better education. Small departments have no chance to alter their competitive position on these dimensions. If athletes could be paid directly, there would be less money going to facilities and coaches, but *the proportion* of money being spent between large and small departments should not change much.

If anything, there is an outside chance that there would be more balance! There could be a change in how athletes make decisions, based on direct pay as opposed to amenities such as facilities and coaches. Paying athletes might be the only way that small schools can attract *some* of the best athletes. The bottom line is that balance might improve a bit, and there is really no reason to expect it would get worse, but the effect should be very minimal.

IMPACTS ON WOMEN'S SPORTS

A common pay-for-play fear is that the ability of football and men's basketball to support the rest would be reduced. If one believes that paying college athletes will bankrupt the athletic department, or at the very least put an even bigger strain on the athletic department's financial situation, then perhaps low revenue-generating women's sports will be the first to get cut. There might be similar effects on other low-revenue men's sports such as wrestling or baseball.

However, since the impacts will largely be a transfer from coaches and facilities to players, there would be little impact on other sports. Regardless of whether athletes are paid or not, decisions should be made based on all of the benefits and costs associated with each team. If it makes sense to have a women's gymnastics team with no pay-for-play, then is should make sense to have a women's gymnastics team with pay-for-play. The value of the women's basketball team to the athletic department does not change because money needs to be redirected from coaches and administrators toward football players.

One additional feature also is typically ignored in the argument that women's sports will be under the knife in a pay-for-play world. Federal and state laws require athletic departments to ensure gender equity. The penalty is threatened federal spending and lengthy, expensive, and embarrassing legal action. Thus the value of women's sports is much higher than the revenues they generate, and the cost of cutting them is much higher than ever has been admitted.

By the way, the same argument goes for lower-revenue men's sports without the legal kicker. If it makes sense to have a men's wrestling team without pay-for-play, it makes sense to have one with pay-for-play. Redirecting money from coaches and administrators to football has nothing to do with the value of the wrestling team. Indeed, as grant-in-aid costs, spent disproportionately on football and men's basketball, have risen over time, there has been no widespread move to reduce sports participation.

DIFFERENTIAL PAY

Athletes in lower-revenue sports may generate less for the athletic department directly, and the university at large, than other athletes. In the usual competitive market way, they would make less than athletes that generate more. This is a problem for those that want all athletes to be paid the same amount. As we all know, this issue is not unique to college sports in the fantasy world of pay-for-play we discuss here. Instead, it is a basic fairness argument about how people are paid in general. The sentiment is perhaps more impactful in college sports since universities are typically held to impossible standards as beacons of social progress. Ernie Chambers, a former Nebraska state senator that favors paying all athletes equally, captured the essence of it for college players (Aaronson, 2010): "It's not more for a skill position, less for a lineman, more for an offensive player, less for a defensive player." Even though he favors paying the athletes, he sees problems with differentiating the pay, going on to say, "They're all in it together. And whether they ride the bench or ride the shoulders as conquering heroes after the game, they all get paid the same amount."

Of course, those that do not hold the equal pay paradigm may ask, "Why not 'more for a skill position, less for a lineman'"? If that is what the market would decide, adherents to this view would see no problem with different pay for different college athletes. A backup kicker probably does not contribute as much, in terms of additional revenues, as the starting quarterback, and the differences between sports are even more severe. Turning to professional sports, athletes are "all in it together," but they don't get paid the same.

As always, fairness is subjective. After all, across the rest of the university, professors, administrators, and coaches are not paid the same. Further, scholarships of different amounts are offered to different potential students. In fact, we do not think of any industry where all workers are paid the same. Aside from differences driven by gender and race discrimination, this is a generally accepted outcome. Besides, even if you want a fairer way of paying athletes, you at least want them to be paid—and that is the central pay-for-play issue.

INFINITE VALUE OF A FREE EDUCATION

Some critics of pay-for-play finally reach the end of their rope, throw their hands in the air, and cry, "Enough already! They're already being given a free education!" (or logically equivalent, training for the next level). And the truly evocative version usually throws in "a *priceless* free education." It's true that grants-in-aid are all about the educational side of the student-athlete. Having their tuition, room and board, and books covered allows them the chance to earn future income and enjoy the nonmonetary quality of life of a college graduate. But used as an argument against pay-for-play, this has at least three shortcomings.

First, what's so "free" about this "free education"? The life of a scholarship athlete has been cast by Gary Funk in *Major Violation* (and observed by your authors, first-hand over the years) as equivalent to that of students who must work full-time in order to pay their way through school. In addition to their course load in pursuit of their degree, all spend the rest of their waking hours working on their sports, 24/7/365. As another interesting aspect of how people think about college sports, this is viewed as commendable for the athlete and despicable for the coaches that require it. Other classmates with full-time jobs also are viewed as commendable, but their bosses are not vilified for the requirements put on these students. Anyway, at least from the student-athlete perspective, there is nothing free about their education.

The second shortcoming is that the argument takes as given that *all* athletes value the educational opportunity in the first place. Even the casual observer knows that this is true for some athletes but not all athletes. While this irritates some people, the preferences of those athletes that are only in it for the sports opportunity cannot be invalidated just because some people think they should value it more. Some may judge this as a fatal flaw in college athletics, but, as it stands, that is just the way it is. For these athletes, compensation in the form of educational opportunity is worth little. In fact, for all students, athletes and their classmates, the value of an education is an entirely subjective exercise. It follows then that for all students receiving them, athletes and their classmates, they are the only persons who can know the value of their individual scholarships. And if you think that a college education is "priceless," think again. If the price of tuition increased 20 percent, some sizable portion of the general student population that could still afford the higher price would still not pay it.

This word "priceless" often leads to astonishing judgments by those wielding it. Take the case of the college athletes that leave school early to take their shot at the pros. They are simply assessing the value of staying in school, including both the enhancement to their nonsport and sports earnings plus any quality-of-life values, versus moving on to the usually short-term but high return at the pro level. In fact, Jason Winfree and Eastern Washington University economist Christopher Molitor (2007) show that an astonishing percentage of baseball players make their college decisions based on expected lifetime earnings. Whether they value their education highly or not, often the size of pro returns swamps staying one more year. And, a propos one of the most basic logical components in economics, it is unfair to judge the decisions of athletes *after the fact* if they should not work out. At the point in time that they make their decision, there is clearly a price of continuing on with their college education. And that price is the lost income of their pro shot.

There is certainly nothing wrong with some people placing a value of "priceless" on education. However, it becomes a problem when those values are imposed on others in order to make the case that they should not be paid. After all, even if the benefit of an education were infinite, the cost is still the price of tuition plus the opportunity cost of the student's time. So it is difficult, and a bit hypocritical, to claim that the value given to the athlete is infinite when the university has literally put a price tag on it. Surely it is the case that some athletes are not generating revenue in excess of tuition, but it is also surely the case that some athletes are generating much more revenue than their tuition bill. The bottom line is that most of us would not be happy if our employer used our paycheck to send us to school or as an extracted payment for the on-the-job training we obtain.

The third shortcoming is that even the people making the argument would not want it to apply to them. Just ask people making this argument if they would be willing to accept less than the competitive outcome for themselves. That is, would they be willing to accept a world where they must take less than they are contributing to the value of the firm in which they work? Most would cry foul. But that is exactly what they are pushing onto student-athletes with their argument that a free education is enough compensation. Some of those athletes contribute more than the dollar value of their grant-in-aid compensation. Arguing that the grant-in-aid is enough is just a value judgment, and a hypocritical one at that.

RECRUITMENT PROCESS

Some have argued that one drawback of paying college athletes is that it might lead to an even more exploitive recruiting process. As it stands now, colleges are becoming increasingly competitive in signing high school recruits. Two years ago, USC accepted a commitment from an eighth-grade quarterback, and this year LSU and Washington offered scholarships to eighth-grade youngsters (Sherman, 2012). This leads some to worry that with actual signing money waved in their eyes, parents of young athletes will offer them up at an even younger age, robbing them of even more of their childhood. This seems completely backward to us, especially since it is already happening without pay-for-play.

As it stands now, college coaches enjoy both a program building value and a direct monetary value from recruiting. For the former, recruiting a strong athlete makes a better team. For the latter, recruiting a strong athlete generates a higher revenue value for the athletic department. Under the amateur requirement, the athletic department keeps that value over and above the grant-in-aid. Part of that net value goes to the coach. Under pay-for-play, that portion going to the coach would go back to the player. Since the value of the players *to the coach* would be reduced, so is the value of intense recruiting, and that activity should be reduced.

Related to this point is that much of the policing of colleges and universities by the NCAA would be superfluous under pay-for-play. As with any enforcement issue, making something legal reduces enforcement costs by definition. A whole host of so-called sleazy practices would go away. For example, college basketball head coaches sometimes hire the relative of a prized recruit as an assistant coach. Under pay-for-play, if players choose to put part of the value that would otherwise go to them in the hands of a relative, that would be up to them. Of course, these by-products of pay-for-play are only attractive in the sense that pay-for-play would eliminate the amateur aspect of college sports in the first place.

CONCLUSIONS—SHOULD COLLEGE ATHLETES BE PAID?

One seemingly reasonable argument against pay-for-play is that it would change the nature of play; fans would perceive it to be professional, just like the pro sports leagues in North America. The implication, typically unstated, is that the value of college sports would fall. And it might. But this is really just a value judgment disguised as an argument: The amateur version of college sports is somehow fair or otherwise desirable, and the claim follows directly from this assertion that any other form would be worth less. So the deciding issue is not the differential value that might ensue, but what is more desirable in the first place. This is the realm of value judgment that also governs the question of whether college athletes should be paid more than their grant-in-aid.

Paternalistic justifications are of the same variety. Some might argue that athletes just don't know the value of their education very well, especially the nonmonetary values of good citizenship. Some might believe that college athletes are too young to know what to do with all the money they would make under pay-for-play. But young people in other lucrative entertainment industries are not viewed the same way, and not since the demise of the "studio contract" have there been anything akin to restrictions on their pay.

Economics is not the realm of dueling value judgments. Economists speaking from their own value judgment position might voice their opinions. Some might say that college sports are already viewed by fans as highly professional, and the damage done by pay-for-play won't be significant. Some might say that paternalistic justifications are overblown. After all, we are talking about (for the most part) legal adults responsible for every single one of their other choices. In addition, it is all well and good to try to protect young people, but we don't protect them from criticism on the field, sometimes to the point where they are humiliated in front of national TV audiences. But these are all just opinions, not economic logic or reasoning.

The best economists can do is to illustrate the effects of different economic conditions or policy choices. So economics cannot answer the question of whether college athletes should be paid. Instead, we can address the "what if" question: What if pay-for-play is instituted? Our first finding is that pay-for-play will not bankrupt college athletics departments. The values generated by college athletes that would constitute their additional pay are already being spent by athletic directors on coaches' salaries, administrator salaries, and facilities. Pay-for-play would just send that money back to athletes.

In addition, we are able to address the common arguments against pay-for-play, most of which follow from the "bankruptcy" argument. Pay-for-play won't harm competitive balance. There is no reason that pay-for-play will harm women's sports (or men's lower-revenue sports). If pay-for-play operates in an economically competitive fashion, differential pay should result. The so-called free education is enough argument misses the boat because there is nothing free about it, and the argument really is just imposing a value judgment, somewhat hypocritically, on athletes. Finally, rather than increasing the intensity of recruiting, pay-for-play should reduce recruiting intensity.

We end with our opening—we are agnostic on whether players should be paid more than their grant-in-aid. But we are far from noncommittal on the myth being foisted on fans and the general public. It is certainly one's right to believe that college athletes should simply not be paid more than their grant-in-aid (if at all!), but both the value to those espousing the view and the ramifications of such a view should also be made plain. On the former, it is no accident that those foisting the myth are also those who earn very high return if it is believed—athletic directors and college coaches. It would be naive indeed to ignore that the entire machinery of the NCAA has been brought to bear to see to it that the amateur requirement is maintained.

On the latter, the myth that pay-for-play will bankrupt athletic departments is used to justify player compensation restrictions. While this fairness issue is important, we think, there is also something missed by focusing on fairness only. From society's perspective, the myth leads to overinvestment by athletic directors in coaches' pay and facilities relative to their actual values to the university. If resources are not to be wasted, people should understand that the result of not allowing pay-for-play is that it inflates the salaries of other employees in the athletic department and results in more spending on facilities.

This brings to the fore the question of what to do with the money generated by college sports. Perhaps a sincere debate on the question would generate the result that athletes continue on with just their grant-in-aid. But busting the myth that pay-for-play will bankrupt athletic departments would shed new light on such a debate. It might even send the money to other worthy causes at the university besides coaches' pay and facilities dedicated to varsity athletes.

And remember that we seldom hear from the players that don't make it big. There are thousands of former players that generated thousands, if not millions, of dollars for their alma mater and never really saw any tangible benefit. Injuries may have precluded the big payoff for some, while others simply never made the cut at the next level. It is true that there are amenities that are associated with being a college athlete. That may be a good reason not to pity college athletes, but it seems to us a weak reason to allow a large part of the revenues they generate to go to administrators and coaches.

6 TITLE IX COMPLIANCE MUST COME AT THE COST OF MEN'S PARTICIPATION

INTRODUCTION

Critics of Title IX argue that some men's sports are cut to satisfy its requirements of more equal participation opportunities for women. This belief is based on an assumed "zero sum budgeting" and a bit of arithmetic. First, cutting a men's sport frees money to spend on women's sports. Second, for the same number of women's sports, a decrease in the number of men's sports makes access look more equal. Under this belief, the executioner's ax is ready to swing on men's wrestling, tennis, gymnastics, swimming, and track.

The examples cited include the following. The University of Kansas athletic department cut men's swimming and tennis to stay in the black, saving about $600,000 per year and reducing participation by fifty male athletes (Lee, 2001). Among the reasons cited for the cuts were increasing scholarship costs, a 115 percent increase in team travel costs for the other sports, and increases in coaches' and administrators' salaries. The Kansas athletic department also noted that the cuts were made in order to meet gender equity requirements. The same logic was pronounced over the elimination of baseball at Northern Illinois (Watson, 2009). Most recently, the University of Delaware announced that it was cutting men's track because it feared that it would not be able to meet the requirements of Title IX in the future, even though it was about to add women's golf (Thomas, 2011a). Irony of ironies, some of the threatened men's track team members filed a complaint with the Office of Civil Rights (which oversees Title IX), claiming discrimination. According to the author:

Delaware is one of dozens of universities that have eliminated low-profile men's teams like wrestling, gymnastics and swimming in an effort, the universities say, to comply with Title IX, the federal law that bans sex discrimination in education.

But dueling anecdotes from some of the "dozens of universities" suggest that something isn't quite right with this belief. First, take the case of James Madison University. Effective July 1, 2007, the athletic department cut seven men's sports *and three women's sports*, stating flatly that the cuts were made for the sake of Title IX compliance (Brady, 2007). But clearly no women's sports had to be cut if it was solely about equal access; seven men's sports relative to three for women goes quite overboard, and immediately criticism arose that the AD was just shifting money from women's sports *and men's sports* to football and men's basketball. Second, there is the case of Ohio University. The 2007 season was the last for men's indoor track and field, men's outdoor track and field, men's swimming, and *women's lacrosse* for the same reasons—budget balancing and Title IX compliance (Znidar, 2007). Once again, note the imbalance of it and the fact that cutting a women's sport wasn't required for Title IX compliance.

Even more interesting, except for an acknowledgment that they were driven partly by Title IX considerations, the massive cuts just occurring at Maryland do not fit the bill. Four men's sports and two women's sports were cut (the Department of Education does not recognize the other "sport" that was cut, competitive acrobatics and tumbling, originally added to the Maryland offering under the name "Cheer") (Giannotto, 2012). Again, this is entirely overboard from the Title IX perspective and, again, no women's sports needed to take the fall for Title IX compliance. The simple fact of it is that everybody recognized that the Maryland athletic department was headed for a $17 million deficit by 2017, and these are the cuts that met the university-mandated balanced budget by 2015. By the way, the reason for the deficits was a dramatic fall in football and men's basketball revenue, so naturally one would reduce . . . Nope! Not football and men's basketball but other men's sports—swimming, tennis, cross-country, and indoor track—plus women's swimming and water polo.

So, simply by example, on the one hand some would have it that Title

IX compliance must come at the cost of men's sports. Athletic departments have typically been break-even propositions, financially. While nowhere does Title IX require equal spending, it is one of the criteria often referred to and, on top of that, if an AD is to try to create equal opportuntiy, then funding has to be found. So cut men's sports, move the money to women's sports, and that's how it goes. All well and good, except for the fact that this type of financial rearrangement cannot explain the cases at James Madison, Ohio, or Maryland.

In addition, there are other options open to ADs, some reasonable and one a bit sneaky. The reasonble other options comprise the bulk of our argument in the rest of the chapter. The sneakier option includes simply inflating female participation at nearly no cost. Katie Thomas (2011b), writing for the *New York Times*, documents how a few athletic directors have increased the number of spots but not the actual participation of women; squad sizes are increased with athletes that will never actually be competitive with scholarship athletes. Apparently, there are also "loopholes" that allow ADs to report some *male* practice players as female participants.

So, examples hardly uniformly support the view that Title IX compliance must come at the cost of men's participation. In addition, there are other options employed by ADs and others that are not even put on the table by ADs in order to comply. So it's a myth. The understanding we have developed in preceding chapters of the relationship between university administrators and the athletic department shows how this myth is perpetrated. ADs simply have discretion over their budgets. In schools where there is no university support, this discretion is complete. In schools where there is university support, the discretion also involves money coming from the university. So, actually, complying with any demand, as a result of fiscal exigency or federal law such as Title IX, is a discretionary act. And discretion in this case is against some men's *and women's* sports. It doesn't *have to be these sports*, but that's the choice that ADs clearly are making.

The myth is easily busted, but before we get there, let's remember an important thing. People use outcomes to bolster their beliefs and to change policy to be consistent with those beliefs. If one is hostile to gender equity, so that Title IX is a target, critics will use anything to do battle. If one wishes to do battle against Title IX, so be it. But that should be done on the basis of whether it is a good idea or not. That college sports resources are rearranged from men's sports to women's sports is the whole idea. Arguing that Title IX fails because it does so is a bit silly. Just listen to it—Title IX dictates that resources go from men's sports to women's sports, but Title IX fails because resources are going from men's sports to women's sports.

The rearrangements dictated by Title IX remedy what society has proclaimed through law as an inefficient allocation of resources engendered by discrimination. So spending is too high on all of the other areas in the athletic department and too low on women's sports, from the perspective of the law of the land. Rather than argue against Title IX because it is actually doing what it was intended to, critics would be more believable if they just took Title IX straight on. For example, it seems that fans prefer men's sports, most of the time, by attendance, viewing, and by spending. Further, survey data suggest that women are less interested in playing sports than the originators of Title IX might have thought. But the popularity of women's sports and arguments about the validity of Title IX are not our point. Given that Title IX exists, the question is how ADs have dealt with it and why they have chosen the methods we observe.

Now for the myth busting. The choice to reduce sports offerings rather than to rearrange spending away from the actual beneficiaries of gender bias—namely, overspending on men's sports, athletic directors, coaches, and facilities—is made by ADs. But as one would expect, given the incentive facing ADs, the entire array of possible spending that could be cut is never put on the table. It is extremely interesting that AD salaries, coaches' salaries, increases in football spending from increased revenue generated by that sport, or spending on facilities primarily for men's sports never seem to make it into the discussion of where to find money for Title IX compliance. Thus, Title IX compliance could come from other spending areas and not just reduced spending on men's sports. So men's sports do not necessarily have to be cut in the first place. Indirectly, ADs demonstrate that this is true when they cut women's sports as well as men's, as in the cases of James Madison, Ohio, and Maryland.

In addition, university administrators are complicitous in this outcome, since they accept the student aid payments from the athletic department (grants-in-aid) and enjoy other benefits created primarily by football and basketball and also benefit, relatively, when minor men's sports are cut. Typically, Americans view universities as a bastion of fairness (especially gender fairness), and yet university administrators do not engage their ADs over their decisions to cut men's and women's sports. As a result, it is equally interesting that university administrators do not pitch in for the sake of the law of the land. They can do so by directing ADs to make other choices or by reducing their take from the athletic department and dictating that it be spent in the name of gender equity.

The myth is particularly destructive because it pits men's and women's sports against each other, and the impacts on women athletes and the efficient allocation of revenues by athletic department directors are swept aside in the wave of emotion, both pro and con Title IX. The myth is also a back door ploy by gender equity critics against Title IX, rather than against the choices made at universities in the face of the law. Of all places, the myth casts universities as a seething battleground over society's perception of the fair distribution of resources and access for women in sports.

BACKGROUND

What is this Title IX that creates all the fuss? Title IX of the Educational Amendments of 1972 states, "No person in the United States shall, on the basis of sex, be excluded from participation in, or denied the benefits of, or be subjected to discrimination under any educational program or activity receiving Federal financial assistance." Because almost all schools receive federal funds, Title IX applies to nearly all education institutions. Title IX recognizes that discrimination can be about access as much as it can be about pay or hiring.

Compliance can be tested in any of three ways, coined the "three-pronged test of compliance":

1. Providing athletic participation opportunities so that participation opportunities for men and women are "substantially proportionate" to their respective undergraduate enrollment. OR

2. Demonstrate a history and continuing practice of program expansion that is responsive to the developing interests and abilities of the under-represented sex (typically female). OR

3. Full and effective accommodation of the interest and ability of its female students even where there are disproportionately fewer females than males participating in sports.

Spending parity isn't required under Title IX, but rearranging resources toward women's sports will be one of the ways that improvement will be generated under the three-pronged test.

Three things are quite clear concerning relative spending. First, the amount of money spent on football swamps all other considerations. But so do football revenues. This gives rise to the setting for our earlier myth that men's revenue sports pay for the rest of the sports. Second, in terms of revenues generated, women's sports pale in comparison. Third, ADs spend the most money on men's sports. The logic appears to be that sports that make the money get to spend the money.

Even thirty years after the passage of Title IX, equity remains elusive. Inequality has evolved over a long time, and very well established interest groups like the way that money has traditionally been spent. Boosters, athletic directors, and coaches all are doing quite nicely under the traditional arrangement, thank you. So are university administrators when you come right down to it. Student aid paid back to the university (grants-in-aid) in the millions and the other benefits across the rest of campus all go to them. It should come as no surprise that the shriek from the athletic department is clearly audible, and protests by university presidents are barely audible, when gender equity crusaders make the scene.

Addressing the main economic argument against Title IX clarifies everything. That argument is simple: Where will the money come from? ADs argue that they barely break even as it is, and that (in most places) only after university support is included. Therefore, to pay for gender equity, either nonrevenue men's programs will have to suffer or revenues will have to come out of men's revenue sports, primarily football. The compound part of the argument goes that diverting money from football could so weaken the ability of the football program to continue to prosper and subsidize other sports that all of the sports at any college could be worse off.

BUT HERE'S THE TRUTH OF IT

The facts are completely against this argument. First, while it's true that athletic departments typically break even, their revenues at the median and at the top have grown considerably and constantly since the late 1960s, when the NCAA began keeping track (recall the presentation in our chapter on the arms race). So it is a bit disingenuous to paint any picture of a fixed revenue pie for college sports. It's also true that costs have risen, but remember that is the job of the AD—to spend all of the money that comes in. And where that money is spent across the athletic department is at the discretion of the AD.

Second, football and men's basketball actually generate enough revenue to cover all of the rest of the sports in only a very few athletic departments. We went through this in our chapter busting the myth that football and men's basketball generate enough revenue surpluses to pay for the rest of the athletic department. It simply is not true and, thus, pulls one of the foundations out from under those foisting this myth that men's programs must be cut to meet Title IX. Typically, the men's programs that are cut did not make enough money to cover their own operating costs in the first place.

But to make an important point quite clearly, let's go ahead and suppose that Title IX had granted immunity to men's sports from its inception (it didn't, but suppose it did). Under this fantasy, all amounts to fund gender equity would have to come from "somewhere else." Where could that somewhere else be? The answer is, of course, the "other spending" that we just saw, and a hefty bit of "other spending" is on salaries, recruiting, event management, and facilities. We expect all of these to be somewhat bloated because of the fact that athletes are not paid. In addition, the university takes the student aid payments on all athletes. The sum of these is easily the few million dollars needed to fund gender equity.

The basic understanding of athletic department budgeting and spending used in previous chapters serves us well here. Athletic departments do not really break even, because they adjust their budgets to spend any excesses within budget periods. The money to fund gender equity is already there in the athletic department and in the student aid sent from the AD back to university administrators.

But let's return to the fantasy that men's sports are untouchable for gender equity purposes. If discrimination has reduced investment in women's sports below the amount preferred by those taxpayers supporting Title IX, then there may have been overinvestment in other areas in these departments. Equalizing the resources devoted to men and women will just reduce these overpayments. So there is no reason to leave men's sports untouched in the first place, and part of the point of Title IX is to alter this past overinvestment in men's sports that may have occurred in the past.

Now, we would be poor economists indeed if we thought that current beneficiaries of the pre–Title IX college sports funding model would throw off their old ways. It is perfectly predictable that those who currently benefit from past distortions in spending will not be happy about reallocations that will come out of their paychecks. As always, a true myth serves the purposes of identifiable beneficiaries, and it is easy to see why they have adopted the protectionist approach to men's sports.

Perhaps that most compelling evidence of this protectionist behavior comes when we switch gears away from Title IX, toward the threat of the general recession to athletic departments, and still find it as the AD's "go to" response. Take the episode at Stanford University; faced with unexpected budget shortfalls resulting from the recent recession, they planned to cut $5 million in 2009 (the Maryland situation described in the introduction would do just as well, but let's spread the coverage around a bit more for the sake of generality). The analysis in what follows is based on the OPE data familiar to our readers from the chapter on athletics as a drag on the university budget.

Stanford's athletic department spending in 2009 was about $75 million, so the $5 million represents about a 7 percent cut. Men's spending was $27.4 million and women's spending was $16.5 million. The highest spending for women was $2.5 million on basketball. Stanford spent $14.9 million on football and $14 million on all other women's sports combined. "Spending on athletes" in men's basketball was $681,000. As we understand it, this was the student aid that went back to the university. Total spending on men's basketball was $3.3 million. The balance is salaries, travel, recruiting, and the like. For football, the numbers were $2.8 million on athletes and $14.9 million total. Basketball topped the list for spending on women players at

$420,000, while total spending was $2.5 million. No other women's sport showed spending on athletes even equal to the $390,000 spent on men's baseball, so we'll disregard them in what follows except to point out that the Stanford AD would have had to cut quite a few sports, men's and/or women's, at $390,000 or less to get to $5 million.

Suppose Stanford's AD holds participation dear and looks only at spending that is not on athletes. The difference between spending on athletes and the total spending on their sports was: $3.3 million – $681,000 = $2.6 million for men's basketball; $14.9 million – $2.8 million = $12.1 million for football, and $2.5 million – $420,000 = $2.1 million for women's basketball. But that's just spending by sport. The rest of the Stanford athletic department spending not allocated by sport was $30.9 million (including, it must be pointed out, the AD's own salary). So without even touching money spent on athletes, the total was ($2.6 + $12.1 + $2.1 + $30.9) = $47.7 million.

Of course, we all understand that the AD had to pay his coaches. And some of the money from football (but not as much as most people think) spilled over to other sports. So the full $47.7 million was not really on the table. But it was the starting point for considering budget cuts that preserve participation.

Proportionally speaking, $3.3 million on men's basketball (not on athletes) was just over 4 percent of total athletic department spending. Some $14.9 million on football (not on athletes) was just under 20 percent of total spending. And $2.1 million on women's basketball (not on athletes) was under 3 percent of total spending. The rest of the budget, $30.9 million, was just over 41 percent of total spending. In total then, these items represented 68 percentage points. If the cuts were allocated according to their spending proportions of the 68 total points (e.g., men's basketball was 4/68 = 6 percent of the $5 million cut), then the cuts would have been as follows: $300,000 in men's basketball, $1.45 million in football, $200,000 in women's basketball, and $3 million for the rest of the budget. Rather than a general 7 percent cut, if the entire $5 million were allocated only across all spending not on athletes, the cut rises to just under 10 percent for each target area. There is easily $5 million in the Stanford athletic department budget in other areas besides athlete participation.

The first thing out of everybody's mouth is cutting staff and student participation and the subsequent leap to arguments over Title IX. But, again, let's parse this out. As suggested by the data presented above, staff and participation cuts would have to be deep indeed. On the other hand, why isn't any of the rest of the budget being discussed? These seem insightful observations before dragging the Title IX baggage into the discussion.

There are two reasons why ADs respond as they do. First, outside observers seldom track the relative availability of funds to cut. It didn't take us long to research and write this chapter, but, apparently, the relative benefits and costs of generating the type of information in this chapter see few doing the same. Without such an effort, however, it is missed that cutting staff and athlete participation goes hand-in-hand with preserving the salaries of revenue-generating coaches and the AD, as well as the program-enhancing investment in facilities.

The second reason ADs respond as they do is that college sports are structured to produce that result! If the point is to maximize revenues, then all players are treated as inputs to that process. Those less valuable at the margin when revenues fall—namely, athletes in the programs that generate less revenue—go by the wayside. Nonrevenue sports that are more about excellence in participation for the sake of that participation are now obviously and predictably expendable. And in the current structure where massive rents generated by players accrue to mobile inputs such as coaches, don't expect any single AD to commit suicide by doing anything else, like cutting coaches' salaries. To expect different behavior by ADs is to miss the point that college sports are, literally, big business.

We come then to the final rallying cry against equalizing the resources devoted to men's and women's sports—any individual AD is correct to point out that unilaterally moving "other spending" to women's sports will just force them to reduce the quality of their program because the coach will leave and their facilities will fall behind. In econmic jargon, any single AD pursuing such an approach is committing suicide because mobile resources will flee.

Now, college sports are interesting and different from pro sports in many ways. One of them is that university administrators and ADs have designed collective action organizations to handle just this type of issue—namely, conferences and the NCAA. So there is a clear and obvious (to us) response to this last rallying cry—coordinated action is the solution. If members of the NCAA can structure that organization to enforce the amateur requirement, they also can structure that organization to enforce gender equity across the entirety of college sports. In the name of that most sacred of NCAA precepts, institutional control, and partly out of the necessity to protect federal research funding in jeopardy if bad decisions are made about cutting women's sports, university administrators can act through the NCAA to explicitly tax the salaries of coaches and ADs and facility spending. Not in the collusive way they did against assistant coaches a while ago, running afoul of the antitrust laws to the tune of $67 million (*Law et. Al. v. NCAA*, 1998), but in a genuine way that requires gender equity advancement without reducing partcipation by men. (By the way, if members of the NCAA, universities all, truly are committed to Title IX, university administrators can also contribute to the cause by waiving athletic department student aid payments for athletes as long as the AD documents that those funds are spent enhancing women's sports.)

We are not so naive as to believe that the NCAA membership will actually do this. But that failure changes nothing about the analysis. We simply put this finishing touch to our job of undoing all arguments that somehow men's sports must be sacrificed to Title IX compliance. The basis in fact is not there, all of the arguments supporting this myth fall apart, and there is a clear way to get it done. Acting in unison through the NCAA to comply with Title IX is not an act of antitrust. It is an act of trust, a united act of compliance with the law of the land.

CONCLUSION—A FABLE FOR THE AGES ("THE MONEY IS ALREADY THERE")

We frame our conclusion in the form of a little fable. Once upon a time . . .

* * *

The rulers of the Kingdom of College Sports issued a royal decree that made all college athletes amateurs. The grand viziers, the athletic directors, formed together to enforce this decree. This did nothing to change the vast millions generated by college athletes, but it did make it illegal for the athletes themselves to receive the full benefit they help create. The royalty kept almost all of the money for themselves. They were wise enough to know that a happy serf is a productive serf, so they provided education and room and board for the athletes. But this was very cheap, compared with the actual amount that the athletes generated. And of course a bit had to go to the viziers.

The rest was spent on what the royals liked best—generating the best athletics program they could afford. Lavish training facilities for athletes were maintained so that the best would always want to participate. And, of course, under such a system the royalty found that much of the spoil went right back out again to retain the best coaches. But there was plenty of money generated for an opulent lifestyle for themselves as well.

Fans loved the athletic competition dearly. But they loved men's competition the most. And they paid the most for that kind of competition. So men's competition is just what the royalty gave to the people. And coaches of the most popular men's sports enjoyed the most opulent lifestyle of all. There were lesser men's sports, as well. And there were some fans who enjoyed women's sports (and one of the members of the royalty had an athletic daughter), so there was some, but relatively less well financed, women's athletics.

And so it went for many years. Men participated at higher rates and levels than women. Coaches of very popular men's sports lived lavishly, and the royals kept the rest. But one black day, invaders from a distant land appeared on the horizon. They were ruled by a strange religion that dictated equal opportunity for men and women. The invaders had swept through all of the neighboring kingdoms, spreading gender equity wherever they went. And now they lay siege to the Kingdom of College Sports, offering a zealous ultimatum. Either the Kingdom of College Sports would implement gender equity in athletics or face annihilation.

Since the invaders had proven themselves in battle, the royalty begged time to comply. And it was granted. Some of the royals, either in fear or sympathy, simply begged the rest to pour out their treasury into gender equity. Once enough had been spent to ensure equal participation, surely the invaders would be appeased? But others grumbled that they shouldn't have to bear the whole burden. After all, coaches were living a far richer lifestyle than they actually would accept and still remain in their profession. Let them help pay. An argument started over just how large the coaches' share was to be.

But a few royals, calm and collected, quieted their panicky relations. They argued that there was no reason at all to entertain the idea of offering up much of anything at all to the invaders. The following diversion had worked in the neighboring Kingdom of the Workplace. Low-level positions held by men had simply been replaced by women. The numbers added up to equal participation, but the lavish positions of the rulers of the Kingdom of the Workplace had been preserved.

With this example to guide them, argued the calm and collected contingent of royals, all they had to do was tell the invaders the following. The vastly popular men's sports were the golden egg-laying goose. None of the support for those sports could be reduced, since that would reduce the overall amount available to achieve the ends of the invaders. After all, where would the money come from to support all of the weaker sports? "Clever!" shouted the rest of the royals, but in guarded tones they all whispered to each other, "Where indeed, besides our own treasury and the wealth going to coaches." Soon it was agreed that they would sacrifice a few lesser men's sports, a sort of equality by reduction approach, and transfer the freed resources wherever they wished. The calm and collected were immediately appointed to take the plan to the invaders.

In the conquerors' tents, the plot unfolded. The calm and collected poured out their subterfuge in knowledgeable, sincere, and respectful tones. They were careful to pay homage to the invaders and their worship of gender equity. At the end of their plea, the invader council sat quietly. Then the obvious battle leader spoke. "This sounds quite like the plan that was offered to us by the royalty of the Kingdom of the Workplace. Indeed, I wonder if some of them are among you. But no, that can't be." Laughing as she strode to the far side of the tent, the invader threw back a tapestry and revealed the heads of the royalty of the Kingdom of the Workplace displayed on a neat row of pikes. "None of you can be the former royalty of the Kingdom of the Workplace, because they all are here. We discovered their subterfuge, and retribution was sure and swift. Would you care to revise your plan?"

Horrified, the negotiators surrendered and pleaded for mercy under the following plan. Since men's athletics generated the most money in the first place, that endeavor would continue to be strongly supported. And in order to increase the opportunity for women, the royalty would stop their lavish spending on themselves and their athletic programs. The reduction in their own wealth, plus the reduction in spending on the viziers and their minions, would be redirected to the sincere and ceaseless quest for gender equity. And the royalty of the Kingdom of College Sports were as good as their word, remembering the pike-riding heads of their neighboring (former) royalty.

And so it went in the Kingdom of College Sports. Since it continued to be strongly supported, nothing changed about men's athletics. Since there was no better opportunity anywhere else, the viziers and their minions grumbled about their reduced circumstances but stayed put. (Except for one that went into broadcasting and another that went on the motivational speaking circuit. They were both easily replaced.) More than enough money was available both to maintain the high level of performance in men's sports and to move women toward equal participation. By the way, once they received greater exposure, women's sports grew in popularity in the kingdom, an unexpected bonus. The invaders were appeased and the Kingdom of College Sports, although its royalty and coaches were less wealthy than they used to be, lived generally happily ever after (since, after all, they managed to keep their heads).

* * *

And the moral of our story is . . . It's time for those genuinely concerned with gender equity to wise up, just as the members of the invader council did concerning the rulers of the Kingdom of the Workplace. There is plenty of money already present to pursue gender equity. It's simply being spent on football and men's basketball, athletic directors, coaches, facilities, and recruiting. The President's Committee of the NCAA should be sharpening their poles and looking for heads to hoist. Or at least planning how to implement a competition neutral directive to take and redirect the revenue to fund Title IX. We prefer the heads-on-pikes approach. It's an age-old, tried and true incentive mechanism. University admiminstrators are also partly on the hook here, since they collect student aid from the athletic department and enjoy other benefits produced by college sports. It may well be time for them to put their money where their mouth is as well and leave some of that collected student aid as additional scholarship money for women athletes.

In the meantime, we live with the destruction caused by the myth that gains to gender equity must come from nonrevenue sports. Until the truth is recognized about the actual spending in the athletic department, belief in this myth will continue to pit men's and women's sports against each other. The impacts on women athletes and the efficient allocation of revenues by athletic department directors will continue to be swept aside in a wave of arguments that have no grounding in fact. Universities, of all places, will continue to evade (in the true sense of the difference between that word and its weaker cousin, "avoid") society's dictate of the fair distribution of resources and access for women in sports. And it just doesn't have to be that way. A simple agreement to reallocate money across college sports to gender equity is all that is required. We repeat, this is not an act of antitrust. It is an act of trust and genuine adherence to the law.

7

THE FBS PLAYOFF WILL BE BETTER THAN THE BCS

INTRODUCTION

Since the title of this chapter embodies another myth, we will present just why it is that the FBS playoff that kicks off in 2014 is not necessarily better than the BCS. Yosemite Sam, that bellicose Warner Bros. Cartoons standby, often uttered the challenge, "Them's fightin' words!" and we fully anticipate that some of our readers will draw their pistols like Sam and order us to stand and deliver. But before any of that, we state immediately that *neither of us prefers either of the alternatives*, an FBS playoff or the BCS, to the other. While we run the risk of being labeled un-American, both of your authors actually prefer the old-style, pre-BCS determination just by polls and catch-as-catch-can postseason bowl games. It made for fun arguments through the winter and spring. So our coverage of this myth is not motivated by our own preferences on the matter at hand.

The issue is much older than most know, judging by the focus just on the BCS. Scanning the Internet, even prior to the BCS, when two polls determined the champion, a Gallup Poll in 1990 showed more than two-thirds of the public believed a championship playoff would add interest to college football. After three years of the BCS approach, 54 percent of college football fans wanted to scrap the BCS for a playoff according to a 2001 CNN/USAToday/Gallup Poll. By 2007, a Gallup Poll found that 85 percent of fans prefer a playoff to the BCS system. Momentum seemed to be growing, but a Quinnipiac University survey in 2009 showed 63 percent in favor getting rid of the current system, while 26 percent want to keep it. But preferences rebounded strongly, if they ever really did change, since a recent *Sports Il-*

lustrated poll found that more than 90 percent of sports fans oppose the BCS. Every year in December and January, commentators discuss the merits of a playoff system in college football. Some critics, such as Dan Wetzel, Josh Peter, and Jeff Passan (2010), have even gone so far as to wish mortal harm to the BCS.

Indeed, this had become a full-time rallying cry of some fan action groups. From its "Agenda," one of sportsfans.org primary concerns is an FBS playoff:

> Unfortunately, the NCAA outsources the postseason of its most popular sport to corrupt bowl committees and the BCS. Not only is the method of determining the champion inequitable, the way the revenues from the postseason are distributed are inequitable, leading many athletic departments into debt. A college football playoff would be fairer to the fans and the taxpaying public.

We sincerely hope the reader can see the multiple myths on college sports finances from the preceding chapters woven into this careful tapestry of misinformation, but on the issue of an FBS playoff the excerpt is representative of the feelings of many on the issue. An official federal political action committee, playoffpac.com, puts it this way in "Our Purpose":

> The Bowl Championship Series is inherently flawed. It crowns champions arbitrarily and stifles inter-conference competition. Fans, players, schools, and corporate sponsors will be better served when the BCS is replaced with an accessible playoff system that recognizes and rewards on-the-field accomplishment. To that end, Playoff PAC helps elect pro-reform political candidates, mobilizes public support, and provides a centralized source of pro-reform news, thought, and scholarship.

By the way, the 2009 Quinnipiac survey cited above found that 48 percent of respondents said it's a "bad idea" for Congress to be involved. But of course Congress did get into the act, and it is easy to see why the particular elected officials involved chose to lead the way. Congressman Gary Miller (R-California, in the USC area code) introduced H.R. 599 in January 2009, to bring about college football playoffs. The Miller bill is straightforward and simple:

- It prohibits receipt of federal funds by any school with a football team that participates in NCAA Division 1 Football Bowl Subdivision unless the national championship game is the culmination of a playoff system.
- It is the responsibility of the 120 FBS schools to develop and implement the playoffs.
- There are no restrictions from incorporating existing bowl games into playoffs or a national championship. Nor are there restrictions from nonplayoff teams playing in nonplayoff postseason bowl games.

Not to be outdone, Congressman Joe Barton (R-Texas) introduced H.R. 390, the "College Football Playoff Act," later that year in December 2009. TCU had been passed over twice before for BCS game selection (2000 and 2005) but also just prior to this bill in 2008. About this same time, after the University of Utah Utes were denied a championship game despite going undefeated in 2008, Senator Orrin Hatch (R-Utah) started the Senate investigative ball rolling in 2009. Barton from Texas struck again just recently on December 16, 2011. This is certainly no accident either, since after its Rose Bowl victory over Wisconsin in 2010, and a final #2 ranking, the Horned Frogs felt they should have been higher. The aim of his H.R. 3696 is to "prohibit, as an unfair and deceptive act or practice, the promotion, marketing, and advertising of any post-season NCAA Division I football game as a national championship game unless such game is the culmination of a fair and equitable playoff system." The perennial snubbing of Boise State goes right along with the fact that Congressman Michael Simpson (R-Idaho) was a cosponsor of this bill. And what good would possible legislative intervention be without its own PAC? BCSreform.org has the stated purpose of getting bills like this into action:

> BCSReform is a grassroots alliance of college football fans and former players joining together to lobby Congress to pass legislation to implement college football playoffs. We are open to legislation that will lead to a college football playoff tournament.

The result of all this legislative attention and pressure was a "dialog" opened in 2011 between the Department of Justice and both the BCS and the NCAA. The most telling remark for those interested in the move to a playoff is NCAA Mark Emmert's response to the assistant attorney general for the antitrust division at DOJ, Christine A. Varney:

> The BCS system is composed of the eleven conferences, plus Notre Dame, that are members of the FBS . . . . Other than licensing the postseason FBS bowls, the NCAA has no role to play in the BCS or BCS system . . . . The NCAA conducts 89 championships in 23 sports annually, and each of those championships has been created at the request of the Association's membership. At no time in the history of the FBS or its predecessor, Division I-A, has a formal proposal come before the membership to establish a postseason football championship in that subdivision . . . . Without membership impetus for a postseason playoff, the NCAA has no mandate to create and conduct an FBS football championship.

There is a simply beautiful statement of the actual issue involved in this response by Emmert, but it is actually one of the original questions posed by Varney of the DOJ: "Have you determined that there are aspects of the BCS system that do not serve the interests of fans, colleges, universities, and players? To what extent could an alternative system better serve those interests?" None of the arguments we have seen anywhere worry about these truly fundamental issues.

The first fan also called publicly for a playoff. Here is what President Obama said on *CBS*'s *60 Minutes* on November 16, 2008:

> This is important. Look. I think any sensible person would say that if you've got a bunch of teams who played throughout the season and many of them have one loss or two losses and there's no clear decisive winner that we should be creating a playoff system. Eight teams. That would be three rounds to determine a national champion. It would add three extra weeks to the season. You could trim back on the regular season. I don't know any serious fan of college football who has disagreed with me on this. So I'm going to throw my weight around a little bit. I think it's the right thing to do.

Well, we are two serious college football fans and while, technically, our ambition is not to disagree with the president, there will be some very strong logic that calls the superiority of a playoff into question.

Generically, the welfare of fans, colleges, universities, and players is determined by the same basic factors, whether under the BCS approach or a playoff—the selection process, seeding the games (that is, filling in the initial playoff bracket), and then the issue of head-to-head determination through one or more rounds. In addition, the welfare of the BCS—really equity conferences and the ADs of member institutions—is determined by the distribution of the value created by the playoff. Two things are truly striking to us about the cry for an FBS playoff.

First, there really is no guarantee that any system of determining the final champion necessarily identifies the best team that season, whether this is polls, the BCS system, or a playoff. All any system can do is identify the best team as determined by that particular approach. We can think of no better example than the 2012 BCS Championship Game. During the season, LSU beat Alabama, and for the championship Alabama beat LSU. In another sport, how many times have we heard that "the real championship game" is in some quarterfinal or semifinal in March Madness? Or, remember the original grumblings of purists about including wild card teams in pro play-offs? Regardless of the process that generated the outcome, head-to-head competition gave us a result that cannot answer which is indisputably the better team. Given that we are restricted in the number of games that teams can play, so that longer seasons cannot settle the issue, a playoff does give us more information about the teams, but it also admits the possibility of the best team getting unlucky and losing the championship.

The second truly fabulous aspect of an FBS playoff is that all of the focus has been on increasing the number of rounds over the "single round" BCS "playoff." While FBS playoff proponents seem to be on a crusade to look more like FCS football and Division I basketball, there are good reasons for second thoughts about expanding the new playoff beyond the 4 + 1 that will be in place in 2014. The other crucial elements of an expanded play-off format—selection and seeding for fan welfare and the distribution of value for athletic department welfare—have received nearly no attention. The importance of this inattention can be seen in how the presidents of the major college conferences and ESPN, or what used to be called the BCS, responded to playoff demands.

Lest we forget, the same conference presidents and ESPN still hold all of the cards. They have announced that the BCS is out and, starting in the 2014–15 season, it will be replaced by a "plus one" format that is just a two-round playoff among the top 4 teams; 4 plays 1, 2 plays 3, and the winners meet to decide the championship. So far we have seen nothing concrete about the selection process, the seeding, or, and especially, the distribution of the revenues. These are all completely crucial to making any judgment about the superiority of any system over another. The critical questions that remain are how this new "playoff" will actually do what everybody claims it will do—select the best teams, structure the seeding to guarantee that the best team bubbles up, and then distribute the value created differently than before.

In the case of this myth, in particular, we are mindful of a variety of cautions about change. Pioneering social psychologist Kurt Lewin offered the following admonishment, "If you want to truly understand something, try to change it." English novelist Arnold Bennett cautioned, "Any change, even a change for the better, is always accompanied by drawbacks and discomforts." We have never read a nicer statement of benefit-cost impacts. But our favorite is the African proverb, "When the music changes, so does the dance." With few exceptions (for all of you Pareto Optimality fans), one thing is almost certainly true about change: some fans, university administrators, ADs, and players will be better off and some will be worse off. Rallying cries that presume to speak for all fans are, quite simply, unbelievable in such a setting. To our knowledge, there is no analysis anywhere of the impact of a move to a playoff, short of the type of vagaries we see above, such as "fairer to fans and the taxpaying public." In what follows, we expose both the myth and the motivations of its purveyors.

First, we make sure that we are all on the same page by describing the BCS and why it did what it did ("If you want to truly understand something, try to change it"). Then we move on to consideration of just what is different about a playoff compared with the BCS approach ("Any change, even a change for the better, is always accompanied by drawbacks and discomforts"). Finally, our conclusion makes it plain that some fans and organizations want change, but surely they cannot speak for the welfare of all fans ("When the music changes, so does the dance").

IF YOU WANT TO TRULY UNDERSTAND SOMETHING, TRY TO CHANGE IT

The BCS is not really a difficult thing to understand. The common belief (we'll add to this shortly) is that its original formation as the Bowl Coalition in 1992 (for the 1993 bowl season; six conferences and Notre Dame, six bowl committees) rose out of the dissatisfaction with the polling process, based on regular season and bowl season outcomes, which previously governed the crowning of the (then) Division I-A (now FBS) football champion. In those days it was rare that the teams ranked 1 and 2 going into the bowl season ever met each other, because of conference commitments to the major bowl games. So the champion named by the polls in this system always caused arguments that lasted all the way to the next season (the arguments we admitted to enjoying so much in the introduction). Indeed, the polls didn't even always name a single champion. Just prior to the formation of the Bowl Coalition, there were split national champions in 1990 (Colorado and Georgia Tech), 1991 (Miami and Washington), and 1997 (Michigan and Nebraska).

The new Bowl Coalition was supposed to pit 1 and 2 against each other and crown undisputed champions. With some rough spots along the way, eventually all of the major conferences and bowls joined in the effort. Steps along the way were the Bowl Alliance for the 1996 bowl season (down to four conferences and Notre Dame, three bowls) and, finally, the Bowl Championship Series for the 1999 bowl season. The BCS is (until 2014) composed of all eleven FBS conferences and the independents—Army, BYU, Navy, and Notre Dame—plus the organizing committees of the Fiesta Bowl, Orange Bowl, Rose Bowl, and Sugar Bowl. Now, individual teams have the rights to their games, but the management of media rights is granted to the conference directors. Thus the conference directors have the legal right to the games, and that is why their commissioners form the backbone of the BCS. Oh yes, let's not forget their broadcast partner, ESPN.

So, that's what the BCS *is*, but what does it *do*? Well, for starters the BCS has made good on its promise always to pit number 1 against number 2. The BCS included four games with 1 and 2 rotating between the Fiesta, Orange, Rose, and Sugar bowls through the 2005 bowl season. An additional BCS

Championship Game, for a total of five games, was added for the 2006 bowl season. This game rotates between the same four bowls. This is somewhat a hollow victory, since the BCS also decides the ranking in the first place, and their choices are not always universally accepted. In addition, the BCS has almost always crowned an undisputed champion. The exception was 2003, when, despite rules that were supposed to preclude such an outcome, LSU and USC split the poll results (a few coaches received stern letters, and the selection process was altered to eliminate this possibility in the future).

If this was all the BCS did, it is unlikely that any of the complaints listed in the introduction would ever have been voiced. It is easy to characterize the rest of what the BCS does around our main factors identified earlier—selection, seeding, the number of rounds, and the distribution of the values created. While seeding doesn't matter much in the current BCS because there are no subsequent rounds, the rest of this characterization serves to emphasize the points of contention with the BCS. (Seeding will matter big-time in the next section where we evaluate a playoff.)

The BCS selection process is a bit lengthy, can be found elsewhere, and we don't repeat it here because the outcome is the point. And that outcome is that the BCS selection process simply and effectively excludes any team outside the so-called automatic qualifier conferences (AQ conferences for short, which include the ACC, Big East, Big Ten, Big 12, Pac 12, and SEC) from enjoying the fruits of major bowl payoffs. Since the technical inception of the BCS for the 1999 bowl season, non-AQ teams have been selected for only seven BCS games—Utah, 2005 Fiesta Bowl; Boise State, 2007 Fiesta Bowl; Hawaii, 2008 Sugar Bowl; Utah, 2009 Sugar Bowl; Boise State and TCU, 2010 Fiesta Bowl; and TCU, 2011 Rose Bowl. That makes a six-year inaugural streak (1999–2004) with only AQ teams and only AQ teams again in 2006 and 2012. To put another spin on it, there have been eight BCS bowl seasons with four games (thirty-two games over 1999–2006) and six with five games (thirty games over 2007–12), for a total of sixty-two games and 124 selection chances for teams. The seven selections of non-AQ conference teams represent only 5.6 percent of the chances, and none have ever been selected as either 1 or 2, despite the fact that every one of them was undefeated at the time they were selected.

Adding insult to injury in the eyes of their fans, there have been undefeated non-AQ teams ranked highly in the BCS that were not even selected
for a BCS game five times. Boise State suffered this dubious distinction
twice (the 2004 and 2008 BCS bowl seasons). What's more, the Broncos
were not selected for a BCS game at 11–1 in either the 2011 or 2012 BCS seasons, relegated to back-to-back appearances in the lowly Las Vegas Bowl.

Back in Chapter 4, we detailed the explicit BCS formula for the distribution of the value it creates. We don't reprise it here, but remember there are
a few key observations. The value distribution is guided by the simple principle that conferences in the BCS bowls receive the largest portion of the
revenues. Non-AQ teams rarely make a BCS game, and most of the money
goes to those that make it in the first place. For the yet to be announced distribution of the 2012 BCS game outcomes, we show in Chapter 4 that if the
AQs should get about 90 percent, the non-AQs about 7.5 percent, the FCS
conferences about 1.1 percent, Notre Dame about 1 percent, and the rest 0.2
percent. This concentration of the value on the AQs does not happen by accident and is the result of careful design by the members of the BCS.

So it actually is pretty easy to see why the BCS has been so unwilling to
change, and why the move to a playoff is such a small, truly incremental
step to 4 + 1. Really, the distinguishing feature of a playoff is that it generates
more uncertainty about who will win the championship. Fort and his colleague, retired California Institute of Technology economist James Quirk
(1995), showed this in a seminal sports economics paper for the addition of
a championship round for the NFL. Intuitively, the idea goes as follows. The
total revenue generated under the current BCS approach is, indeed, smaller
than might be generated by a full-blown playoff. However, the chances that
equity conference members will get to the money are larger under the BCS
approach. So those controlling the FBS postseason could go to a playoff
now, with its higher total revenue, but the amount of money each equity
conference could hope for would fall. So the equity conference members
stuck with the BCS approach as long as they could and now offer up only
the smallest appeasement to the playoff proponents in the form of another
completely controlled 4 + 1 alternative. We stress again that the details of
the distribution of the return remains to be announced, but we will buy the

drinks if that distribution strays much from the current 90 percent take for the AQ conferences, minus (probably) the Big East, which seems unable to hold on to its members. After all, its new configuration will simply be a conglomeration of primarily Conference USA (CUSA) and Mountain West teams. The real lords of football, the members of the other five AQ conferences, might think nothing at all about reducing their number to five. As Forrest Gump reminded us, "One less thing."

Put another way . . . What form of final competition would the BCS heavies like to see? The answer is, the form of final competition that maximizes *their revenues*, not the most money that could be made from the variety of possible ways that a champion could be determined. Thus, the BCS maximizes the revenues that can be made while determining a national champion from among the top athletic departments in the six AQ conferences. Not surprisingly, minimal access under the rules of the BCS is allowed to the rest of the FBS athletic departments. If you are the best team in the country (or at least the number one ranked team in the country) you don't want a playoff, and it is most likely (given history) that the top teams in the country are from the AQ conferences. Thus the largest revenue pool possible for the best AQ conference teams is generated by the BCS system, not the most that could be made from some alternative way of crowning a national champion.

The foregoing should make it quite clear that the BCS is really the AQ conferences scooping up heaping helpings of the major bowl payouts. The way the BCS has chosen to structure itself over time makes plain that this is purposeful behavior. This also suggests a clear line of reasoning that governs just when the BCS would choose a true playoff structure over its current approach, and by this we mean many more rounds than the measly 4 + 1 successor to the BCS. We turn to that next, but provide the following segue.

It is clear to us that the non-AQ squawk over access to a shot at the championship masks a more fundamental discontent over the distribution of the value created. Only a very occasional non-AQ team would ever have a shot under any format. We do not mean that Utah (now moot with their move to the AQ Pac-12), Boise State, TCU, or Hawaii is somehow undeserving, just that they represent a very small proportion of the forty-eight programs in the non-AQ conferences. But the economics of it are much broader. Making it to a BCS game isn't really worth much to any non-AQ athletic department. The last "best" non-AQ conference, the eight-team Mountain West, brought in $4.6 million in bowl revenue on top of the likely $5.0 million it will receive in BCS distributions, a total of $9.6 million. As of 2010–11, the MWC shared all postseason football equally (Mountain West Conference, 2010) so this represents about $1.2 million each. If one of the best teams had made a BCS game, the distribution would increase to $10 million, but then the alternative $1 million bowl game would not be played, so the net is $9 million. This would push the total to $13.6 million, or $1.7 million for each MWC team. The net gain of getting a BCS game is $500,000.

Is all this fuss really about the chance for another half-million dollars to any member of the MWC, plus the kudos for a champion? We think not, and it's highly likely that the people behind the BCS don't think so either. Indeed, all the BCS would have to do to squelch the noise is up the sharing formula a bit to appease everybody, if that were the case. But they have not done so. No, surely it is about an even larger redistribution away from the BCS.

CHANGE, EVEN A CHANGE FOR THE BETTER, IS ALWAYS ACCOMPANIED BY DRAWBACKS AND DISCOMFORTS

This quotation simply says there are good things and bad things, compared with the current setting. Pareto told us all about this a long time ago, and the only way out is actually to assess the amounts of the good and bad. It can't be just saying that more people want it—majority rule guarantees only the welfare of the majority, after all, and the losses to the rest could outweigh. And it cannot be denied that there are both gains and drawbacks. (We abstract from the impact on athletes, not because we do not care or because there won't be any, but because very few observers ever consider their welfare in this discussion, beyond token lip service.)

The potential gains are pretty easy to conceptualize, again along the lines we proposed earlier. Critics get some of these gains, but they do not get a full slate, because of their fixation only on expanding the number of playoff rounds. The selection process might be biased in a way that can be changed, to the detriment of the equity conferences and their members but to the improved welfare of everybody else. Right now, it includes some truly bad teams even by the BCS's own rankings, because equity conference champs are guaranteed a game. Examples in 2012: West Virginia and Virginia Tech. The form of at-large selection is also suspect in the same way, biased toward equity conference members. (The interesting fact that some equity conference members are passed over because of the "no more than two" rule, as with Arkansas and Kansas State, does not change this; it is still bias toward equity conference compared with the rest of the FBS members.)

The seeding might also be fixed to the delight of the rest of the FBS and some fans, even though the opposite would be true for fans of the BCS and the equity conference members. This is revealed mostly in the usual gains under an expanded playoff—best against worst, through subsequent rounds, to the winners, as opposed to 1 v. 2, 3 v. 4, and a haphazard subjective set of seeding after that.

The number of rounds works for everybody else and against the BCS by simple expansion. As we showed in the last section, while there is a lot more access, the chances of bad teams moving up are small, but they do matter in terms of whether the top-ranked teams advance.

Finally, changing the distribution of the value created can almost certainly benefit some teams at the expense of the current equity conference members and the independents (Army, BYU, Navy, and Notre Dame). But this is not a given and depends on the form of redistribution. For example, suppose the rallying cry of redistribution is "One for all and all for one!" Three Musketeers redistribution would divide (for 2012) $136.7 million equally. At the level of the eleven FBS conferences, that's $12.4 million each. At the level of 124 FBS teams, that's $1.1 million each. Right now, even some of the rest of the FBS conference members make more than that, so an equal redistribution would hurt them.

The drawbacks are, first and foremost, the always-possible tyranny of the majority—even if a greater number of people vote for a revised playoff, it is possible that the smaller number of people impacted have a greater total value of harm. For example, in the Quinnipiac Poll of 2009, 26 percent of those asked wanted to keep the BCS. It is possible that this minority values their satisfaction more than the majority 63 percent in favor of getting rid of the current system. It cannot be said, without in-depth marketing analysis, that the revenues would be larger under a playoff than under the current BCS. Even if they were, that does not necessarily mean that welfare will follow suit.

Let's think of the examples. Will fifty thousand Michigan fans (or Alabama fans, or LSU fans, or what have you) really travel more than once to watch their teams work their way through the playoff bracket? It need not even be true then that the revenue potential really helps, since part of the payoff to each participant is ticket sales revenue (some claim that they already take a beating here and have to, horror of horrors, sell their bowl ticket allotment to the opposing fans). In addition, this will reduce the travel to the cities that host bowl games, reducing development dollar results, thereby reducing the incentive to host them in the first place.

Here's another example. A playoff system would certainly create some games that generate a lot of revenue, since television ratings would be high. However, a playoff system would also mitigate the excitement of the regular season, and might even mean fewer other games, such as conference championships. As it stands now, some teams play twelve games, plus a conference championship game. Even one additional bowl game makes fifteen games for two teams. One likely outcome might be that conference championship games would be eliminated to alleviate these tensions. This would mean eliminating four games that currently generate a large amount of revenue. If these games generate even half of the revenue of a playoff game, then a playoff might not increase revenue at all.

More generally, while playoffs increase the number of games played by some teams, playoffs also limit the total number of games. The longer the playoffs, the sooner some teams stop playing. If we take the point of view that there is some maximum number of games that teams can play, the number of total games by all teams is maximized with no playoffs! In addition, playoffs make more sense in professional sports because fans start to tune out when their favorite team has had their championship hopes dashed. In college this is less true. Given that a large number of fans have an association with the university, either as a student or an employee, demand is less dependent on the probability of winning a title and more on the conference championship. A larger percentage of college fans are willing to watch games with no championship implications. Therefore, for these fans (remember our original drawback, tyranny of the majority), it makes more sense to maximize the number of games even for teams that will not ultimately be the best team in the country.

No matter how many teams make the playoffs there will be interest in which teams get in, just as there is interest in which teams make the basketball tournaments—but there will not be the same anticipation of top-ranked teams playing each other. Subsequently, while a playoff system would increase some revenues, it would also decrease other revenues. So the argument that a playoff would increase the size of the pie, so maybe more teams could win financially, is not a sure thing (and we have already shown that it all depends on how the money is divided in the first place). At the very least, it is not as big a thing as some would have it.

And still another example concerns the fact, as we show in previous chapters, that an athletic department generates other benefits across the university, in addition to a bit of revenue paid back through "student aid" (grants-in-aid) by the athletic department. Athletic success can have an effect, albeit small relative to the entire university budget, on enrollment or donations. The bottom line is that participating for a national championship can generate valuable exposure to a university. Now, only so many teams can have athletic success at the level of championship play. Expanding access to the championship through an expanded playoff format will raise the chances of success for some teams, but only at the expense of other teams. The chances are it might come at the expense of an AQ conference team. The case of the FCS is completely instructive on this point, and we follow the evolution of that tournament for its clear lessons for the upcoming FBS tournament.

In football, Division I was separated into Division I-A and Division I-AA in 1978. Later, in 2006, they were renamed the FBS and FCS, respectively.

The FBS postseason has been run by the BCS in various forms, as described above. The FCS, on the other hand, is just another one of all of the rest of the sports whose postseason is run by the NCAA. The Big Sky, Big South, Colonial Athletic Association, Ivy League, Mid-Eastern Athletic, Missouri Valley Football, Northeast, Ohio Valley, Patriot League, Pioneer, Southern, Southland, and the Southwestern Athletic conferences participate; the Ivy League and Southwestern Athletic Conference choose not to participate in the football championship. The FCS championship began in 1978 as a 4 + 1, just as the new FBS tournament will be in 2014; 1 played 4, 2 played 3, and the winners played for the championship. Teams then and now are selected and seeded against each other by the Division I Football Championship Committee composed of select DI-AA athletic directors. Under NCAA by-laws, this committee is subject to review by the NCAA Division I Presidential Advisory Group. The 4 + 1 lasted only three years (1978–1980), and the selection grew to eight teams in 1981 and then immediately to twelve teams in 1982. Again, this didn't last long, and the tournament grew to sixteen teams for 1986–2007. Since 2008 the tournament has included twenty teams and is set to grow to twenty-four in 2013.

So one apparent lesson is that once it started, expansion of the DI-AA football tournament was pretty rapid (we show below how the NCAA Division I basketball championship expanded dramatically over the years as well). It is extremely difficult to believe that anything else would be true for the infant FBS tournament after 2014. There are two other object lessons here as well. First, in the data we could compile, there were thirteen years with both the committee's tournament seedings and poll results for that year—all of the twelve-team years, 1982–85; 1989–90 and 1998–2000 for the sixteen-team years; and all of the twenty-team years to date, 2008–11. The polls matched the top 4 by the selection committee eight of these thirteen times—three of the four twelve-team years, four of the five years where there are data on both selection and polls for the sixteen-team years, and just once for the four current twenty-team period chances. Along with the annual disappointment for nonselected teams that bemoan being passed over in any given year, it is clear that these data show the type of variance in selection and seeding that is bound to drive fans wild. The mechanism suffers the same problems as March Madness in basketball on selection and seeding.

The other lesson, actually pretty easy to see, is just how big the "intrusion" by teams outside the top 4 becomes as the DI-AA/FCS tournament expanded—that is, the Fort and Quirk lesson from above. We refer to it as an "intrusion" because that is exactly how those in control of the FBS post-season would view it. Seeding in the FCS tournament began in 1981. Once it went to twelve teams, the top 4 seeded teams received a bye in the first round, so they can be identified that way. After the tournament grew to sixteen teams in 1986, the top 4 seeds were always identified (we couldn't find a consistent data set on all of these and use the available poll data to fill in 1986 to 1988 and 1991 to 1997). This allows a comparison to just a four-team selection that happened from 1978 to 1980 and also parallels any move that might happen later in the upcoming FBS 4 + 1. (If we could find a consistent set of data on the seedings for all teams rather than just 1 – 4, we could provide even more detail, as we did for March Madness in Chapter 4.)

We see the Fort and Quirk demonstration, or the "intrusion" from the perspective of those in control of the FBS postseason, immediately in 1981. The semifinals have Eastern Kentucky (1) v. Boise State and Idaho State (2) playing South Carolina State (3); only Boise State is outside the top 4. The final is Eastern Kentucky (1) losing to Idaho State (2), so the "intrusion" by teams outside the top 4 was minimal. Teams outside of the top 4 are a bit more of an "intrusion" over the four-year, twelve-team tournament period (1982–85). Teams outside the top 4 seeds occupied 5/16 = 31 percent of the semifinal slots and 3/8 = 38 percent of the final slots. Only one team outside the top 4 seeds actually won the championship during this period—Georgia Southern. The Eagles began what would be a bit of a dynasty, winning the championship in 1985 as a team outside the top 4 seeds. They would go on to win back-to-backs in 1985–86 and 1989–90, and again in 1999–2000. In addition, Western Carolina and Louisiana Tech were two other teams outside the top 4 to make it to the final but lose, in 1983 and 1984, respectively.

The longest single period for comparison is the twenty-two-year sixteen-team championship, 1986–2007. Over that period, teams outside the top 4 seeds occupied 38/88 = 43 percent of the semifinal slots. Half of those advanced, occupying 19/44 = 43 percent of all final slots. However, teams outside the top 4 seeds made their presence felt in that final. They won 9/22 = 41 percent of the championship games. Apparently, this had to do with the fact that the tournament committee simply could not figure out that The Thundering Herd from Marshall and the Youngstown State Penguins really were very good teams. Marshall came first, making it to the final game in 1987 from outside the top 4, losing to Louisiana-Monroe. But the fun really started in 1991. That year, neither team was in the top 4, but they both made the final. The Penguins were the victors. In 1992, they were both outside the top 4 but both made it to the final again. This time it was The Thundering Herd that won. The year 1993 was a repeat of 1991 for the Penguins. Marshall would again make the final game from outside the top 4 in 1995, losing to another team from outside the top 4, Montana. Youngstown State would win the whole thing from outside the top 4 again in 1997 but also lose the final to Georgia Southern after making it from outside the top 4 in 1999. Others that slipped through include Furman (1988), Montana (1995), Massachusetts (1998), Western Kentucky (2002), James Madison (2004), and Appalachian State (2007), all winning the championship from outside the top 4.

Finally, over the last four years with twenty teams, 6/16 = 38 percent of teams outside the top 4 were in the semifinals and 2/8 = 25 percent were in the final. Interestingly, both of those teams from outside the top 4 won the championship, Richmond in 2008 and Eastern Washington in 2010. Moving from eight, twelve, sixteen, to twenty teams in the tournament, it is easy to see that the chance that just the top 4 teams dominate falls as the tournament grows. Thus, if the upcoming FBS tournament moves on beyond 4 + 1, as the history of the other tournaments suggests that it will, the gates will open and more and more teams will have access to the big money.

We note in passing that March Madness is also often held up as an example, but the facts here are far less compelling. The Division I national basketball champion has always been decided by a playoff. Like the FCS football tournament, the field has increased from 8 teams (1939–50), to 16 teams (1951–52), 22–25 teams (1953–74), 32 teams (1975–78), 40 teams (1979),

48 teams (1980–82) 52 teams (four play-ins, 1983), 53 teams (five play-ins, 1984), 64 teams (1985–2000), 65 teams (opening round game for first-round for lowest ranked teams, 2001–10), and finally 68 teams (four play-ins, 2011–present). Playoff proponents point out that smaller Division I teams populate even the semifinals, and Butler University played in the championship game in 2010 and 2011. Of course, Butler was not expected to play in these title games, but having the playoff system gives them this opportunity.

Now, getting carried away with "mid-majors" runs afoul of John Adams—"Facts are stubborn things; and whatever may be our wishes, our inclinations, or the dictates of our passion, they cannot alter the state of facts and evidence." As we show in Chapter 4, since the playoff grew to 64 in 1985, the chances for any real advancement by the lowest seeds are truly de minimis. Since the lowest seeds are typically the smaller programs, it follows that it can be difficult for smaller schools to advance in the NCAA men's basketball tournament. Fort also shows in his aforementioned upcoming book with Quirk that March Madness returns are also concentrated in the hands of AQ FBS conferences. So smaller basketball programs are even less of an intrusion on the major conferences in basketball than they might end up to be in football.

But our story here is that even though it is hard for small schools to be successful in basketball, it is nearly impossible in football. Any argument based on the success of smaller schools in basketball misses the point that none of them even play football, it is cheaper to create strong basketball programs at smaller schools, and only one or two terrific players are needed to make it happen in basketball. Indeed, returning to the case of Butler, they were seeded 5 in 2010 and 8 in 2011 and are actually a strong program over the last decade. Furthermore, it seems difficult to argue that basketball is inherently more uncertain than football and therefore lends itself to small schools competing, since if any major North American sports league has a balance problem, it is the NBA.

Finally, it is a bit hypocritical to knock the current BCS system for its focus on money and, in the next breath, use the argument that there would be even more money under a playoff! It is also hypocritical to argue that it's all about the head-to-head determination, or the unfairness of the initial selection process, when those who demand more access than they now have would also be financially better off under the alternative playoff.

However, for some fans, a playoff champion is somehow more legitimate. The idea that a team could be undefeated at the end of regular season play, and still not be considered in the determination of the champion, rankles the feathers of many fans. Of course a playoff would ensure, or at least make it more likely, that a team could not go undefeated without winning a championship. After all, if a team ends up undefeated and still can't win, they apparently didn't have a chance to win the championship to begin with, which is unfair in the eyes of many. So, to us, the more likely explanation of fan ire toward the BCS is legitimacy, not ensuring the best team wins the championship.

CONCLUSIONS—WHEN THE MUSIC CHANGES, SO DOES THE DANCE

So, for us, it all boils down to comparing one group's happiness with another. That way lies economically invalid comparison except in the most restricted of circumstances. And so we come to our conclusions. The foregoing makes it abundantly clear that some fans and organizations want change, but surely they cannot speak for the welfare of all fans. So the myth: It cannot be that an FBS playoff will necessarily end up making "fans" better off than the BCS, since some fans like the BCS just fine. We have also charted the territory—there are gains and drawbacks, and that would be true of any form of playoff.

This puts the comparison between the upcoming FBS playoff and its predecessor BCS on the same footing as any other comparison—advocates can only know that it will be better for them, and they should confine their claims to that. We also show above just why they *might* be better off but, since so little is known yet about the 4 + 1 alternative, nobody can know the dimensions that will ultimately come into play in any change. Indeed, as the simple accounting at averages shows at the end of the last section, some athletic departments outside of the equity conferences could be financially worse off as well!

This is one of the most self-serving myths in all sports. It leads opponents of the BCS on a merry chase—now they must not only find a system that actually does deliver a "true" champ (not as easy as they think) but also one that the current BCS power brokers (AQ conference presidents and ESPN) will, quite literally, have to buy into. The power comes from the arguments made against a full-fledged playoff of the current FCS variety in favor of the much milder 4 + 1 to replace the BCS determination of the national champion. Those arguments ring hollow, and misdirected skepticism searches for a real alternative—it must be about the money! As always seems to be the case, so the myth goes, a playoff system would make fans better off by having a "true champion."

So, before we can go any further with the idea of an expanded playoff to replace the current BCS version, the alternative needs to be carefully specified and assessed. And hopefully the welfare impacts can also at least be put on the table. One thing is sure. It will be different, and different people will be happier than they are now. But some will be less happy. Without careful consideration of the alternatives, the result could be just changing the happiness of some for the happiness of others, with no net gain to the overall happiness in society. And that's what we are already getting from the BCS and its careful manipulations of the form of the determination of the FBS football champion over the last couple of decades. Put in the context of this section heading, right now the AQ conferences call the tune and enjoy the dance. Any change just changes the tune so that some others can enjoy a different dance. Maybe there are some alternatives where this can be avoided, but not if anybody buys into the myth that an FBS playoff is necessarily better than the BCS.

PRO MYTHS

8 OWNERS AND GENERAL MANAGERS ARE INEPT

What the hell did you trade Jay Buhner for?! He had 30 home runs, over 100 RBIs last year! He's got a rocket for an arm . . . . You don't know what the hell you're doing!
—Frank Costanza proclamation on *Seinfeld*

INTRODUCTION

Many fans and pundits feel that a shockingly high percentage of General Managers (GMs) seem to have very little idea what they are doing when it comes to talent evaluation and crafting a winning team. Since owners hire GMs (and take some of that role upon themselves at times), it follows that owners are inept by association. For those that feel this way, examples of bonehead moves are legion. Harry Frazee sold Babe Ruth to the Yankees after the 1919 season for $125,000, purportedly to finance stage plays (Frazee is, after all, usually referred to as the theatrical promoter that also owned the Boston Red Sox). The Portland Trailblazers drafted Sam Bowie ahead of Michael Jordan in 1984. The Atlanta Falcons took Brett Favre in the second round of the 1991 draft and traded him, after only one season, to the Packers for the 19th overall pick in the 1992 draft. Readers will have their own examples of bonehead mistakes made by the GM of their favorite team.

And if it isn't bonehead choices, then it's boneheaded overpayment. Time and again, proponents of this view drag out the example of the New York Yankees. Let's just review the 2011 season. The Yankees spent $202.7 million on payroll, according to the USAToday.com Salaries Databases. They won the AL East (0.599 winning percentage) but lost the ALDS to Detroit. The Tigers' payroll was $105.7 million, and they took the AL Central (0.586 winning percentage) but lost the American League Championship Series to Texas. The Rangers spent $92.3 million in payroll, won the AL West (0.593

winning percentage), but lost the World Series to St. Louis. The Cardinals spent \$105.4 million on payroll and placed second in the NL Central (0.566 winning percentage).

Adherents to the inept GM view would paint Yankee GM Brian Cashman in the following way. He spent about twice as much as the GMs of these other teams (Dave Dombrowski for the Tigers, Jon Daniels for the Rangers, and John Mozeliak for the Cardinals), had the poorest playoff performance of the bunch, and did only marginally better in winning percentage than the Rangers, who made it to the World Series. Detroit GM Dombrowski did only marginally better, spending 14 percent more than Texas to get one step further than the Yankees into the playoffs but going down 4–2 to the Rangers. Indeed, Rangers GM Daniels would be the star here. He spent 88 percent of what St. Louis GM Mozeliak spent and the Rangers took the Cardinals the full seven games through the series, looking like they might win early and staying even through five innings of that seventh game. For a bit more perspective, the Ranger payroll was only 6 percent above the median (about \$87 million), while the Yankee payroll was 133 percent of the median. And so the conclusion goes that GMs (and owners by association) must not know how to evaluate talent.

This is myth, pure and simple, foisted on fans to make sportswriter/broadcaster careers and to sell newspapers, magazines, and ESPN programming. These sports pundits sell bad economics, exploit weak statistical intuition, and train a selective but very public lens on sports decision-makers. By doing so, they prey on human nature with a destructive myth. There are needless hard feelings created between owners and their GMs, on the one hand, and fans on the other in this callous pursuit of media career self-interest and revenue generation.

BAD ECONOMICS

Quite simply, sportswriters/broadcasters are with few exceptions very poor economists (through personal experience we know that Wayne Drehs, Ron MacLean, Darren Rovell, and Bob Costas are exceptions). This is easy to see through their consistent portrayal of the additional costs of winning as somehow being constant, implying a simple linear relationship between spending and winning. The best example is when payroll spending per win is compared across teams. In fact, the "cost per win" statistic seems to be gaining in popularity with writers everywhere (just Googling "cost per win" generates more than 21,000 hits, including Forbes.com, USAToday.com, espn.go.com, and msnbc.com on the first page). The team with the higher spending per win is up for criticism, but this implicitly assumes that the cost of additional winning is constant, so that the GM for the higher-spending team could get the same wins for lower spending. We will demonstrate that GMs that spend more per win than others are not guilty of bad management. Instead, critics using this argument are guilty of misunderstanding the production of winning. The costs of winning additional games are not constant, and there is a further complication in the fact that fans may be willing in some locations to pay a lot more for small increments in team performance than in other locations.

The idea of constant costs of winning makes the world a simple place. If a team spends twice as much, it should be twice as good (recall our New York Yankees example in the introduction). However, that is both silly intuition and a weak understanding of the complexity of any economic production process. No matter the process—farming, automobile manufacturing, or producing wins in sports—costs of additional output are not constant. The additional costs of production must eventually increase.

In addition to rising costs of additional winning, it can also be the case that, with production that requires scarce talent, fans in some markets simply want to see only the very best players all of the time, even if the cost of getting them isn't justified in terms of added wins. This is the well known "superstar effect" attributed in economics to Professor Sherwin Rosen (1981) at the University of Chicago. If the most that New York or Boston fans are willing to pay can only be collected by the GM by fielding an all-star lineup, then the GM will see to these demands and collect the reward for doing so. Players may be only 5 percent better than the next best that could take the field, but fans may value their performance by more than 5 percent in additional payroll. While this superstar effect might not be as large as some people think, fans will often watch a game to see a superstar play.

While winning has a huge effect on game attendance, even if their team isn't doing that well fans will still go to the games because of some superstar. For example, baseball fans keep their eye on the pitching rotation, and attendance rises when the star is scheduled to take the mound. For another example, when Michael Jordan was playing for the Washington Wizards, he was not helping the team much. However, a lot of fans attended so they could watch him play. So what should owners be willing to pay a player like Michael Jordan late in his career? In this case, helping the bottom line may make owners look like they do not know how to win on the court, but they are winning the battle of the bottom line.

The Yankees had a similar situation in late 2010 when they wanted to sign Derek Jeter to another contract. While it appeared that Jeter's productivity had declined, he was still "The Captain," the face of the Yankees. Therefore his value was not determined only by on-field performance. Thinking only about winning, some argued that the Yankees overpaid for Jeter (even though his salary fell from $22.6 million in 2010 to around $15 million for the next two years). However, if the Yankees do not have Jeter, that completely changes the marketing, publicity, and recognition of the team. Fortunately for the Yankees, they signed Jeter and his performance has been superb since returning from a rehabilitation period.

And let's think about those spending the least, famously represented by the Oakland Athletics by Michael Lewis (2003) in his book *Moneyball* and by Columbia Pictures in the movie of the same name. Part of what Oakland's GM Billy Beane did was to field pretty good teams on a small payroll upon taking the GM job in 1997. After all, in the famed 2000–03 run, the A's never made it out of the LDS; when they did in 2006 they lost the ALCS to Detroit, 4–0. Beane did it by playing inexperienced players that were recently drafted and were not being paid their true value to the team. On the other hand, a team like the Yankees, seeking the very best players (superstars), turns to the free agent market. Now, free agents typically not only give more value to the team but also are able to receive payment closer to their true value to the team. This means that the Yankees pay much more for only slightly better talent. The Yankees aren't overpaying relative to the A's because their fans are interested in more than just the on-field performance differential. Yankee fans also want a superstar lineup. If the Yankee GM did the same thing as Billy Beane, it should be expected that the Yankees would be about as good as the A's but that revenues would fall, because Yankee fans want (1) a better team than the A's, and (2) superstars on the field.

The fact that Billy Beane's skills are highest valued in a smaller-revenue market like Oakland (where he remains, despite his genius), rather than in New York, stands testament to this observation. If Billy Beane were suddenly to replace Brian Cashman for the Yankees, he would be hard pressed to do any differently than Cashman. The Yankees recipe is first, spend more to win more and, as an added kicker, spend even more because fans in New York are willing to pay the most to see the very best players.

In addition, if one focuses only on Billy Beane's innovation, it is the nature of fierce competition that gains from innovation are short-lived. Subsequent work suggests that the innovation was valuable, as Branch Rickey said such things would be, seventy years ago, for about two to three seasons. A study by economists Raymond Sauer and Jahn Hakes (2006) in the *Journal of Economic Perspectives* shows that Billy Beane was able to exploit better statistics for a short time, but the rest of the league caught up.

One misconception is that statistical analysis has been unusually slow in penetrating the sports industry, and a few savvy general managers are able to capitalize on this at the expense of inept GMs. Again, the story of Billy Beane is useful. There is no doubt that Billy Beane was on the forefront of statistical analysis in baseball. However, the sports industry has had a long love affair with statistics. For example, Ben Bernanke actually credits much of his early learning of statistics to baseball statistics. In his thorough biography of "The Mahatma," Lee Lowenfish (2007) points out that Branch Rickey actually hired someone to develop a full statistics profile of players as early as 1947. Today sabermetricians argue that batting average is not that useful of a statistic, but Rickey knew this over sixty years ago. So while teams certainly vary, all major leagues have very sophisticated statisticians working for them.

Poor evaluation of a team's success can also contribute to this myth, and we return to the basic production of winning. It is reasonable to use wins as an output measure, but, as we stress above, increments to winning cannot be had for some constant amount of additional payroll spending. Depending on the sport, it is usually easy to win at least a few games. However, wins get harder and harder to come by for good teams. We show this first and then demonstrate the fallacy of assuming that a win is a win, regardless of how good a team is.

It is crucial to recognize here that wins are harder and harder to come by *for all teams*. If a low spending, low win team wants to improve, eventually improvement will get more and more expensive. It isn't just a comparison of the highest payroll teams to some chosen others; *it is true across all teams*. To see this, take the 2011 MLB payroll data at USAToday.com, sort from lowest payroll to highest payroll, and calculate spending per win. What you will see is consistently explained by the logic we present, above, but runs afoul of the usual inept GM explanation. For example, divide the teams into the top 10, middle 10, and bottom 10, and spending per win rises steadily from $703,000 for the bottom 10, to $1.1 million for the middle 10, to $1.6 million for the top 10. Importantly, the number of wins also increases—79 wins on average for the bottom 10 (0.488), 80 wins for the middle 10 (0.494), and 85 wins for the top 10 (0.525). On average *across all teams*, not just the highest spenders, increased payroll leads to more winning for fans, in particular for those high-spending GMs the critics love to hate.

In addition, the marginal cost of winning follows good economics to the letter. For the teams with the bottom 10 payrolls, spending is ($52.1 million)/(0.488 x 1000) = $106,762 per point. The results of the same calculation for the middle and top payroll groups are 88.1/(0.494 x 1000) = $178,340 per point and 138.4/(0.525 x 1000) = $263,619 per point, respectively. This shows that the average cost per win goes up the more teams win, which also means the marginal cost of additional winning percentage increases. Finally, regarding the "superstar effect," we were not at all surprised by the members of the top 10 group (lowest to highest)—the Tigers, Twins, Giants Mets, Cubs, White Sox, Angels, Red Sox, Phillies (tops at 102 wins), and Yankees. Fans in some of these cities are used to seeing only the best at nearly everything, and why not baseball? We think in particular of New York, Boston, Chicago, and Los Angeles (by the way, the Dodgers were at the top of the middle group of 10). There is very old and very sound economic reasoning here, rather than some off-the-cuff claim that GMs and owners in MLB are somehow inept.

So something else is in operation here besides GM ineptitude, since all GMs face the same rising cost of winning, and the GMs that spend the most per win also get more wins. Put another way, either all GMs are awful (not just the GM of your favorite team), or it is the combination of factors identified earlier—it gets more and more difficult to win at the margin and, for some teams, fans demand as many superstars as GMs think they can afford.

As if the foregoing were not enough, it is also easy to see the real flaw with the belief that winning is linear that underlies the use of cost per win as a metric for comparison among GMs. It all boils down to this—If you're going to take a truly simplistic view of the production of winning, then at least get it right! In Figure 8.1 we offer a plot of wins against payrolls for all MLB teams in 2011. In addition, Figure 8.1 contains two alternative linear specifications that give dramatically different takes on the 2011 Rangers/Yankees comparison we set up in the introduction. The solid line embodies the usual portrayal of constant costs for additional winning; for 2011, the average spending per win was about $1.14 million, and the Texas Rangers were not too far away at $.96 million. Following along with the constant added cost of winning assumption, if a team spends nothing, then they get no wins, but for every $1.14 million they spend, they add a win, from the bottom to the top of the winning outcomes. Again, this is the derivation of the solid line in Figure 8.1.

The constant spending per win argument then goes like this. Teams above the line outperform the expected relationship; their wins are much larger than their spending would indicate. Teams below the line perform below the expected relationship. The Rangers/Yankees comparison follows directly. Given their positions relative to the line, the Rangers won 15 more games than expected by their spending (96 actual wins with 81 expected), while the Yankees had just over half the wins expected for their spending (97 actual wins with 177 expected). Uh oh. Something already smells fishy, since there are only 162 games in the season. The simple constant cost per win extrapolation actually produces an impossible goal that the Yankees

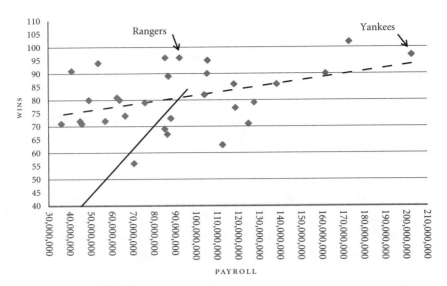

F ig . 8.1. 2011 MLB Payrolls and Wins. Calculated from data at Fort (2012).

can never achieve, not because their GM is inept but because the idea of constant costs per additional win is bankrupt.

The same type of strangeness holds if we look at the bottom of the distribution of spending as well. The teams furthest above the line are the bottom 6 spenders with both the lowest spending per win and the least number of wins! While the Rays and Diamondbacks are in there and did well, so are the Royals, Pirates, and Padres. By this argument, it isn't just that the Rangers shine relative to the Yankees, but especially teams like the Pirates and Padres outshine everybody! But, of course, we never hear the critics extend their criticisms in this direction.

There is a much "better" version of the constant cost per additional win idea that seems to have eluded all adherents. The dotted line is the best linear fit of the data. It gains in realism because it begins not from zero wins for zero spending, but from around 72–74 wins even if a team spends only $30 million or so, as did the Royals. From that starting point, rather than $1.14 million for an additional win, the best linear fit gives $8.74 million per win. Under this more reasonable alternative, the Rangers are still above the new line and generate more wins than expected for their spending. Indeed, for the Rangers, the expectation is almost identical under either specification. They actually won 96 games when this best linear fit suggests 81 expected wins; the Rangers beat this expectation by 15/81 = 19 percent. But the Yankees are now also above the line. They actually won 97 games where they would be expected to win 94 by their spending, 3/94 = 3 percent over their expected winning. Under the best linear fit, we also no longer get the weird result that the Royals, Pirates, and Padres beat expectations at all; instead they are now below the line. We can't resist pointing out that the Oakland A's are also a bit below this more reasonable line (they were just above the earlier less reasonable solid line representation). By this more reasonable linear relationship, the Yankees did just fine. They just didn't do quite as well as the Rangers.

From this perspective, the "inept GM" conclusion really doesn't pass muster. It relies on a linear relationship that clearly doesn't hold for winning. In addition, the untrue linear world foisted on people by this conclusion is a truly weak linear representation to begin with! Another, more compelling linear representation actually reverses the conclusion—the Yankees did better than their spending would have predicted, just not quite as well as did the Rangers. That might not further writing and broadcasting careers or sell papers and TV ad space, but it is much closer to the facts of the matter.

So the point is, it is easy to win a few games, but it often takes a tremendous payroll to have a very good team. Also, we have to remember that in MLB, a team that wins 30 percent more games compared with another team is considered to be much better than that other team. A team that wins 70 games is not very good, while a team that wins 91 games is one of the best teams in the league. We cannot stress enough that our main point is that *any linear analysis is a weak approach to understanding winning.* However, even if one adopts this strictly linear view of the world, there is a right way to do it and a wrong way to do it. The right way gets closer to reality. Even in a linear approximation done correctly, teams with high payrolls typically look more efficient. So teams like the Yankees, Lakers, Knicks . . . OK, the Knicks have still had very poor teams over the last decade with very high payrolls.

But in a world of uncertainty, the Knicks actually prove a nice example. First, how bad can bad get, or how good can good get, just randomly? The answer is surprising. Simple statistics reveals that streaks of 3–4 occur randomly for almost any process. Since economist Gerald Scully (1994) first made the case, it is also well known that sports success is cyclical, and cycles clearly describe the Knicks over their entire history. They enjoyed ten successive playoff appearances from the inception of the NBA, 1946–47, to 1955–56. Then there was a ten-year drought from 1956–57 to 1965–66, interrupted by only one playoff appearance (1958–59). Then the Knicks enjoyed another nine-year streak of playoff appearances, 1966–67 to 1974–75, where they were twice NBA champs (1969–70 and 1972–73). This Knicks heyday was followed by twelve years of spotty playoff appearances, 1975–76 to 1986–87. Note that the "streaks" during this period adhere to our observation of randomness, no consecutive appearances were longer than two seasons, and no consecutive period of playoff absence is longer than three seasons. An astonishing fourteen-year streak of successive appearances ran from 1987–88 to 2000–01. Most recently, in the last ten seasons, the Knicks are back on the downside of their completely cyclical success pattern, with only three playoff appearances, 2003–04, 2010–11, and 2011–12. Cycles should suggest that the Knicks are about to hit it big again.

STATISTICAL INTUITION

The statistical part of the persistence of the myth is actually quite simple to see. The starting premise is that GMs know player skill better than anybody and ought to predict eventual player performance pretty precisely. And yet it ends up that their choices are often wrong. The evidence is that some expensive, top draft-pick or high-priced free agent ends up a bust, while other owners have clearly uncovered passed-over gems. Sportswriters and other pundits point out the errors, and fans generally accept that the GMs (and their owners) under the lens are inept.

But that is not treating the GM's decision problem fairly, either literally or from the statistical standpoint. To treat the decision fairly, one must judge the decision at the point in time at which it was made. In addition, one must examine the decisions by a given GM (and the team owner by association) in total, rather than jumping to comparisons at a point in time. Is the GM under the microscope always worse than the rest of the GMs, or just in this particular instance? And are the other GMs, purported to be so much smarter, *always* better than the GM under the lens, or do they end up under the same attack at some other point in time? Of course, since the entire exercise is really forecasting future performance, very smart people are going to be wrong a relatively high percentage of the time. But the statistical issue is whether anybody else could do any better with the same information set at the point in time that the decision was made. If so, the GM under the lens is indeed making bonehead mistakes. But this is not an easy job.

The greatest lifetime average hitter was Ty Cobb (0.366). In twenty-four seasons, he played in 3,035 games with 11,434 at bats. But the standard deviations of these statistics are 0.038 points, 28 games, and 121 at bats. He hit below his lifetime batting average in ten seasons—that is, 42 percent of his career (on the other side of this variation, he also broke 0.400 three times). This variability, high and low, was for what some call *the greatest baseball player ever*. Indeed, if a baseball player hits .300 over a long career, they will invariably be considered for the Hall of Fame. Why do fans think that GMs are any better at guessing about player success than players are actually able to demonstrate success? Put another way, given the difficulty in actually performing at the major league level, how often will GMs actually be correct? To what standard should GMs be held in a game like baseball where players that fail 70 percent of the time (hitting 0.300) are judged as great?

So let's return to the scene of the crimes referenced above and view the choices at the same point in time that the decisions were made, at least starting from the fair statistical point of reference. First up, Harry Frazee sells Babe Ruth to the Yankees for what ends up to be $125,000 including finance charges in 1919. Many who follow baseball and ownership know the often-cited reason for this sale—Frazee was also a theatrical promoter/producer in need of money to finance his next play. However, as often happens with those wielding a highly selective lens, *all of the circumstances* of history are typically forgotten. Actually, two circumstances led to Frazee selling Ruth to the Yankees. First, Ruth was holding out, demanding double his pay. Yes, *double* his pay. Now he may have been worth that somewhere in the league, but Frazee did not agree he was worth that in Boston playing for the Red Sox. Second, the American League president at the time was no friend of Frazee and convinced everyone but the White Sox and Yankees not to buy Ruth's contract. So Frazee was left with little choice, given his assessment of Ruth's value to his Red Sox. Even though the options were limited, Frazee was able to get four payments of $25,000 ($100,000 total, or around $125,000 after interest payments), which at the time was the most ever paid for a player. In fact, Colonel Jacob Ruppert, part owner of the Yankees at the time, had earlier said, "Who ever heard of a ballplayer being worth $125,000 in cash?" (Wagenheim, 1974). By the way, remember that at this time, Ruth had only switched from pitching to full-time hitting for two seasons and was a far cry from the historic slugger he would eventually become. So was Frazee's sale of Ruth a foolish blunder, or the best business move that Frazee could make, under the gun by Ruth's salary demands and given unfair treatment by his own league president?

Next up, the Trailblazers draft Sam Bowie ahead of Michael Jordan in 1984. Lest we forget . . . while he was no Michael Jordan, Bowie played ten seasons in the NBA and had a respectable career. Let's also remember that the Houston Rockets also passed on Michael Jordan, drafting Hakeem Olajuwon with the first overall pick. Now, Olajuwon also had a long and prosperous NBA career, but somehow sports pundits have never taken the Rockets to task for the same pass over as the Trailblazers. Looking back, Bowie met the needs of the Trailblazers at the time better than Jordan. The Trailblazers already had capable guards and needed a center. It is also true that Bowie suffered from injuries through much of his career. It is hard to know how his career would have ended up if he had been healthy. It is virtually impossible to identify otherwise healthy players that eventually end up injury prone. It is easy to judge after the fact, but the eventual outcome for a given player is not always obvious at the time of the draft. So did the Trailblazers blow it, or did they draft the best they could get according to their needs and end up with a player unpredictably prone to injury?

Finally, the Falcons trade Brett Favre to Green Bay for a first-round pick in the 1992 draft (19th overall). While Atlanta took Favre in the second round, 33rd overall, then coach Jerry Glanville was against it from the outset. Chris Miller was a capable NFL quarterback in the fifth year of his ten-year career. Indeed, under Miller, the Falcons beat New Orleans to make it to the Division playoffs in Favre's first year. Miller was backed-up by Billy Joe Tolliver, who eventually had a nine-year career as a back up. Favre also was a revealed health liability in 1992, diagnosed with avascular necrosis of the hip (the same malady that ended Bo Jackson's career), a condition that led doctors to recommend the trade to Green Bay be nullified. In addition, while he ended up a short-career running back/kick returner, let's remember that Tony Smith, the player that the Falcons drafted (1992–96, the last two with no action at Carolina), was a 1,000-yard/8 TD rusher at Southern Mississippi and Senior Bowl MVP in 1991. Further, in 1992, he was not the unmitigated disaster that he would eventually become. In his first year with the Falcons he rushed for 329 yards and two TDs and just under 4 yards per rush (just behind Steve Broussard on all counts). He also averaged 10 yards per punt return and 25 per kickoff return. By the way, the Falcons did OK with their other first-round choice (8th overall), offensive tackle Bob Whitfield from Stanford. So did Atlanta screw up trading an unknown at that time for a first-round pick? On nearly all counts, it was just another trade at the time, and Atlanta could not possibly see the eventual disposition of Tony Smith.

To wrap it all up, let's return to the epigraph. The character Frank Costanza's rant at the actor playing George Steinbrenner on *Seinfeld* shows why it might be fun to point out teams' mistakes, but it also points out why running a sports team is a difficult job. First, it is easy to see *now* that Jay Buhner became a better player than Ken Phelps, but hindsight is always 20/20. As George Steinbrenner's character in *Seinfeld* replied, "Well, Buhner was a good prospect, no question about it, but my baseball people loved Ken Phelps' bat. They kept saying, 'Ken Phelps, Ken Phelps.'" Second, unfortunately for former Seattle Mariners general manager Dick Balderson, nobody made a sitcom that pointed out his amazing foresight in getting Jay Buhner to Seattle. This is really a nice segue into our next issue, the training of a selective lens on GMs.

THE SELECTIVE LENS

Anytime someone's performance is as public as it is in sports, mistakes are magnified and many people assume incompetence. This is especially true if the mistakes are presented through a selective lens, and that is precisely what happens, much to the confusion of the issue for fans. As we just alluded, sportswriters/broadcasters focus only on the busts for one set of GMs and the bargains for another set of GMs. By this selectivity, almost every GM will make a bonehead play at some time or another and, we guess, they are all inept! At the very least, this makes for a kaleidoscope of ever-changing bad GMs without ever making the relevant comparison—over time, is a given GM a really bad judge of talent or not?

The coverage above helps to make this clear. Frazee did send Ruth to the Yankees. But on the other side of this coin is the genius of the Yankees' owners. But this is never the point in any of the discussions, despite the fact that Ruth had really only been a "hitter" rather than a "pitcher" for a couple of seasons and was far from the historic slugger he would be eventually. The Trailblazers did pass on Michael Jordan. But so did the Rockets, and Jordan going third in the first round to Chicago is certainly no act of genius either. Table 8.1 shows the 1984 picks by both teams. We defy anybody to argue that one team was somehow better than the other at any of these draft stages, and we have already included the first round in our discussion of Bowie versus Jordan for the Blazers.

But nowhere was there any re-aiming of the lens when the top 5 choices by the two teams revealed that Portland actually had quite a nice draft. We've already covered Sam Bowie. Bernard Thompson (five seasons, 2,935 minutes, 1,078 points) and Steve Colter (eight seasons, 9,570 minutes, 3,319 points) became established pros. Jerome Kersey (seventeen seasons, 28,115 minutes, 11,825 points) became a solid star player. Only Victor Fleming never played. Chicago clearly did well with Jordan but traded Ben Coleman (five seasons, 3,612 minutes, 1,494 points) to New Jersey before he played a minute. Tim Dillon, Melvin Johnson, and Lamont Robinson never played in the NBA!

But remember, this is not to pick on the Bulls. The proof is in the long

TABLE 8.1. *1984 Drafts, Portland Trailblazers and Chicago Bulls*

Round	Portland	Chicago
1	Sam Bowie (Kentucky)	Michael Jordan (North Carolina)
	Bernard Thompson (Fresno State)	
2	Victor Fleming (Xavier, OH)	Ben Coleman (Maryland)
	Steve Colter (New Mexico State)	
	Jerome Kersey (Longwood)	
3	Time Kearney (WVU)	Tim Dillon (Northern Illinois)
4	Brett Applegate (BYU)	Melvin Johnson (UNC-Charlotte)
5	Mike Whitmarsh (San Diego)	Lamont Robinson (Lamar)
6	Lance Ball (Western Oregon)	Jeff Tipton (Morehead State)
7	Victor Anger (Pepperdine)	Butch Hayes (Cal)
8	Steve Flint (UCSD)	Brett Crawford (U.S. International)
9	Dennis Black (Portland)	Calvin Pierce (Oklahoma)
10	Randy Dunn (George Fox)	Carl Lewis (Houston)

Source: Compiled from media draft reports.

run eating of this pudding, and we are sure that the Blazers had their previous and subsequent bad years, just as the Bulls did in 1984 (outside of
Jordan, of course). Whether drafting or trading, talent evaluation is a difficult prospect at best. And that is about all that really can be said. Training
a selective lens on one GM in a given year rather than over a career, without
comparison to the rest of the GMs, and without any sense of the history of
GM performance, is simply biased reporting. Why sportswriters/broadcast-
ers should take this approach, contrary to the evidence, can only lie with
either their ignorance or the sensationalistic value of such reporting—that
is, human nature.

THE ROLE OF HUMAN NATURE

It is basic human nature that if something ends up wrong, somebody
should have known better at the outset. Rather than recognize all that we
have presented above, it is human nature to think that GMs should simply
"do better." When they make "mistakes" (judged unfairly with 20/20 hindsight), they demonstrate ineptness, and that simply cannot be tolerated.
From cell phone use while driving, to just plain bad driving, we are all arbi-
ters of other people's behavior. And sportswriters/broadcasters are honking
their horns and shouting the loudest at owner choices.

It is also basic human nature to remember glory and wonder where it went. Returning to the Knicks, despite their cyclical success, they have won the NBA Championship only twice, 1969–70 and 1972–73. They also have made the NBA Finals only those two years and six more scattered during the upside of their winning cycle. But no doubt these appearances in the finals are in the minds of all fans when sportswriters/broadcasters lament the current downside of Knicks performance. We are particularly tickled by this attitude at our own University of Michigan. Aside from Lloyd Carr's AP-only national championship in 1997, Michigan hasn't been national champion since 1948, under Bennie Oosterbaan. However, being in the running under Bo Schembechler through the 1970s and 1980s, along with the ever-present ghost of Fielding Yost (six national championships from 1901 to 1923), made current Michigan fans so bitter about their recent fare under coach Rich Rodriguez that his contract was terminated after only three of its original six years. Perhaps these fans don't need sportswriters/broadcasters reminding them of recent choices by athletic directors, but you know they are doing just that.

On yet another count, it is human nature to discount the role of luck in our lives, both good and bad. Every team in every major sports league knows they are potentially prone to injuries. One injury can make or break a season. But other than being age-related, and that particular motion mechanics that simply cannot be avoided cause them, injuries are nearly completely unpredictable. Furthermore, the ball can bounce the right way or the wrong way. Sometimes it's the breaks of the game that matter, especially in hotly contested races.

It is virtually impossible to tell how much of management success comes from talent and how much comes from luck. For example, consider a situation in which everything is determined by luck. Half of the owners, GMs, and coaches will win more than they lose. A few will win a lot more than they lose and will be able to do this repeatedly. The problem is, we simply do not know what role luck plays in this type of success. So it is nearly impossible to distinguish between luck and skill when it comes to owners and their GMs.

This issue is certainly not unique to the sports industry. For example, very smart people disagree about the efficiency of the stock market. While some people, such as former Federal Reserve chairman Alan Greenspan, argue that the market can have periods of "irrational exuberance" where there seems to be no rational reason for the way stock prices move, other very smart people claim that these prices are efficient, nonetheless. It's not that stock prices are all correct and the people paying the prices can see clearly into the future. It's that prices are completely rational given the available information. There are stockbrokers that have actually made money on stock price movement rather than selling services to their clients and earning their return on commissions. But was this skill or luck?

Of course, even if the market for playing talent is efficient, that is different from saying the average owner is skillful. It could be that all owners and their GMs are equally inept. But given competition over these jobs, this seems unlikely. Besides, usually when owners and their GMs are accused of ineptitude, it is on the grounds that they are relatively worse than others. Our argument is that when owners and their GMs do not perform well, it is more often the result of luck rather than ineptitude.

Finally, it is human nature to want somebody else to do what is best for us, rather than what is best for them. Winning is everything, and that's what owners should always do, win more! This has been true throughout ownership history; most thought Frazee should never be able to use baseball profits to finance other endeavors such as stage plays (surely Boston theater connoisseurs disagreed). But with billionaire owners less reliant on team performance to enhance their wealth portfolio, fans seem to find them wanting even more, recently, in the dedication to winning department.

For example, some research suggests that, relative to other players that contribute more to winning, NBA GMs overvalue players that score a lot of points. This will fundamentally irritate fans who want more wins rather than less. However, it may be perfectly rational to sign players that score a lot of points, since there is also some evidence that fans also like scoring. So it is possible for teams to maximize profit by having players that score a lot of points, and maybe do not play any defense, if that is what the fans who are willing to pay the most want to see the most.

It is evidence like this that leads to smug economists. As long as owners care about the bottom line, we actually can predict that fans will be unhappy if their only satisfaction is in their team's winning. The owner's goal may be different, reflected in the actions of the GM. Trades are another example where profit considerations temper winning. Sometimes trading talented veteran players is simply a profit-maximizing move instead of a winning move. Clearly it is not in the best interest of some teams financially to spend too much on payroll. Of course, this is a fundamental fan irritant, since they want more wins no matter the cost. Fans will not and should not like their team getting worse, and fans of small market teams know all too well that their team often loses their most talented players. However, we should not take this disparity of goals between teams and fans to imply owner incompetence. Some of the moves they make might be exactly the correct move to maximize profits.

In addition to these direct talent choices and profit tradeoffs, fans that care only about winning will also be dissatisfied when owners make decisions about the long-term versus short-term or even the team's place in the owner's larger business conglomerate view. We can take each of these cases one by one.

A long-term strategy by a team can sometimes look like a strategy that is simply giving up, or at least a strategy that minimizes costs. Sometimes it can be hard to tell if a team is investing in the future or simply not trying to win. If a talented veteran player is traded for younger players, it can be disheartening for fans, but sometimes this is the best strategy for the team. That is especially true when a team is aging and sees little hope of a championship in the near term. Given that fans and teams often want a chance to win the championship, it may be worth making the current team worse in order to improve the long-term chances of winning. Thus fans may mistake long-term aims at winning for short-term ineptness.

Turning to decisions about their entire wealth generating enterprise, especially in the era of modern ownership, an owner's goal for the team in the grander scheme of things may lead to dissatisfaction among win loving fans. It is becoming more and more common for sports teams to have complicated ownership structures, and so teams should think about how their performance affects other parts of the business. However, this should not make fans too angry about decisions, because if anything, this should create a situation in which the team wants to win even more. For example, if the team wins and a media outlet owns them, the media outlet increases revenue as well. Still, we should be aware that owners care about their entire wealth-generating business enterprise.

Sportswriters/broadcasters, through the selective lens, play on all of these aspects of human nature. Otherwise, wouldn't they be there cheerleading every time their GM made a good trade? Indeed, it is the beautiful symmetry of the sports talent market that, for every bad trade, there is a good trade. In fact, there are probably more good trades than bad trades, since some trades can help both teams with their particular needs. In the instance where one player turns out to be so much better than the player traded for, while there may have been one GM that made a bad mistake, there was also apparently one genius. But where are the sportswriters/broadcasters then? This is using human nature in a biased fashion as well. The fact that nothing but invalid statistics has already been pounded into fans forever only serves to bolster this observation.

It is certainly true that some owners and their GMs are better than others, at least for a period of time. However, we would argue that the disparity is not as large as some might think, and the overall quality of these team leaders is high. So while it could be possible that one particular GM is not particularly talented, it is a harder argument to make that as a group they just do not get it. To make this point, let's go back one year further, to the 2010 Yankees.

They finished second in their division behind the Tampa Bay Rays. The Rays lost to the Texas Rangers in their ALDS, while the Yankees beat the Minnesota Twins in their ALDS, then lost to the Rangers in the ALCS. So while the Rays payroll was a much lower $71.9 million than the Yankees $206.3 million, the Yankees fared better. They also fared better than the Braves, who lost to the eventual World Series champion San Francisco Giants in the NLDS. So Yankee payroll was 2.4 times larger than that of the Braves, and even larger than that of the Rays, but they got twice as far into the playoffs as either of these.

CONCLUSION—PHYSICIAN, HEAL THYSELF
(FANS ARE NO BETTER AT IT THAN GMS)

Rather than drone through the usual "here's what we have said" conclusion, we instead turn the tables on this myth with a concrete example of how good fans are at predicting talent. If sports leadership is awful at it, then fans should be better at least. Alas, such is not the case.

In the 2011 NCAA men's basketball tournament, the final four teams were #3 seed Connecticut, #4 seed Kentucky, #8 seed Butler, and #11 seed Virginia Commonwealth. Every year the masses predict who will get to the final four on Tournament Challenge at ESPN.com. Well, "only" 23.1 percent of fans correctly predicted that Connecticut would get to the final four. And that was the high point; 8.0 percent predicted that Kentucky would get there, 6.0 percent predicted Butler, and a mere 0.1 percent predicted Virginia Commonwealth in the final four. Correctly predicting final fours teams is not easy, but even if we knew nothing about the teams other than their seeding we should be able to correctly pick a final four team one out of sixteen times, or 6.25 percent of the time. Averaged across the actual final four teams, fans predicted the final four 9.3 percent of the time, and remember, these fans are not picking teams at random. These are the same fans that expect college coaches and professional GMs to be right nearly all of the time about future talent performance.

Perhaps fans are simply not as well informed as those who follow the games more closely—namely, sportswriters/broadcasters and college basketball experts. Alas for those foisting the myth of GM ineptitude off on fans, Espn.com also featured twelve celebrities and college basketball experts as "featured brackets." President Obama, Bill Simmons, Snoop Dogg, Colin Cowherd, Phil Hellmuth, Dick Vitale, Mike Greenberg, Scott Van Pelt, Matthew Berry, Michelle Beadle, and John Kincade picked *exactly zero final four teams correctly*. Mike Golic predicted Connecticut would make it. So out of forty-eight possible picks, this group got exactly one right (2.1 percent).

It is hard to blame fans or experts for the low prediction rates. After all, clearly many upsets happened during the 2011 NCAA tournament. But the point is, *upsets always happen,* and both teams and players often over- or under-perform. While the 2011 final four teams may have been harder to predict than in previous years, it was not *unusually* so. Virtually every year, people predict few final four teams correctly. So can we really blame NFL GMs for not always drafting well, or NBA GMs for making a bad trade? Perhaps the most important question along these lines is, "How often do we reasonably expect capable GMs to be wrong?" The answer is clearly "sometimes," and, indeed, might be "most of the time.

The destructive part of the myth is in the needless hard feelings created between ownership and the fans by sportswriters/broadcasters. And perpetuating this myth is like shooting fish in a barrel. There always will be a GM that, under a selective lens aided by 20/20 hindsight, made a "mistake." Since basic human nature is easy prey in this context, perpetuating the myth builds sportswriter/broadcaster careers and probably sells more papers and magazines. After all, given the success of rotisserie sports, many fans surely feel they are better at judging sports horseflesh than are owners and GMs. Disdain for the application of straightforward business decision-making principles by these perpetrators misleads fans rather than informing them and fuels the antagonistic relationship between fans, sports team owners and their GMs, and college athletic directors.

9 OWNERS LOSE MONEY ON THEIR SPORTS TEAMS

INTRODUCTION

Sports team ownership used to be a personal thing. "Old Tom" Yawkey used to sit in a blanket during his Boston Red Sox practices and "his boys" would all pass the time with him waiting their turn in the batting cage. But ownership has changed dramatically over the last couple of decades to the exclusive club of the fabulously wealthy. Even the identified managing partner in ownership groups earns that position by being the billionaire among multimillionaires. Today, nearly every team is only one element in their owner's wealth-generating portfolios.

As a result, to many sports fans and pundits, it seems that sports teams are now simply toys for billionaires. Part and parcel with this perspective, many reject the usual business and economic models as meaningful ways of analyzing ownership behavior and outcomes. At points in time when they face chances for very large gain, owners oblige this viewpoint strategically to their own ends. As the old joke among owners goes, the way to get a small fortune is to start with a large fortune and then buy a sports team. When confronting players at collective bargaining points or their state and local government hosts at subsidy revision points, owners claim massive losses and call for a "new business model."

So we end up with the usual trappings of myth. Sports fans hear from owners that teams are money pits. Despite the fact that there are perfectly sensible explanations that don't force anybody to abandon sound business and economic principles, mythical "ownership irrationality" somehow manages to dominate the discussion. For example, sports team prices are just a speculative bubble, driven by inflated expectations, destined to pop when a Keynesian "greater fool" can no longer be found (Keynes had argued that assets could continue to be improperly priced as long as a "greater fool" could be found). This myth is swallowed whole, despite the fact that these assets are expensive, rising in price over time, and hotly pursued by some of the wealthiest people in the world.

The myth gains its destructive power in two ways. First, it misdirects attention from the actual value of owning a team. There are many values of ownership that cannot be found looking only at the team's bottom line. Second, explanations based on ownership irrationality are easy to swallow when the economy is in a shambles. And, at the end of it all, comes an extremely expensive result. Following claims of poverty, owners are quick to remind local business interests and politicians that want the flow of value from sports team presence, that subsidies are required. Since subsidies have an opportunity cost, either spent privately or on some other public purpose, the myth can be destructive of the public purse because there probably weren't any losses in the first place. Thus the common belief that owners lose money on their sports teams is precisely the type of myth we want to cover in this book.

We unravel this myth as follows. First, it can make sense to assess the net value of ownership only by identifying all of the values of ownership. Part of the reason owners seem to successfully claim that teams lose money is to focus only on the team's own bottom line. However, there are other values beyond the bottom line. Second, with all values specified, the idea of "losing money" on a team can be put in its proper perspective. It is at this point that the myth begins to unravel, since perfectly rational reasons for observed increases in prices, even in the presence of negative team bottom lines, can be found to replace "ownership irrationality." And, even when prices fall, there's good reason for it.

THE VALUE OF TEAM OWNERSHIP

There is plenty of evidence that the bottom line matters to owners. Fans criticize owners for being rapacious monopolists in their pricing policies, and owners are clearly not in the charity business. Lately, owners have been using the same complicated, peak-load computer simulation ticket pricing approach used by airlines and hotel chains in the pricing of tickets and rooms. Surely they could let just a few of those dollars stay with fans if the bottom line didn't matter. On the other side of the business coin, owners spend massive amounts of money in arbitration and salary negotiations trying to keep the cost side in order. Again, the discipline of the bottom line is in force. Sometimes there is not much there, if positive, and in some spectacular cases the bottom line is negative. But the team bottom line isn't all that matters.

There also is plenty of evidence that ownership is valuable beyond the team's bottom line. One of our favorite classroom examples is the Seattle Supersonics. Howard Schultz, the Starbucks billionaire, bought the team in December 2000 for $200 million. Strictly by the bottom line, over the 2000–01 to 2004–05 seasons, the Sonics bottom line showed losses of $47.5 million, $63.1 million, $46.6 million, $27.6 million, and $33.1 million, respectively. Unadjusted for inflation (because we're not that interested for the points made here), that's a total of $217.9 million. Aside from the greater fool theory, how in the wide world of sports did Mr. Schultz then sell the team in 2006 to Clay Bennett (who then moved the Sonics to become the Oklahoma City Thunder) for $350 million (adjusted for inflation, that's a 6.9 percent real rate of annual growth)?

The answer is simple. First, a loss on the books need not really be a loss. Smith College economics professor Andrew Zimbalist (1992, p. 62) offers one of our favorite quotations on the subject by former Toronto Blue Jays president Paul Beeston: "Under generally accepted accounting principles, I can turn a $4 million profit into a $2 million loss, and I can get every national accounting firm to agree with me." Fort and Quirk (1992) formally showed how the well-known tax allowance for pro sports team owners allows large "depreciation" write-offs on the "roster value" of the team. For the Sonics, these write-offs actually reduce the losses to about $78.5 million. Also under allowed firm structuring for tax purposes, any remaining losses can be passed through to the owner's 1040 Form to shelter other income. And remember, this pass-through shelter is calculated from the bottom line losses.

For a billionaire like Mr. Schultz, paying the highest 33 percent marginal tax rate, that's a shelter of $71.9 million on the $217.9 million loss. Since losses after counting the special sports depreciation are already reduced to $78.5 million, this additional shelter value actually sends the true loss on the Sonics down to $6.6 million over five years, or about $1.3 million annually.

But are these really losses, or an investment in a set of remaining values that are generated by team ownership? Other values of ownership are well known. There are related business opportunities and political clout from ownership. There can be no doubt that Jerry Jones has reincarnated the original Cotton Bowl Game because of his fabulous new stadium. But without ownership of the Cowboys he never would have gotten that stadium with all the trimmings. In addition to related business opportunities, owners can also take profit directly from the team on the cost side. Low interest loans are common, occasionally owners and their family members actually take salaries on the team, and "the team" may buy some services from its owners (e.g., legal services). There also can be revenue shifting tax advantages. Smith College economist Andrew Zimbalist (1998) relates how Wayne Huizenga's "loss" claims on the Florida Marlins relied on strategic allocation of resources between the team, stadium operations, and the regional broadcaster all owned partly by Huizenga himself. Sometimes ownership is enough to catapult a related media enterprise, such as the relationship between the New York Yankees and YES Network.

From this perspective, the clear question to ask Mr. Schultz is whether it was worth $1.3 million annually to gain these additional values that do not appear on the Sonics' bottom line. More to the point, observed behavior suggests that these additional values were quite large, given the incredible increase in value to his sale to Mr. Bennett. A real annual rate of growth equal to 6.9 percent is twice the typical real annual growth rate of the economy at large, and Mr. Schultz gave up this type of growth at sale.

In baseball at large, previous work by Fort (2006) shows that these additional values, including the tax advantages, are worth upward of 20 percent of purchase price. So, suppose you buy a team for $400 million. Twenty percent is $80 million. At $1 million per year in terms of losses (ignoring discounting), you'd run out the value in eighty years! What seems much more likely, instead, is that the returns outweigh the costs if you look in the right place for the returns.

It is certainly true that sports franchise values have dramatically increased over the past couple of decades, or even the last century. For example, the Duluth Kellys, which later became the Washington Redskins, were bought for one dollar, and the new owner assumed the liability of the team's debts. Even if the team's liability was large at the time, this seems like a pretty good investment, given that the team is now worth roughly $1.5 billion according to recent estimates at *Forbes*.

Now, it is worth a note on the *Forbes* values before we go any further. First, in our opinion, while the *Forbes* data on revenues is probably in the area code and can be cross-checked in numerous ways, the same is not true of the cost estimates. Thus it should come as no surprise that owners often reject the income-expense statements portion of the *Forbes* data. Padres president and COO Tom Garfinkel took exception with one Forbes report as follows (Center, 2011):

> The financial numbers in the *Forbes* article are inaccurate. I'm not sure where they get financial numbers for 30 private businesses without simply manufacturing them. The team lost money on a cash basis in 2010. Their valuation methodology is flawed and their numbers are inaccurate. Therefore, their valuation conclusions have no merit.

Second, given the past work just mentioned, it is most appropriate to think of the *Forbes* estimates as referring to stand alone team values ignoring all of the "other values of ownership" mentioned above. Indeed, the *Forbes* estimates have been taken to task for being too low, for example, by Ted Leonsis, owner of the NHL Washington Capitals (Scheck, 2008):

> *The Wall Street Journal*: You still have a ways to go, right? *Forbes Magazine* said in November that the Caps are worth $145 million—28th out of the 30-team NHL.
> Mr. Leonsis: The *Forbes* numbers are the biggest [expletive] joke I've ever seen, but we bring it upon ourselves because we don't publish our numbers. A banker who did our numbers, based on comparables, said our value would be $225 million to $250 million.

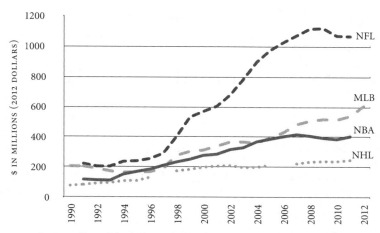

F I G. 9.1. Average Franchise Values. Created using Annual Team Valuations at
Forbes.com.

More recently in 2012, the Dodgers sold for around $2.1 billion, and Forbes
valued the Dodgers at $1.4 billion in 2012 and only $800 million in 2011.

In any event, these estimates are one useful piece of data created by observers who have been producing them since 1990 (back at the now defunct
Financial World magazine). Figure 9.1 shows the average team values given
by *Financial World* or *Forbes* (henceforth, FW-F) for each league. Even adjusted for inflation, team values have risen dramatically. Table 9.1 shows
most team sale prices over the last decade in the NFL, MLB, NBA, and NHL,
and how they stack up against the contemporaneous FW-F team valuation
estimates. Some of the actual transactions include other assets than just the
team. For example, there can be various deals that involve related properties, including the stadium or other capital. Trying to be fair to the FW-F
estimates, Table 9.1 shows the average of the percentage differences that fell
within plus or minus 40 percent of the actual sale price. Thus, when they are
closest to the actual value by this arbitrary (but fair) choice, FW-F estimates
are between 7 and 11 percent below actual sale prices. The understatement
is largest for the NBA, about 11 percent for sales over the last decade. This
is completely in keeping with the explanation in this section (and observations like those offered by Mr. Leonsis)—values to owners are actually in

TABLE 9.1. *Team Sale Prices Compared with Financial World/Forbes Estimates (2001–10, $Millions)*

Year	Team	Price	% Purchased	Implied value	Financial World/ Forbes	% Difference
	MLB					
2004	Cincinnati Reds	6.1	7%	91	245	169.23%
2001	Colorado Rockies	35	24%	148	334	125.68%
2004	Colorado Rockies	20	14%	143	285	99.30%
2002	New York Mets	150	50%	300	483	61.00%
2003	Anaheim Angels	184	100%	184	225	22.28%
2004	Los Angeles Dodgers	371	100%	371	399	7.55%
2007	Atlanta Braves	450	100%	450	458	1.78%
2006	Cincinnati Reds	270	100%	270	274	1.48%
2006	Washington Nationals	450	100%	450	440	−2.22%
2005	Milwaukee Brewers	220	100%	220	208	−5.45%
2002	Montreal Expos	120	100%	120	108	−10.00%
2002	Florida Marlins	158.5	100%	159	137	−13.84%
2009	Chicago Cubs	845	95%	845	700	−17.16%
2010	Texas Rangers	593	100%	593	451	−23.95%
2002	Boston Red Sox	700	100%	700	428	−38.86%
Ave.						*−7.13%*
	NBA					
2001	Atlanta Hawks	184	100%	184	199	22.28%
2004	Charlotte Hornets	65	35%	186	225	20.97%
2001	Seattle Supersonics	200	100%	200	200	12.50%
2004	Atlanta Hawks	208	100%	208	232	8.17%
2004	New Jersey Nets	300	100%	300	296	−25.00%
2003	Charlotte Bobcats	300	100%	300	225	−25.00%
2006	Seattle Supersonics	350	100%	350	268	−35.71%
2002	Boston Celtics	360	100%	360	274	−37.50%
2005	Cleveland Cavaliers	375	100%	375	356	−40.00%
2004	Phoenix Suns	401	100%	401	356	−43.89%
2010	Golden State Warriors	450	100%	450	315	−50.00%
Ave.						*−11.03%*
	NFL					
2004	Baltimore Ravens	325	51%	637	776	21.82%
2005	Minnesota Vikings	600	100%	600	658	9.67%
2003	Washington Redskins	200	20%	1,000	952	−4.80%
2008	Miami Dolphins	550	100%	1,100	1044	−5.09%

Year	Team	Price	% Purchased	Implied value	Financial World/ Forbes	% Difference
2009	Miami Dolphins	550	45%	1,222	1015	−16.94%
2002	Atlanta Falcons	27	5%	540	407	−24.63%
2001	Atlanta Falcons	545	100%	545	338	−37.98%
Ave.						−8.28%
	NHL					
2001	Florida Panthers	104.7	100%	105	115	9.52%
2003	Buffalo Sabres	92	100%	92	95	3.26%
2004	New Jersey Devils	125	100%	125	124	−0.80%
2007	Tampa Bay Lightning	206	100%	206	199	−3.40%
2006	St. Louis Blues	150	100%	150	144	−4.00%
2008	Edmonton Oilers	200	100%	200	175	−12.50%
2001	Montreal Canadiens	183	80%	228	182	−20.18%
2007	Nashville Predators	193	100%	193	143	−25.91%
2006	Vancouver Canucks	150	50%	300	211	−29.67%
2009	Montreal Canadiens	575	100%	575	339	−41.04%
2004	Atlanta Thrashers	250	85%	294	106	−63.95%
Ave.						−6.67%

Sources: Created from sale prices and *Financial World/Forbes* valuation data at Fort (2012).
Notes: Averages are for Percentage Difference with absolute value less than or equal to 40%. Brewers 2005, Sharks 2002, and Thrashers 2004 some debt assumed. Forbes year estimates are different as follows: Charlotte 2004 is 2005; Charlotte 2003 is 2004; GS 2010 is 2009; St. Louis Blues 2006 is 2007; Vancouver 2006 is 2007.

excess of the simple bottom line of the team. This result casts doubt on the idea that owners lose money on their teams. In the next section we show that basic finance tools dispel this myth as well.

BASIC FINANCE AND THE VALUE OF TEAM OWNERSHIP

The first basic financial insight is that the value of a team should reflect the discounted stream of all returns over time; nobody would pay more for an asset than it can generate for them over time. In what follows, we take advantage of this basic finance insight to see if sports teams represent a poor investment or not. We do this by generating approximate price to earnings ratios for pro sports teams, but also remembering the fact that there are other values generated by team ownership, as portrayed in Table 9.1. Actual sale values are larger than the FW-F team valuations by 7.1 percent in MLB, 11.0 percent in the NBA, 8.3 percent in the NFL, and 6.7 percent in the NHL. This shows that actual sales values are difficult to estimate, but it also gives evidence that Forbes is not taking into account all of the many different types of values created from a sports team.

But let's start with just the values generated by the team, itself. Starting here, the point of analysis from basic finance is the discounted stream of profits. Unfortunately, as is often the case with sports, profit data is either scarce, or only a rough estimate can be provided. While we have some income statements from a few teams, there is no comprehensive source for the profits for all teams. This makes knowing this part of the value of owning a team difficult, but we can gain insight into profits using the FW-F estimates of revenues and information from the occasional released financial statement.

Unfortunately, profit data are typically unavailable in sports (but there are some data). This makes the FW-F data one of the very few sources of a twenty-year series of profit data. Figure 9.2 shows the ratio of the total of all franchise values divided by the *Forbes* estimate of earnings before interest, taxes, depreciation, and amortization (EBITDA) for the entire league. The figure shows these values over the last decade for each league. Over this period, the ratios in the different leagues range from 20 to about 60. Some of the values are not reported in the graph because the *Forbes* data include years of very small to negative EBITDA. In MLB and the NHL, in the omitted years, EBITDA is nearly zero, so that the ratio is uninformative. In addition, the NHL did not play its 2004–05 season. In the last couple of years, these ratios have gone up a bit. In 2011 (the 2011–12 season for the NBA and NHL), the ratio was almost 34 for the NFL, about 57 for the NHL, and 67 for the NHL. In 2012, the ratio was 42 for MLB.

Given the misgivings that many have with the *Forbes* data, we check some of it against the few actual statements that are publicly available. For example, Green Bay Packers financial statements are publicly available because the team is publicly owned. In addition, in 2010, Deadspin.com obtained and released financial documents for the Pittsburgh Pirates, Tampa Bay Rays, Florida Marlins, Anaheim Angels, Seattle Mariners, and Texas Rang-

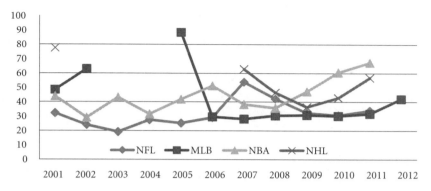

FIG. 9.2. Value Divided by Operating Income. Created using Annual Team Valuations at Forbes.com.

ers. The nature of the publicly reported data for these few teams allows us to make the relevant comparison with the Forbes EBITDA estimate.

As Table 9.2 shows, on average the Packers reported net income (in this case, profits *after* interest, taxes, depreciation and amortization) is about 76.0 percent of the *Forbes* EBITDA estimate. Table 9.3 shows that the over-statement is much more dramatic for baseball teams. On average, the net income reports from deadspin.com are only 35.8 percent of the Forbes EBITDA estimates for these baseball teams over the tabled years. So for the NFL and MLB we can adjust the *Forbes* EBITDA estimates to estimate the price to earnings ratio. If we adjust these ratios for the existence of other values of ownership as suggested in Table 9.1 and for the issues with the *Forbes* EBITDA estimates relative to the Packers and MLB, as just noted, we get Table 9.4. Table 9.4 shows value divided by EBITDA and estimates for value divided by profits for MLB and the NFL. Since profits are less than EBITDA, the value to profits ratio is higher than the value to EBITDA ratio. Since we do not have good estimates of EBITDA to profits for the NBA and NHL, we do not estimate the value to profits ratio for those leagues. We continue on with these ratios and compare them to price to earnings ratios in other industries.

Table 9.5 shows price to earnings ratios for various industries. We notice that the ratio of value to profits is higher for each league, compared with the

TABLE 9.2. *Packers EBITDA, Operating Profit, and Net Income, 1997–2009 ($millions)*

Year	Forbes EBITDA	Forbes Operating Profit (Loss)	Packers Net Income
1997	−1.2	8.05	6.72
1998	16.4	6.99	6.47
1999	−1	−0.42	2.67
2000	9.4	2.77	5.63
2001	2.7	3.27	3.76
2002	30.4	23.2	15.52
2003	23.4	29.15	20.77
2004	35.4	33.73	25.44
2005	22.3	20.93	18.03
2006	20.3	34.25	22
2007	21.9	21.42	23.36
2008	20.1	20.11	4.02
2009	9.8	9.79	5.2
Ave.	16.15	16.4	12.28

Source: Created using Annual Team Valuations at Forbes.com and Packers webpage.
Notes: Packers Net Income is before expansion revenue.

TABLE 9.3. *MLB EBITDA and Net Income, 2007–09 ($million)*

Team	Year	Forbes EBITDA	Net Income
Pittsburgh Pirates	2007	17.6	15
Pittsburgh Pirates	2008	15.9	14.4
Tampa Bay Rays	2007	29.7	11.1
Tampa Bay Rays	2008	29.4	4
Florida Marlins	2008	43.7	29.5
Florida Marlins	2009	46.1	3.9
Anaheim Angels	2008	10.3	7.1
Anaheim Angels	2009	12	10.7
Seattle Mariners	2007	10.1	17.9
Seattle Mariners	2008	3.8	−4.5
Texas Rangers	2008	17.4	−10.4
Texas Rangers	2009	4.7	−12
Ave.		20.1	7.2

Source: Created from deadspin.com leak data at Fort (2012).
Notes: EBITDA are from Forbes.com annual team valuations. Net income is from the deadspin.com leak.

TABLE 9.4. *Adjustments to Approximate Price to Earnings Ratios*

League	Range (Fig. 9.2)	2011–12 Value/ EBITDA Ratios	Adjustments		2011–12 Value/ Profits Ratios
			Other Values (Table 9.1)	MLB & NFL (Tab. 9.2 and 9.3)	
MLB	28–89	42.0	0.071	0.358	117.3
NBA	29–52	67.4	0.110		
NFL	19–53	33.9	0.083	0.760	44.6
NHL	36–78	56.9	0.067		

Sources: deadspin.com leak data at Fort (2012).
Notes: EBITDA are from Forbes annual team valuations.Net income is from the deadspin.com leak.
Example calculation of adjusted ratios: For MLB 2012, Adjusted 2012 Ratio is 42/.358 = 117.3.

TABLE 9.5. *Price to Earnings Ratios of Other Industries, 2012*

Industry Name	P/E ratio	Industry Name	P/E ratio
Maritime	286.65	Hotel/Gaming	57.37
		NFL	44.61
IT Services	165.14	Healthcare Information	43.87
MLB	117.32		
Publishing	102.49	Public/Private Equity	6.65
		Total Market	*42.56*

Source: Damodaran (2012).
Notes: Price to earnings ratio is the price of common stock in the industry to earnings per share. The
data are for January 2012.

average industry in 2012, which had a p/e ratio 42.56. However, the differences are not that dramatic. MLB had a ratio of 117.3, but this is quite a bit less than IT services. The NFL had a ratio of 44.6, which is comparable to the healthcare information industry. All in all it seems fair to say that price to earnings ratios can be high in sports, occasionally comparing to the top end of other industries in America.

Price to earnings ratios, or value to profits ratios, should depend on expected growth rates. So while the value of sports teams does seem to be a bit high when compared with their profits, if owners expect profits to increase, then these ratios should be high. Whether team owners should expect high growth rates into the future is beyond our analysis, but we can at least look at past growth rates. From 2000 to 2010 (2000–01 to 2001–11 for the NBA and NHL) the most recent reported data, adjusted for inflation, average EBITDA grew annually as follows: 5.1 percent in the NFL, 9.0 percent in MLB, and 4.8 percent in the NHL. However, EBITDA in the NBA has not quite kept up with inflation, and their real growth rate from 2000 to 2010 was –1.0 percent. These growth rates were quite a bit higher before the recent recession. After all, over the same time period, the U.S. GDP per capita growth barely kept up with inflation, the real growth rate was 0.4 percent. If we calculated these rates before the economic downturn, league growth rates would still surpass GDP per capita growth (with the exception of the NBA), but all rates would be higher.

So if we used these past growth rates for profits as estimates for future growth rates, and then put these estimated growth rates into a financial valuation model (like the constant growth model, for example), it would not be hard to argue that current franchise values actually underestimate the value of the team. Certainly it depends on the reliability of the data and what we should consider our depreciation rate, but if MLB profits rise anywhere near 9 percent in the long term, these teams are vastly undervalued. So then the question becomes, how likely is a 9 percent growth rate in the long term? Admittedly, this an unusually high growth rate, but we should remember that sports teams have done very well over the past few decades in terms of increasing profits. Any statement that teams are undervalued relies on the argument that profits will not rise anywhere near the growth rates of the past.

While it is certainly possible that manufactured housing or wireless networking could expect high growth rates, it might not be crazy to think that MLB or the NFL could do just as well if not better. Also, let's not forget our earlier point. These profits that are on the books are not all of the benefits that the owner receives, so these p/e ratios should be a bit high.

CONCLUSIONS—TWO FAMOUS EXAMPLES

Our punch line, of course, is that characterizing sports teams as a losing investment couldn't be further from the truth revealed by both the logic of ownership value and the simple finance of actual ownership value outcomes. Two additional examples make this point abundantly clear. *Forbes* valued the New York Yankees at $1.6 billion in 2010. Even if we disregard their operating profits strictly from team operations, Richard Sandomir (2007) of the *New York Times* reported in 2007 that the YES Network alone was valued at $3 billion. Since *Forbes* does not divulge all of their data, it is not obvious how much of the YES Network is included in the $1.6 billion. The Yankees do receive annual payments from the YES Network in the form of broadcasting rights, and the Yankees also own about one-third of the network. The bottom line is that the YES Network would not be worth nearly that much if it were not for the Yankees.

The Dallas Cowboys are another interesting case. In 2012, *Forbes* valued the Cowboys at $1.85 billion, which might seem high considering what franchise values were three or four decades ago. However, *Forbes* also estimated the Cowboys' EBITDA at $119 million. Applying the adjustment factor for the Packers, we would generate a price to earnings approximation as follows: $1,850/(119*0.76) = 20.5$, about the same as biotechnology. This seems low, but remember that Cowboys owner Jerry Jones recently incurred significant debt to build the new Cowboys Stadium, which will impact future profits. On the other hand, there surely are values galore beyond the Cowboys' own bottom line. Cowboy Stadium has hosted other events, such as college football games, the resurrected original Cotton Bowl, and the NBA All-Star game. These other revenues would not have been possible without an NFL team as the permanent resident of the new stadium.

The upshot of all of this is as follows. Even though there has been a dramatic increase in pro sports franchise values, it appears completely warranted since both team profits and the "other values of ownership" have been rising. Given the increase in profits over the last two decades and other financial benefits of sports ownership, these increases in franchise values are far from "irrational."

Speaking of "irrational," we can't help but return to the "speculative bubble" view of sports team valuations to make our point about the damage done by this myth. A few years ago, Tom Van Riper (2009) at Forbes. com correctly posed the bubble idea as a puzzle: Is the rise in the value of pro sports teams a bubble? The answer, like many things in life, is that it is difficult to tell. But let's at least start with an understanding of a speculative bubble.

A speculative bubble is characterized by trade in high volumes at prices that are considerably at variance with intrinsic values. Thus, during a bubble we would observe a rapid run-up in prices caused by excessive buying that is unrelated to any of the basic, underlying factors affecting the supply or demand for the underlying asset, in this case pro sports franchises. Most would agree that such a bubble is caused by exaggerated expectations of future growth. Bubbles are not well understood beyond this set of descriptions plus the identification of exaggerated expectations. Indeed, the only thing known for sure about bubbles is that they eventually burst.

Worshippers at the altar of "irrationality" have decided that the bubble of their own invention has indeed burst. For example, Dan Weil (2010) voices the following:

> Team owners have been able to live high on the hog thanks to an unprecedented three-decade boom in team values: the Jockstrap Bubble. As the financial exuberance of the 1980s, 1990s and whatever-we're-calling-the-last-decade mounted, hot money, ego and new revenues from sponsorships and luxury boxes combined to kick-start a boom in professional sports-team ownership. And once the notion took hold that teams would perpetually rise in value, it wasn't long before owners began blowing through the new cash in ever more extravagant ways. . . .
>
> Sports teams were caught up in the same bubble that enveloped financial markets, real estate, art and virtually every other asset that could be exchanged by humans.

He justifies the sports ownership part of it on the idea that sports teams lately have been selling at a loss—that is, for fewer dollars than the original purchase price, an occurrence that hasn't been witnessed since the 1970s.

Now, if one views the entire world as a bubble, it is small wonder that sports team values also are included. But there are very real problems with this view. First, it simply is not true that "teams are selling below their purchase price." In the same book cited earlier, James Quirk and Fort (1992) documented this far back in history and, in the same paper cited earlier,

Fort (2006) documents that, while a very few teams declined in price occasionally, by and large sports team ownership is a pretty safe investment. Our Figure 9.1 also backs this up. Second, a decline in value that is based on a drop in the value of the underlying fundamental contributors to value is not a "bubble" bursting. Even housing need not have been a bubble, since optimism was fueled by cumulative fraud in the so-called mortgage-based asset market.

What we have shown is that the fundamentals of finance provide a straightforward explanation of team values and, thus, the value of owning teams. Further, when the value of a given team does fall, it is much more likely that recessionary periods impact the price of all assets, including sports teams. The fundamental sources of their value—sponsorship and luxury boxes, and TV revenues (reduced because fan demand is down for almost everything in a recession)—slip, and so do team values. Rather than "irrational," this outcome is just fundamental finance in operation.

But that doesn't stop others from grabbing on to the idea that irrationality drives the world of sports team ownership. Unfortunately, the misuse of "irrationality" belies a more fundamental underlying issue. It's appealing emotionally, especially for the vast majority of people who believe that owners are idiots in the first place. If everybody believes that irrationality rules in pro team ownership, many who hate owners now have earned their place at the podium. In addition, those who think focus on sports is overblown now have ammunition.

This does not mean that all owners generate huge returns on their investments. As we'll describe in the next chapter, if previous owners expect large future returns, then current owners have already paid for all of the associated benefits of owning a sports team in the form of the sale price. On the other hand, this also doesn't mean the owners are losing money.

The myth is destructive because it misdirects attention from the actual value of owning a team. This is important information not just for owners to know, but also for taxpayers to know, both at the state and local level, and at the federal level, since often this is used as an argument for increased subsidies for owners.

10 PLAYER SALARY DEMANDS INCREASE TICKET PRICES

It bothers me enormously that no longer can a family of four see a game. What's happened is the [player] salaries are so high, we have to keep raising ticket prices. I don't want to raise my prices again.

— Abe Pollin, former owner of the Washington Wizards and Capitals

(Heath, 1997)

INTRODUCTION

If even an owner says it, shouldn't it be true? No wonder fans bemoan what they think are the facts. First, fans bemoan that tickets are too expensive. The Fan Cost Index is a sort of CPI for live attendance at North American pro sports games published by Team Marketing Reports (www.teammarketing.com). Their "sports market basket" for two adults and two children includes tickets, refreshments, parking, and souvenirs. While not all fans incur all of these expenses every time they attend, the index is useful for comparison between teams and over time. We choose the NFL because it is the most expensive (the most recent Fan Cost Index data are for 2011). The New York Jets topped NFL average ticket prices for 2011 at $120.85, and the New England Patriots topped premium ticket prices at $566.67. Adding in the rest of the basket, the price of the 2011 sports market basket for the NFL ranges from Jacksonville at the bottom, $316.50, to the Jets at the top, $628.90 (the average was about $427). Taking the average family to some pro games looks more like a trip to Disneyland than the trip to the stadium their parents might remember as kids.

Second, what do fans observe at the same time? Players continue to enjoy huge salaries and salary increases over time. (As long-time observers of the player pay scene, we agree that this is true.) With the help of statements by team owners (see the epigraph), and laments by sportswriters/broadcasters about the "corporatization" of sports attendance, fan arithmetic jumps to two plus two must equal four; player pay must be the cause of the increased prices they face. The easy explanation is that players are greedy (or at least tough negotiators) and that the only thing owners can do is to pass the expense on to fans. How else can owners still make a go of it in the face of these staggering results for players?

This myth rests on a complete misunderstanding of the most basic Econ 101 reasoning. The root cause of higher ticket prices and everything else in the sports market basket is not player salary. Player salaries rise because fans over time have shown a remarkable willingness to pay ever-increasing amounts for sports attendance over time, both at the gate and on TV or over the Internet. In other words, fans don't face increasing ticket prices because salaries increase. Salaries increase because increases in willingness to pay for sports characterize fan demand over time. The data bear this out and refute the myth as well.

Three other Econ 101 mistakes are as follows. First, as is generally human nature, no comparison is ever thrown into the discussion of what "high" price even means. Without any context, this is the same error that people make lamenting the high price of gasoline. Is it really (in the economic sense of the word) higher historically, or compared with other goods? Second, before fans get too carried away, they should sit down with economists and ponder this. There is a good economic reason that prices should be even higher (!) in leagues in which there are sellouts. Finally, despite the fact that many owners generate nifty profits from their teams, it is the case that owners would lose money—that's right, *lose* money—rather than just take lower profits by lowering some ticket prices.

The destructive power of this myth is that it drives an even wider wedge of resentment between fans and players than already would exist without the myth. Some begrudge high pay to those who receive it, and sports fans are no different. Just listen to fans when "bonus baby" rookies or newly acquired star free agents fail to perform up to expectations. The heckling invariably includes shouts of "overpaid!" It is clearly the sentiment of many fans that players are overpaid during contentious collective bargaining episodes, such as those that have plagued every sport over the last fifteen years.

The myth that this then also means fans are paying more adds insult to injury. This wedge of resentment serves owners well during collective bargaining, where sometimes judicial and even political intervention, fueled by public sentiment, can enter into the process.

MYTH BUSTING

Even intuitively, those who buy into the myth should feel a sense that something is wrong. If owners could simply raise ticket prices to cover some cost increase (such as an increase in salaries), why wouldn't they raise ticket prices even without any cost increase? And one simple data comparison adds to what should be a bothersome intuition. Figure 10.1 shows that player salaries have far outpaced ticket prices. Data are not available over a long enough period to make any long-term conclusions in the NFL and NHL, but data from the NBA and MLB show that since the 1950s and 1960s player salaries are now about ten times higher relative to ticket prices. So while ticket prices and player salaries have both clearly been on the rise, something else is certainly going on with player salaries. If owners were increasing ticket prices to cover player costs, then fans would be very fortunate that teams have been able to come up with other revenue streams, especially media revenues, because if those revenues were not available they would have had to increase ticket prices by much, much more to cover player salaries.

Before we move on, it is important to acknowledge (remember) two things about pay in pro sports. First, if we were to look over an extensive period of time, the advent of free agency has dramatically affected player pay. Under "reserve clauses" in sports, the only time players could change teams was to follow their contract. Through litigation and collective bargaining, these reserve clauses were modified to create free agency for players after a certain number of years in the league. As one would expect, once players are able to sell their services to the highest bidder, salaries increased. But this is an "earthquake level" event in salaries, shifting all pay, rather than the type of annual change over time that is the point of the myth.

The second overarching factor to consider is that player pay is tied by

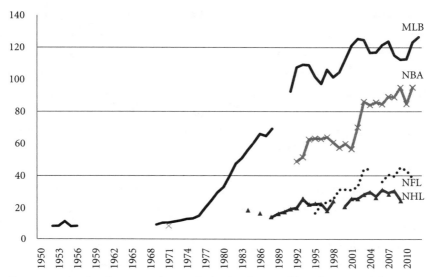

FIG. 10.1. Ratio of average player salaries (in thousands) and average ticket prices. Created from average salaries at USAToday.com. Salary Data Base and ticket prices from Team Marketing's Fan Cost Index.

formula to revenues in three of the major leagues (all but MLB) through payroll caps. Through collective bargaining, owners and players decide how to split up sport revenues. The share that goes to players is then divided equally across all teams, and that is the so-called payroll cap. So players are restricted in their salary demands by the room that any given owner has under the cap in any given season. This is a nice segue into our main point: it is revenues that determine player salaries.

The chain of economic occurrences goes like this. Owners determine how much more fans are willing to pay for games and related goods and services (concessions, parking, memorabilia) at the gate and for games on TV. In Econ 101 terms, this is an increase in demand for *the final sports product* at the gate and on TV. Note that if nothing else happened, prices at the gate and for TV viewing would rise just because of this shift in demand. This has nothing to do with player pay at all . . . yet. But there is more.

With a modicum of competition for player services, owners use this increase in revenue to bid among each other for player services, bidding up pay to players. In Econ 101 terms, this is an increase in *the derived demand for player services.* (One interesting thing about pro sports talent is that its availability doesn't change much with a change in price, so what fans typically see is the same players paid more than were previously. While this can be a head-scratcher, we all love it when we are simply in higher demand and our pay goes up while we do the same job.) So it is true that ticket prices and player pay go up at about the same time. But the causality is from revenues to player pay—that is, from the fact that fans are willing to pay more in the first place.

Now, the culmination of all of this is that player pay represents a cost to owners. So the final step in the economic chain of events is that the cost function for owners shifts up as well. So in addition to the fact that increased fan demand raises prices to fans, the increase in cost is partly passed on to fans as well. It is a bit of a technical issue, but owners cannot pass on the full cost of the payroll increase; demand slopes down, price rises, and owners don't raise price to *all* fans because some fans buy less as the price increases.

So the outcome is, as fans see it, that both prices and salaries go up. But the causality is not at all as portrayed by some owners and taken for granted by fans. Rather than salaries causing ticket price increases, it is ticket price increases that cause salaries to rise. The same is true for television and the growing presence of sports through streaming media, by the way. Increases in fan willingness to pay for games under the standard fee structure and under premium fee structures actually raise the price of those TV offerings. Players will also earn a part of this increase in revenues, but it is the increase in willingness to pay that starts the whole chain of events in motion.

As is always the case with myths, the data reveals this one for what it is. First, let's look at just recent history, sport by sport, where "recent" is defined by the latest available average salary data at USAToday.com or ticket price data in Team Marketing's Fan Cost Index. For MLB, recent is 2011 and 2012. MLB average salary changes ranged from a decrease of $1.6 million for the Cubs to a $2.2 million increase for the Marlins, with an average change of $96,916. The average percentage change across all the teams was 11.3 percent. Changes in the Fan Cost Index average ticket price ranged from a decrease of $11.67 for the Angels to a $10.56 increase for the Tigers. The average change was only $0.06, and the average percentage change across all teams was only 2.1 percent. Finally, the correlation between average salary changes and average ticket price changes across all teams for these two years was 0.01, essentially zero.

Looking behind these summary statistics shows why. Of the seventeen teams that showed average salary increases, four actually lowered their prices in nominal terms and, with inflation right around 2 percent, five more owners did not increase their ticket prices by greater than the rate of inflation. Thus, in total nine of the seventeen teams with increased payrolls actually lowered their prices. Of the thirteen teams that lowered their payrolls, four raised ticket price by more than inflation, counter to the requirements of the myth. Thus, in total, thirteen of the thirty MLB teams (43 percent) behaved counter to the myth for the 2012 season.

Performing the same comparison for the other three leagues generated the following results. Average NBA salaries (recent is 2009–10 and 2010–11) fell 14.2 percent, ticket prices fell 2.6 percent, and the correlation between payroll changes and ticket price changes was a negligible 0.24. Sixty percent of NBA teams behaved counter to the myth. In the NFL (recent is 2009 and 2010), average salaries fell 2.6 percent from 2009 to 2010, average ticket price fell 1.5 percent, and the correlation between payroll changes and ticket price changes was still small, at 0.38. Forty-one percent of NFL teams behaved counter to the myth. Finally, payrolls rose 5.8 percent in the NHL (recent is 2010–11 and 2011–12), average ticket price fell 1.0 percent, and the correlation between payroll changes and ticket price changes was a strong 0.78. Thirty-seven percent of NHL teams behaved counter to the myth. In summary across the leagues, between 37 and 60 percent of teams behave counter to the myth in the most recent data on average salaries and ticket prices. Any correlation between changes in average salaries and changes in ticket prices is small in three of the leagues. In the other, the NHL, the high correlation attests not to the myth but to the fact that ticket revenues are the largest proportion of total revenues in the NHL, compared with the rest. Rest assured that this summary also is true for a significant number of teams in each league back in time.

In fact, even earlier reports by USAToday prior to the Internet, show that the average MLB player salary was $19,000 in 1967, and it was $1,895,630 in 2000. So in nominal terms the average player salary was one hundred times what it was thirty-three years earlier. Again, getting reliable data is an issue, but it appears that ticket prices increased by less than ten times (still in nominal terms) over the same time period. If ticket prices must rise to cover ever-rising salaries, there is quite a large deficit issue revealed here. Other sports tell a similar story. For example, Fort (2011, ch. 7) has shown in his textbook the history of the behavior of salaries and ticket prices over the years for the pro teams in Boston. The same myth busting result occurs—over different periods of time for different sports in Boston, real ticket prices either stay constant or fall, and salaries continue to rise (the most startling example is the NHL's Boston Bruins). The relationship between salaries and ticket prices required to support the myth simply is not there.

Thus, rather than appeal to weak argument and claim that the rest of the teams at least behave according to the myth, the Econ 101 explanation explains these other teams as well. All you have to do is turn to the rest of the revenue streams, as we alluded to for the NHL. Salaries increase at much greater rates than ticket prices because ticket prices represent only a part of the revenue streams that players help to generate. When increases in TV and Internet revenues are added to the picture, it is easy to see why salaries outpace ticket price. The data tell us that player salaries tend to increase when players gain free agency, or when revenues dramatically increase with a big new media contract. So the Econ 101 explanation explains it all, while the myth explains at best a share of the outcomes for teams in pro sports leagues.

Looking at team-by-team payrolls within a league also helps confirm the causality we show. Within a league there is a correlation between market size, ticket prices, and player salaries. Places like New York and Los Angeles tend to have higher ticket prices and higher payrolls because they are larger markets. Certainly players are not greedier in bigger markets. Owners in large markets are not wealthier, either. For example, the wealthiest sports owner, Paul Allen, owns the Portland Trailblazers, not exactly the largest NBA market. The reason payrolls and ticket prices are higher in large markets is that those markets have higher demand. There are more fans willing to pay high prices to go to an MLB or NBA game in New York than in Toronto. Therefore ticket prices are higher, which creates a greater incentive to win, which creates higher payrolls. Furthermore, demand for the NHL is high in Toronto. And guess what, the highest ticket prices in the NHL are in Toronto, followed by another hockey crazed city, Montreal. While this has not translated into the highest payroll in the league (this might be explained by Maple Leaf fans going to games win or lose, thus reducing the team's incentive to win), higher ticket prices in Toronto shouldn't be blamed on high player salaries. There are typically counterexamples to these situations, but most of the time large markets create more fan demand, which leads to higher ticket prices, which leads to higher payrolls.

THREE OTHER MISTAKES

So, Econ 101 reasoning busts the myth that rising player salaries cause rising ticket prices. But there were three other related issues raised earlier as well . . .

What does "high" price mean? Here we bring both a sense of history and the simple but exceptionally important economic tool of inflation adjustment into play. For example, in the NFL case in the introduction, perhaps it has always been true that a trip to the stadium has cost about the same as a trip to Disneyland. And perhaps the actual cost of either one hasn't risen any more than most other things. The only way to know is to look at history and inflation. For example, New England at $117.84 is right behind the Jets' top ticket price, but the Patriots have not changed this price since 2008–09. So ticket price did not rise even though player pay surely did over the last few years, and, actually, this represents a decrease in price adjusted for even the low inflation we observe lately. As another example, adjusting for inflation, the average fan cost index in both the NBA and NHL was *higher in 1998 than 2010.*

It is surprisingly difficult even to know how ticket prices have changed over the past few decades, because while we know some of the ticket prices for sporting events long ago, we do not have complete data sets. Even if we had an "average" ticket price for each sports team for each year, that does not tell us what every fan paid to get into the game. Not only are there different prices for different types of seats, but there are also a lot of discounts given by teams.

Furthermore, ticket pricing in sports is becoming much more complex. Teams are starting to differentiate ticket prices by which opponent they play. Sometimes prices are different depending on when the fan bought the ticket. It is also becoming much more common to bundle a ticket with other goods. For example, in some baseball parks teams sell certain tickets with all you can eat food to go along with it. In these situations, it is actually hard to determine what is paid just for admission.

However, we can at least use some of the data we do have. For example, in 1958 the New York Yankees charged $3.15 for box seats, $2.10 for a reserved grandstand seat, $1.30 for general admission, and 75 cents for a bleacher seat. According to Team Marketing's Fan Cost Index, the average ticket for the Yankees is $51.55 for a game in 2012; the average premium seat price is $305.11. Of course, when the new Yankee Stadium opened in 2009, the $2,500 that some fans had to pay for premium seats grabbed the headlines. No question that $2,500 is out of most people's budget, but this was only for a few seats. During the season the Yankees did not sell all of those tickets and cut the price from $2,500 to $1,250, clearly still expensive seats. But if we stick to the average ticket price, it seems to be about twenty-five times as much in 2012 as in 1958 (2012 average ticket price compared with a 1958 reserved grandstand). If we adjust for inflation though, ticket prices are 3.1 times as much. For other teams the increase is less. For example, in 1958 the average MLB ticket price in Kansas City (then the A's) was around $2.00 ($3.00 for box seats, $1.85 for reserved grandstand, and $1.25 for general admission). In 2012, the average ticket price for the Royals was $21.84. After adjusting for inflation, the Royals' average ticket price is only 1.4 times higher than in 1958. So it is true that ticket prices are increasing, but maybe not as much as some people would think in many locations.

Figure 10.2 compares average ticket prices with per capita GDP over the last few decades. Again, reliable data over the time span for each league is not easy to come by, but the graph does show some interesting results. Over the last six decades, per capita GDP has actually outpaced the average MLB

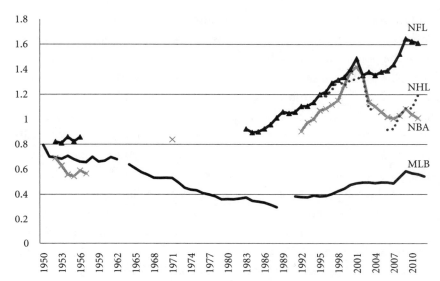

FIG. 10.2. Ratio of average ticket prices and United States GDP per capita (in thousands). Created from ticket prices at Team Marketing's Fan Cost Index and GDP series available at the Department of Commerce, Bureau of Economic Analysis (http://www.bea.gov/national/index.htm#gdp).

ticket. While the NBA and NHL saw a surge in ticket prices in the late 1990s, prices have come back down relative to what fans are earning. The NFL is the only league that has seen a significant increase in ticket prices compared with per capita GDP.

The next question then becomes how much *should* ticket prices have changed over the last few decades? There are a lot of different ways to look at this. In 1958, the average movie ticket price was 68 cents, and in 2012 the average movie price is $8.15 or, adjusting for inflation, 1.47 times the 1958 price. So Kansas City Royals tickets compare directly to movie tickets in the amount they have increased. But if we look at the market structures of sports leagues compared with most other industries, including movies, it might be surprising that teams have not increased prices far more than most other industries. Most professional sports teams are local monopolies and can restrict other teams from coming into their territory. Most other businesses, such as movie theaters, do not have this luxury.

One result of this power is a restriction on access to professional sports. While the number of teams in leagues has increased, it has not kept pace with the population, and it has fallen even further behind compared with total disposable income. The reason this might not be true with movie theaters is that as populations increase and incomes increase, people will build more movie theaters, or at least have more screens. In fact, the number of movie screens increased 73 percent from 1987 (the first year of available data) to 2009, which is a far bigger increase than the number of major professional sports franchises over the same period. With population and incomes increasing, but access limited, one might expect dramatic increases in something like sports ticket prices. Sports teams and leagues have monopolies, and one would expect them to respond to an increase in disposable income with higher ticket prices.

Another way to look at the issue is to examine how much bigger the markets have become. For example, in 1958 the U.S. GDP was $467.2 billion, and in 2011 it was $15.1 trillion. So in 2011 the GDP was thirty-two times what it was in 1958. As a percentage of GDP even tickets for the Yankees have not increased. It might seem odd to compare a ticket to a Yankees game with GDP, but we should remember that going to a Yankees game is a unique experience. While many fans might root against the Yankees, it is hard to deny that for many people there is no other close substitute for attending a Yankees game. If a constant percentage of society wants to go to Yankees games, then fan demand would depend on population and income. Since GDP represents a combination of population and incomes, it may seem reasonable that ticket prices to Yankees games and GDP increase in a similar way over the long run.

On the other hand, when we look at trends in prices over the past few decades, there are a lot of things that could change. For example, maybe baseball is now relatively less popular than the movies, compared with 1958, or maybe not as many people want to go to Yankees games. Maybe the quality of movies has increased faster than the quality of baseball. This is apples and oranges, and one could certainly argue that the product on the movie screen has increased its quality faster than the quality of play on the field, court, or ice. However, it is hard to deny that buying a ticket to a major modern sporting event comes with many amenities. For example, most stadiums and arenas are now built specifically for one sport, which was not true a few decades ago. This can lead to a better fan experience. Also, things like concessions, luxury seating, and other entertainment at the game have improved. Most modern stadiums actually have less seating but take up more space, which means they are more luxurious. Some stadiums and arenas have amazing features, such as a retractable roof or sixty-yard television screen. So going to a game in the 1950s or 1960s was an all around different experience than today, and one might expect that the ticket prices are going to be higher.

There is a good economic reason that prices should be even higher! In leagues in which sellouts are common, economists remain puzzled as to why owners don't raise prices even more. In the face of a sellout, the usual economic idea is that raising price by a dollar would reduce the length of the line but still result in a sellout; the stadium can be filled at higher revenue but no higher cost, and profits would rise. But sellouts are continually the case for some sports, especially football. (While some waiting line is optimal for some events, that is not the same thing as explaining why very long waiting lists in pro sports might be optimal.)

While it is instructive to see how ticket prices at sporting events have changed over time and how they compare with other industries, at the heart of the matter is the question, "What should ticket prices be?" Economics tells us that decreasing ticket prices will (a) lower the cash inflow for each ticket sold, (b) lead the team to sell more tickets, which increases cash inflow, and (c) increase certain variable costs because there are more fans at the game. In sports, however, the additional costs of getting more fans to the game are typically negligible, so we can pretty much focus on the change in revenue. So a change in ticket price should balance the change in revenue from each ticket with the change in tickets sold, and most businesses will raise prices until the benefit of increasing prices equals the cost of raising prices. The research in sports economics usually tells us that if teams raised their ticket prices there would be a small decrease in attendance, so that revenue would be higher if teams raised their ticket prices. In some circumstances that is obvious. For example, if the

NFL increased ticket prices for the Super Bowl by $10.00, would they not sell out? Other fans buy tickets to sporting events because they're guessing that they will be able to sell or scalp them at a higher price later. The teams know this kind of behavior happens. So in some cases ticket prices are clearly "too low."

In fact, we should ask ourselves why teams don't raise their ticket prices even more. Some NFL teams have season ticket waiting lists that are ludicrously long. Why not just charge higher prices? There might be a slightly smaller waiting list, but ticket revenue would increase if ticket prices rose. Even in sports or leagues in which it is uncommon to sell out games, raising ticket prices does not seem to have a large effect on the number of fans that go to the game. Fans that buy scalped tickets understand that sometimes teams' prices are too low and face value does not represent the full value of the ticket.

There are actually quite a few reasons teams would set ticket prices lower than the short-term ticket revenue-maximizing price. For example, if lowering ticket prices got more fans to the game, the team could sell more beer and concessions. Also, advertising space inside the stadium becomes more valuable if more people are in the stadium. Maybe more important in the long term, slightly lower ticket prices might mean growing a fan base. Higher ticket prices might scare away new fans that could become fans for life. Also, if a team can get fans to the game one time, there is a decent chance they will come back.

Sometimes teams sell out games because it helps their reputation. If fans know that a team usually sells out, it becomes a selling point. For example, when the Yankees were not selling some of their $2,500 tickets, that was bad publicity. No team wants to show empty seats on television in a brand new stadium. In fact, owners or television crews are always trying to show excited fans on camera. Some evidence suggests that it helps generate a larger television audience if there is a raucous crowd. Another great reason to have lower ticket prices is that it might generate some good will with fans. Since teams are such a public business, it should be important to them to do things to help the fans. This can be especially true if the team is trying to get a public subsidy, or maybe even if they just did receive a public subsidy.

The animosity of the fans can be compounded if they just helped pay for a new stadium or arena.

Of course, many fans are well acquainted with these arguments for lower ticket prices while they face higher ones instead. But it might help fans if they remember this. If owners raised their ticket prices, they would more than likely increase their short-term ticket revenue. More important, the players should certainly not be blamed for the level of ticket prices. For many decades sports teams and owners have generated as much revenue as possible, just like most businesses. That revenue is then split between the owners and all of the suppliers of inputs to the team production process. If their determined share of revenue did not go to the players, owners would certainly keep it.

One reason that fans understandably get annoyed with ticket price increases is that they lose consumer surplus—that is, the difference between what fans are willing to pay and what they have to pay falls. If ticket prices increase, that is money out of their wallet when they do go to the game. They are willing to pay it, but they are not as happy about their consumption. Also, inescapably, when ticket prices rise, some fans attend fewer games. So fans often remember when ticket prices were much lower, and it is easy to forget about inflation, market structures, or purchasing power. In the same way that drivers get angry when gas prices increase, fans get angry when they are forced to pay higher prices for the tickets they do buy and resent that they can no longer afford as many games.

It should also be noted that the discussion so far concerns a lot of average ticket prices. Some teams are far above the average, and others have had periods of massive ticket price increases. Nearly all teams now offer premium seats, which can be quite expensive. So while most teams offer relatively cheap tickets for some seats, part of the frustration of the fans comes from the fact that it can be difficult to get good seats without paying an arm and a leg. Furthermore, while baseball ticket prices may not have increased as much as some fans think, some leagues, such as the NFL, has seen quite an increase in their tickets.

What may compound this problem is that sports fans want results. If fans are paying high prices and players are being paid millions of dollars, fans want to see a quality team. When players fail to perform when they have large contracts, it is easy to see why fans become perturbed, especially in places where winning is scarce over time (we think of the Cubs and Mariners in baseball; Clippers and Warriors in basketball; Bills, Browns, and Raiders in football; and Maple Leafs and Oilers in hockey). Economically, it is easy to explain how no change in quality can still be rewarded with higher pay as long as demand continues to rise, but that doesn't mean fans understand it—especially when they are already being distracted by the purveyors of this myth.

Owners would lose money rather than just take lower profits by lowering some ticket prices. More knowledgeable fans base this demand on the idea that team owners are local monopolists and earn excess profits. So it would be a bit charitable for owners to lower some ticket prices, but they can afford to do it. We warned that it would be a bit complex to explain, but here we go—if pro sports team owners lowered ticket prices according to this claim, they would not just suffer lower profits, they would actually not be able to cover costs.

This is because fans and sportswriters/broadcasters always forget the logic behind the purchase of an asset, and that owners must recoup their initial purchase price or fail economically. Nobel prize winner James Buchanan and his famous coauthor Gordon Tullock described this all for us long ago in the literature on "rent seeking" behavior. Theirs is really an extension of the most basic of finance principles to all forms of value generated because of market power (sometimes a true monopoly, but usually a superior position in a market that generates more than the competitive return).

The most that anybody will pay for an asset is the discounted present value of the profits it will generate. The price of a sports team (and the logic extends to initial buy-ins through expansion franchises) should then reflect the current owner's best estimate of the future value that the franchise will generate. And here's the crucial part. Profits that accrue over and above the competitive rate of return, generated by the fact that owners occupy a position of market power, will be included in this flow of value. So the purchase price of a sports franchise will be all of the money that can be made from operations, plus the value of any tax advantages of ownership, plus the value of all related business that is enhanced by franchise ownership, *plus the value over and above the competitive rate of return*. Note that this last value also includes any return over and above the competitive rate generated by national media and memorabilia sales by the league.

This logic simply undoes the argument that rich, monopolist sports team owners can afford to take a bit less profit and price some seats at less than the highest monopoly price. Buchanan and Tullock offered the insight that the actual value of owning such a franchise all probably accrued to the original owners in the league. But we're happy enough to point out that at least the current owners all had to pay all of the profit that their predecessor thought their teams would generate, up front, in the purchase price. And so we get to the punch line. Since they were all charged the full market power value of their franchises, current owners would fail to recoup their purchase price if even a single seat is priced below the market power rate. This isn't just "less profit" but an economic failure to recoup their initial investment price.

Now, we are talking about billionaire owners. Perhaps their sense of philanthropy would lead them to take a true economic loss (not just reduced profit) on their initial purchase of the team. But we don't find that very likely. Further, sportswriters/broadcasters and fans should recognize that they expect philanthropy in their demand for "family friendly pricing" or some such.

CONCLUSIONS—MYTH AND THE WEDGE OF RESENTMENT

Player salaries do not cause ticket prices. Indeed, the causality is just the opposite. When fan demand increases, raising ticket prices, players become more valuable to owners. Competition leads to an increase in player pay (even though players do not improve in their contribution to wins). Further, when viewed in their historical context, properly adjusted for inflation, and compared with the rest of the economy, ticket prices have not really risen all that much. In addition, given the prevalence of sellouts, it is reasonable that ticket prices should be even higher! Finally, pleadings that wealthy owners with market power should find it in their hearts to keep some ticket prices "family friendly" are truly appeals to philanthropy. If owners do not charge the prices that their market power position allows, they will fail to recoup their initial purchase price investment.

The destructive power of this myth is that fans start to resent players for high prices, what we referred to in the introduction as the "wedge of resentment" between fans and players. We realize that the wedge is already there. Unlike other entertainers, fans actually do begrudge players their high pay. No parallel myth is spun that high priced movie stars cause increases in movie ticket prices. And "flops" don't generate the same hard feelings. Mel Gibson's recent movie, *The Beaver*, flopped miserably. While we see plenty of press wondering, "What went wrong?" we see nothing clamoring that Gibson is a greedy, overpaid bum because this movie flopped. In sports, it is quite the opposite and, we argue, fan sentiment does have power.

The myth that this then also means fans are paying more adds insult to injury. For example, politics, surely based on fan sentiment, can enter into sports outcomes directly. The 1994–95 MLB strike is a perfect case in point. The second part of the 1994 season, plus the playoffs and World Series, were already lost when Douglas Jehl (1995) reported for the *New York Times* as follows. In January 1995 (between seasons), President Clinton ordered a federal mediator to bring the two sides back to the bargaining table. If they failed to do so, he warned, he would order the mediator to make the decision for them. This was based on the president's observation that the strike was "trying Americans' patience." Sentiment was also growing for an antitrust investigation of baseball in Congress. Then Senator Bob Dole was quoted as follows: "If the players and owners are unable to find common ground and find it soon then we will have to find some way to empower those who are the most important element in the baseball equation, the fans themselves."

Surely owners were glad to have the fans on their side, especially as the episode escalated into a political ruckus. Poll results show that this was the case, precisely, according to Jeffrey Jones (2002), reporting for Gallup. He presents Gallup data for January 1995 showing that 50 percent of fans favored owners during the strike, 28 percent favored players, and 22 percent responded, "Neither." The same was true of fan preferences in 2002 when it looked as if there may be a repeat strike. In August 2002, 43 percent of fans favored owners, 30 percent players, and 27 percent neither.

There is certainly no law demanding that fans accept current ticket price levels. People are entitled to their opinion about how people should be paid. However, understanding the economics behind this situation may lessen the resentment between fans, players, and owners. And wouldn't that make the world a much happier place?

11 FAILURE TO ACT ON THE ISSUE OF COMPETITIVE BALANCE IS HURTING SOME SPORTS LEAGUES

INTRODUCTION

For some leagues, such as MLB and the NBA, many argue that smaller-revenue market teams have no chance of winning in today's environment. For now, we leave this idea under the general name of "parity" or "competitive balance," although further definition will be absolutely essential to the discussion. From Mike Bianchi (2011) at the *Orlando Sentinel*:

> The NBA may like the short-term buzz it is getting from superstar players moving to major markets, but it will reach a point long-term where fans in the smaller markets will abandon their teams, stop buying tickets, quit watching the NBA and find something more productive to do with their time and money.

This, some claim, is in stark contrast to the glory days when (at least) hope sprang eternal in the heart of all fans that their team had a chance at post-season play. To these nostalgia buffs, it seemed that outcomes were less dependent on the disparate economic conditions of owners or cities. Without league intervention, these pundits see a lack of parity leading to financial ruin in the long run.

In still other leagues, the argument is just the opposite, such as the NFL and NHL. Parity has run amok, and it ends up to be pretty much a coin toss as to which teams will make the playoffs. From Troy Aikman (Pedulla, 2003):

> There is no question the level of play has decreased. Now, do games become more exciting? Are teams more evenly matched? No question. Is that

good for the game or not? I don't know. I really don't know. I ask that question all the time.

Here, a return to yesteryear involves the stability of the strong teams that made league legends. As Canadian broadcasting legend Ron MacLean has often been heard to say, "When I go see the Beatles, I want John, Paul, George, and Ringo, not John, Paul, and two other guys they could afford this year." Tangled up in this outcome is the clear incentive (for adherents to this view) to field a mediocre team; why put more into it when the outcome is the same?

In either case, the concern is about fan enjoyment and willingness to pay—that is, about the future economic welfare of leagues. If a league lacks balance, some teams (specifically, smaller-revenue market teams) have no chance before the season starts. In the limit, just rank teams by payroll and you will know who will make the playoffs. This drives the fans of perennial losers away from their team and the game, itself. If there is too much balance, mediocrity is the order of the day, and fans are driven away (at least until the playoffs). After all, the basic premise of a league is that there is serious competition between teams and believable chances for postseason play. This is hardly a novel concept. In his fabulous biography of Branch Rickey, Lee Lowenfish (2007, p. 820) quotes Robert Hedges on his sale of the Browns . . . *in 1915*:

> The biggest danger in baseball is the presence of so much money behind certain clubs. There are in both leagues men who can buy winners. If they allow that ability to run to extremes, the game will suffer greatly. The weak fellows have no chance against men who can bid up to the skies for players.

The inimitable Bill Veeck (U.S. Senate, 1958) sounded the alarm again for baseball . . . *in 1958*:

> It's too late merely to view with alarm the mess into which baseball has managed to get itself. The time has come to sound the alarm before the national pastime, as it still calls itself, collapses under the weight of its own archaic rules, mismanagement, lack of leadership, greed, and plain stupidity . . . . The symptoms of near disaster are plain enough: the Yankees make an almost annual farce of the American League pennant race—a most un-

healthy condition . . . . Interest in big-league ball is on the downgrade. So is attendance, generally.

And for once, academics were not far behind! In the first famous sports economics paper, "The Baseball Players' Labor Market" (*Journal of Political Economy*, 1956), Simon Rottenberg summed up the relationship between "outcome uncertainty" and fan willingness to pay quite nicely.

While all of the foregoing makes it clear that the level of parity is clearly a concern for sports league members (that is, individual team owners that compose the league), it is interesting to us that, despite the existence of mountains of work on competitive balance, nobody actually ever goes through the methodical assessment for a given league prior to claiming that "something must be done" about it. Some anecdotal observation serves as the rallying call without any appeal at all to what we actually know about balance in any given league.

Equally interesting to us is that somehow there is a belief that rules and impositions in the labor market can change these outcomes. Backing into this notion is this from NFL commissioner Roger Goodell (2011):

> Is this the NFL that fans want? A league where carefully constructed rules proven to generate competitive balance—close and exciting games every Sunday and close and exciting divisional and championship contests—are cast aside?

Goodell was referring to revenue sharing and the payroll cap that had governed the NFL up to the labor crises that led to a 135-day lockout of the players prior to the 2011–12 season. But do these "carefully constructed rules" actually contribute to balance?

And we arrive at the myth. Balance is no worse because of the failure to act by pro sports leagues. Indeed, it is no better because of the choice to act in some cases by pro sports leagues! The first reason this is a myth is that it does not seem to be the case that competitive balance actually is getting worse. The second reason this is a myth concerns whether anything actually can be done about balance. In theory, it is easy to identify impositions that can impact balance and those that can't. Those most highly touted by leagues can't, and the one that can is so emasculated as to strip it of its theoretical power. So even if there were a "problem" with imbalance, it surely is not because of absence of effort to do anything about it.

This myth is destructive because, under fan, press, and congressional insistence, leagues may choose the wrong level of balance. Fans of a particular team, its press supporters, and its members of Congress may care more about the chances for their team without any thought of the consequences for the rest of the league's fans. In a sort of fallacy of composition, making weak teams better may improve balance, and those teams may be glad of it, but the resulting increase in balance could hurt the league, generally. It also ends up that every league policy imaginable to improve balance will also, at the same time, decrease player pay. The short-term consequences are labor-management acrimony. The longer-term consequences are quite possibly a lower level of absolute talent in the league. Young athletes make their decisions about which sport deserves their time and energy investment based on expected returns. The lower the returns, the more likely that a potential big-league pitcher turns into a basketball player. In the very short term, such as we invoked for our discussions in Chapter 10, talent is what it is in any given season. But over time, the composition of that supply of talent is precisely the result of decisions just like this by young athletes.

In what follows, we begin by defining terms. This may be the most important part of any discussion of balance, since it matters whether the discussion is about uncertainty of a game, playoff uncertainty, or dynasties over time. Too many times, people talk at cross-purposes because they don't define their terms from the outset. We then take a look at the facts (what a novel idea). What has happened to balance over time—that is, where can we identify a balance problem? In that same section we examine the notion that balance can somehow be "managed" in the way that seems so commonly taken for granted in the whole discussion.

DEFINITIONS

Just what is meant by the somewhat nebulous terms we ignored in the introduction, "parity" and "competitive balance"? The basic idea of competitive balance is that teams are equal in terms of team quality, so that every team has about the same chance to win. Another way to look at it is that there is a large amount of uncertainty as to which team will win a game or championship. The determinants are differential revenue potential, coupled with the never-ending pursuit of both effective and innovative management (think *Moneyball* on the latter). It is important then to remember that population demographics and willingness to pay are the primary determinant of competitive balance in a league.

We have made some headway in our academic work on competitive balance with the following separation. First, there is uncertainty over the outcome of individual games, or Game Uncertainty. How close will a given game be? For example, how close are the odds that Team A beats Team B today? Second, there is uncertainty over the regular season outcome, or Season Uncertainty. How close was the pennant race? How many races were decided by the final game? Finally, there is uncertainty across season, or Cross-Season Uncertainty. This last is the point of discussions about who occupies the playoffs and the impact of dynasties.

These distinctions are important if, for no other reason, they help structure discussions about balance. More than once we've been involved in discussions in which everybody in the room was talking about one of these definitions, but nearly none of them were talking about the same definition. All matter in the general sense of describing parity. But for a given discussion, it seems taking them one at a time makes the most progress. We follow our own experience and advice and do just this in the next section.

To us, one of the most interesting things about discussions of balance is the complete absence of any discussion about what the balance target should be for any given league. Typically, only superficial attention is paid to this question, defining the obvious boundary to the discussion—both one team winning all the time and a complete craps shoot (the only truly even game) are equally unacceptable. This casual boundary setting leads to "squeaky wheel" policy attention. Somebody says that there is not enough balance in the NBA, this is taken as given without much investigation, and those squeaking for more balance get the attention. Somebody says that there is too much balance in the NFL, so something must be done. And a confounding factor is that the level of balance is actually dictated by the choices of member owners acting together as a sports league. The number and location of teams, and thus the revenue potential facing each team, are a centralized, nonmarket decision.

Economists have made some headway here, but not a lot. Suppose that the number and location of teams were competitively determined, instead. What we know is that teams would move or enter those markets where the profits are highest, most obviously New York, the Eastern Seaboard, and Southern California. Entry would reduce the value of talent to the teams already in these locations, driving the price of talent down. Talent would then be spread around a bit more, and there would be more balance. This would happen in all leagues, but the route would involve one more step in, say, the NFL. There, as Commissioner Goodell fears most, given his quoted remarks above, the first thing that happens is that the league abandons its "carefully constructed rules" in the face of competition. After that, the same story we just told unfolds for the NFL.

So Econ 101 insights about what competition would do to the distribution of talent are straightforward. Essentially, if sports resources were allocated like most resources, through voluntary exchange, and resources are not to be wasted as measured by willingness to pay by particular fans, we would not expect an equal distribution of sports talent any more than we would expect an equal distribution of anything else. Everything from shopping opportunities to opera is unequally distributed according to revenue potential around the nation. Just as truly, there are more fans in larger population markets and, typically but not always, revenue potential is also larger. So more fans will be happy if larger revenue market teams win more often.

We also have a few insights into some conditions that would hold in ticket markets and for fan purchase of tickets under such a competitive situation, so that the actual conditions could be compared with these in order to determine if balance needs to increase or decrease in order to mimic the competitive result (your author Fort and his long-time coauthor, James Quirk, have two papers on this subject, 2010 and 2011). This provides one avenue for analyzing which leagues have too much balance and which leagues not enough. That this is even true suggests that a one-size-fits-all policy of increasing balance will not necessarily make fans in any given league better off. Of course, whether or not the competitive result is the actual aim of balance policy is the shortcoming of this type of analysis.

So the economic insights are subject to criticism for their choice of a welfare criterion. But that does not get observers of balance off the hook for their sloppy lack of any criterion at all! What is truly important here is that the critical question still receives nearly no attention. Which league is overbalanced, which underbalanced, and by how much? We raise the issue.

THE ACTUAL BALANCE OUTCOMES

There are plenty of economic studies about the impact of Game Uncertainty on fan attendance. However, we know of no treatment of Game Uncertainty that allows us to say anything about whether it has increased or decreased over time. One could try to assess game score outcomes. Alternatively, perhaps the posted odds for games could be assessed. The undertaking is too large for us for our purposes. Further, in our opinion, while it is interesting to know whether games are getting closer, typically people seem more interested in the other forms of outcome uncertainty from the perspective of "doing something" about balance.

Season Uncertainty is much more heavily studied. If a league is becoming less balanced, there is less uncertainty for individual games, and there should be a bigger difference between teams in the standings. So, if we look at the dispersion of winning percentages at the end of the season, this should give us a reasonable measure of balance in a given season. The easiest way to do this is to calculate the standard deviation of winning percentages at the end of the season and adjust it for season length. A well-known measure that accomplishes this is the Noll-Scully Ratio of Standard Deviations. Without going into the details, the ratio compares the actual league standard deviation with the standard deviation of an idealized, perfectly balanced league. If the ratio equals 1, then the actual league has the standard deviation of the idealized league. As the ratio gets larger, the league is farther away from this perfectly balanced construct. The measure allows comparison of leagues over time or across leagues, since it controls for any difference in either the number of teams or the length of seasons.

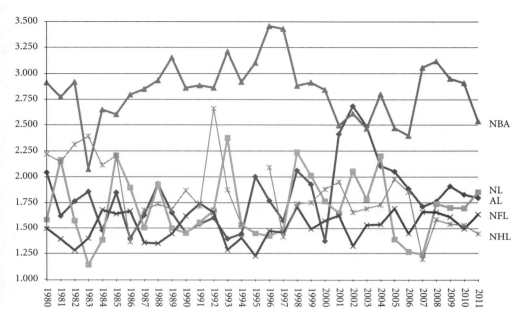

FIG. 11.1. Within-Season Competitive Balance. Created from data at the Sports Reference.com site. MLB strike in 1981 resulted in a "split season" but the data here combine those (AL: before the strike 1.78, after the strike 0.90; NL: before the strike 1.77, after the strike 1.27).

Figure 11.1 shows the Noll-Scully Ratio from 1980 to 2011 for MLB (both the AL and NL), the NBA, NFL, and NHL (the end of the 2011–12 season for leagues that span years). If competitive balance is getting worse, there should be an upward trend. While balance has worsened at times in this way, no trend in this direction exists in any league. The decade averages decline slightly in the AL, from 1.72 in the 1980s to 1.68 in the 1990s, but then rise and overtake the original 1980s level to 2.04 in the 2000s. Overall this is an 18.6 percent increase. The opposite occurs in the NL, 1.69 in the 1980s, 1.72 in the 1990s, and then back to 1.68 in the 2000s. The same thing happens in the NBA, only at a higher level (2.76 to 3.05 and then back to 2.72). The NHL actually shows a decline in decade averages (1.99 to 1.85 to 1.69). Joining the AL in baseball, the NFL shows a chance of worsening Season Uncertainty over time (1.47 to 1.51 to 1.57, a 6.8 percent increase overall) but it occurs at the smallest Noll-Scully Ratio values of any league. Even taking a truly short sighted look at Figure 11.1, the ratio has increased in the AL and slightly in the NFL, but fallen in both the NBA and NHL. In our opinion, none of these are unprecedented in the thirty-plus years shown in Figure 11.1.

Figure 11.1 tells us a couple of things. First, except in the AL, teams are no more likely to dominate a season lately than they were over the last thirty years. (Figure 11.1 cannot tell us whether *a particular team* does so, but we get to that shortly.) In fact, the level of balance within a season seems to remain remarkably constant over time, with the Noll-Scully Ratio around 1.8 for the AL, 1.7 for the NL, just above 2.8 for the NBA, right around 1.5 for the NFL, and just above 1.8 for the NHL. This is true regardless of the imposition of league policies ostensibly justified on competitive balance grounds (e.g., national TV sharing, local revenue sharing, luxury taxes, the draft, and salary caps). We have much more to say about this in a subsequent section (and delve into the details of caps and drafts in Chapter 12).

Second, Figure 11.1 shows us that while Season Uncertainty doesn't seem to change much in a particular league, there are clear differences *between the four leagues*. The NBA is always the most unbalanced (except for 2002–2003 compared to the AL and 1983 compared to the NHL, and we have no explanation for that). The NFL, while not always the lowest, is typically so and shows the least variation in this measure. Baseball and hockey battle it out for the number 2 and 3 most balanced leagues.

Since the imposition of policies like revenue sharing, luxury taxes, drafts, and salary caps haven't had any real impact, the biggest determinant of Season Uncertainty seems to be simply differences in the sports themselves. Star players are most important in the NBA, given that rosters are smallest in league. If there are not enough stars to go around, basketball should be the most unbalanced (and it is). The pitcher-hitter duel defines baseball, but there are more star pitchers and hitters than there are basketball stars, and similarly for hockey relative to basketball. Roster sizes are the largest in the NFL. Further, while the Noll-Scully measure controls for it across leagues, season length may be a defining characteristic of Season Unbalance; one game in the NFL's 16-game season is more important to winning percentage than it is in the 162-game baseball season. Thus it might be that the NBA can never achieve the level of within season balance in the NFL simply because of the nature of basketball versus football. This observation leads us to urge caution when making generalizations about balance. It is possible that MLB does not have to worry about Season Uncertainty, but it could clearly be worthy of more attention in the NBA.

Regardless, the main point to take away from Figure 11.1 is that season balance does not change much over time. One of your authors, in his textbook (Fort, 2011b, p. 169), summarizes it over a much longer time period, roughly as follows. "The forces determining the distribution of team quality and the resulting outcomes over the regular season have not changed much in any given decade since the 1940s, and not at all over the last three decades." Other work by one of your authors and his colleague, Young Hoon Lee, applies careful time series techniques to this same standard deviation idea for all four North American leagues (on MLB, Lee and Fort, 2005; on the rest, Fort and Lee, 2007). That work covered the entire history of balance in these sports, but conclusions about the last thirty years can easily be drawn.

Balance in MLB has gradually improved without any shift at all since 1980. This does not rule out that changes in MLB's revenue sharing in the mid-1990s and early 2000s contributed to the trend, but neither did the trend improve or shift in any way with these alterations. Balance in the NBA gradually declined from 1980, with a shift improvement in 1995. The net impact on balance of expansion in 1995, the imposition of a harder cap in 1999, and the influx of international talent correspond to this shift improvement, but balance resumed its gradual decline after that. Balance in the NFL has been literally constant from 1980 on, reinforcing that revenue sharing changes in 1984 and the eventual imposition of true free agency and the salary cap in the early 1990s had no impact on balance. For the NHL, balance was constant, with a shift improvement in the mid-1980s. The move of Colorado to New Jersey plus the influx of European players coincide with the shift improvement, and balance in the NHL has been constant since, reinforcing that the imposition of the salary cap in 2005 had no impact on balance.

Consecutive-Season Uncertainty also is the point of much attention. Even here, however, we return to our earlier observation. Exactly what are we talking about? Is it getting to the playoffs? Is it some degree of playoff success? Is it winning the league championship? People trying to take one side or the other on the balance issue often flit from one to the other as if it doesn't matter. But it does matter. Let's take the first idea first.

One of your authors has actually done an exhaustive study of Conference Championship in the modern NFL, from the merger in 1970 to 2010 (Fort, 2011a). It is, of course, arbitrary to choose the conference level to investigate, but it has a couple of virtues. The choice evades the one-game tie playoffs that occurred in the old NFL (prior to 1970) and sets the bar higher than just competing for the division title. The measures were turnover year to year in the teams that make it to the playoffs—the number of nonrepeat teams from the year before and the average number of years between appearances for those teams playing for the Conference Championship. This stops short of success through the playoffs, but we partly cover this in the remaining examination to follow.

For nonrepetition, the most frequent outcome was four new teams pursuing the Conference Championship (nine different times, about 22 percent of the time). There was never an occurrence where all four teams repeated from one season to the next. Indeed, three teams repeating happened only six times in the modern NFL (14.6 percent of the time). There were five episodes in which there was equal turnover for three or more years in a row, and most often that involved three teams. This is hefty turnover, annually. This conclusion is bolstered by the average number of years to the last playoff. Nearly all of the numbers were large rather than small (two years or less, for example).

It sure does appear that the NFL has been quite balanced in terms of playoff access, but there was also a look at playoff droughts to show that a very small number of teams appear to be nearly completely excluded. It ended up that the average drought was 8.2 years. Oakland, Tampa Bay, and Tennessee all sat at the average. More important, the median drought was 5.5 years, indicating quite a skewed distribution of droughts. The average drought for those below the median was 2.7 years, and the four tail occupants (Colts, Vikings, Saints, and Jets) all had droughts of one year. The average drought for those above the median was 13.75 years, and the worst droughts were Cincinnati (22 years), Cleveland (21 years), Washington (19 years), and Detroit (19 years). This concentration of long droughts (and very short ones) does indicate hopelessness for the fans of a few teams, even though there appeared to be high-level access among the rest of the teams.

What many fans care about, and what many sports writers write about, is whether or not their team has a chance when a new season begins. The idea that all fans need at least some hope at the beginning of the season is very intuitive. We can try to quantify this type of balance by seeing if winning percentages are correlated year after year. If winning percentages were uncorrelated from season to season, this would imply that each team has an equal chance of winning when the season starts. Figure 11.2 shows the correlation of winning percentages across seasons for MLB (the entry for 1980 is the correlation between winning percentages in 1979 and 1980, and so on). From the early 1980s to the mid-1990s, it appears that the correlation was falling (implying increasing parity), but it has increased since then (implying less parity). While MLB might make the best case for worsening balance across seasons, we would argue that Figure 11.2 does not make that point obvious. It is interesting that MLB's Blue Ribbon Panel Report, with its prestigious list of authors—Yale economist (and president) Richard C. Levin; Senator George J. Mitchell, who brokered peace in Ireland; former chairman of the Fed. Paul A. Volcker; and syndicated columnist George F. Will (2000)—called for more balance in baseball all the way back in 2000. Data from the 1990s are used in many of the figures shown in that report. Figure 11.2 does show that across season balance did worsen over that time, but it did not happen before that time period or after that time period. In other words, what may have seemed like a horrific "trend" for baseball fans was really more a short-term decrease in parity.

Figure 11.3 shows the correlation of winning percentages for the NBA. It appears that balance across seasons has not changed really over three decades. However, if you compare the correlation values with that of MLB, the NBA certainly does have less turnover from year to year than the MLB. So this does seem to validate what some fans suspected—it is easier to predict which NBA teams will be successful than for MLB. Nonetheless, it has always been that way. The talent level of basketball teams simply does not

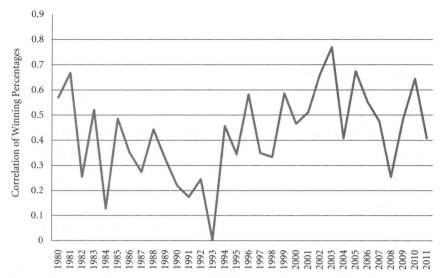

Fɪɢ. 11.2. Across-Season Competitive Balance for MLB. Created from data at the sports-reference.com site.

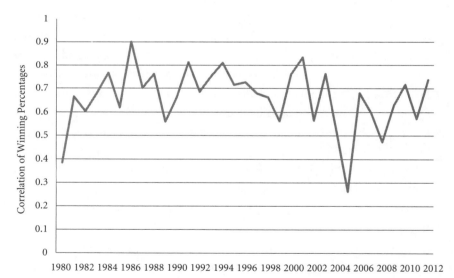

Fɪɢ. 11.3. Across-Season Competitive Balance for NBA. Created from data at the sports-reference.com site.

change as much as that of baseball teams. We do not show the charts for the NFL and NHL, but if anything the correlations suggest increasing Consecutive-Season Uncertainty in those two leagues. It is not obvious that any of these leagues have actually had any dramatic changes regarding balance or parity across seasons.

Finally, for another look at Consecutive-Season Uncertainty, we'll look at the number of different teams that win the championship. While this also measures balance across seasons, it gives us a different measure. To the extent that fans only care about championships, this could be the most important measure. We should note that leagues can manipulate this type of balance quite easily. For example, suppose a league is not balanced and the same team is the best team year after year. The league can certainly change the probability of the best team winning the championship. If after a long regular season, the league has the two best teams play for the championship in a nine game series, the best team has a pretty good chance of winning. If, on the other hand, the league puts thirty-two teams in the playoffs and each series is a one game series, it would be tough for the best team to end up winning the title (remember the lesson from Chapter 7). A league could also change the rules of the game so that winning a game becomes more random, thus introducing more balance. The data show that leagues have become more successful in crowning different champions over time, at least in part because of putting more teams in the playoffs and also because there are simply more teams.

For instance, by definition the average probability of a team winning the championship is one divided by the number of teams in the league. In 1960, when there were thirteen teams in the NFL, the average probability of each team winning was 7.7 percent. Now that there are thirty-two teams in the NFL that probability is 3.1 percent. This means that fans are less likely to have their favorite team win the championship. Put another way, there will be a longer time span between championships for teams. It is becoming more and more common for teams not to have won a championship during the lifetime of many of their fans. Also, in 1960, the NFL and MLB did not have a playoff system. Those leagues simply took the top team from each league or division and played the championship. The NHL had a playoff system, but it was only four teams. There were six teams in the NBA playoffs. Today, MLB has ten teams in the playoffs, the NFL has twelve, and the NBA and NHL have sixteen teams in the playoffs. So the increase in teams decreases the chances of each team winning the championship, and the increase in the number of playoff teams makes those chances more even between teams.

It is relatively easy to see that it is hard to create a dynasty in today's sports world. While many baseball fans despise how many World Series titles the Yankees have won recently, they used to win more. From 1996 to 2000 they won four out of five World Series. From 1936 to 1962 they won sixteen out of twenty-seven titles. The turnover of champions does not seem to have changed much since the Super Bowl began. Instead, the teams have just changed. The Packers, Dolphins, Steelers, 49ers, Cowboys, Broncos, and Patriots have all repeated as champions, but there is no obvious trend. The NBA seems to have the least amount of parity in championships. Only nine different teams have won a championship from 1980 to 2012. However, this does not mean that balance is getting worse. After all, the Celtics won every championship from 1959 to 1966, and they won eleven of thirteen titles from 1957 to 1969. The biggest improvement of championship parity may be from the NHL. After all, from 2003 to 2010 there were seven different champions for those seven seasons (2005 was canceled). From 1976 to 1983 either the Canadiens or Islanders won the title. The Canadiens also won five in a row from 1956 to 1960. Again, one of your authors summarizes playoff outcomes as follows (Fort, 2011b, p. 169):

> Which teams have larger-revenues can change over time, as with the Atlanta Braves and Seattle Mariners in MLB. But larger-revenue market teams simply always have dominated the playoffs in pro sports leagues.

And behind the scenes, there is the previous work on the NFL again (Fort, 2011a). In the modern NFL there were fifteen or sixteen teams in each conference, so an equalized outcome would have teams winning their Conference Championship every fifteen or sixteen years. Actual outcomes could not be much further from this equality. Pittsburgh, Denver, Buffalo, and New England simply ruled the AFC Championship through 2010 (with

Miami and Oakland not far behind). By decade, Pittsburgh won the AFC Championship four times in the 1970s, Denver won it three times in the 1980s, Buffalo won it four times in the 1990s, and New England four times in the 2000s. In the NFC, overall dominance was by Dallas, San Francisco, and Washington. In the 1970s, Dallas won the NFC Championship five times, San Francisco won it four times in the 1980s, Dallas again in the 1990s with three wins, and New York twice in the 2000s.

Of course, that then raises the question of just what is a dynasty in the NFL? If it is Conference Champion dynasties, it seems safe to say that they exist in every decade in the AFC, but for different teams. Turning to the NFC, the chance at a dynasty has declined each decade to the point where there wasn't one in the 2000s.

Moving on to the Super Bowl (updating to include the most recent in 2012), just with the modern NFL from 1970, the AFC won nineteen Super Bowls and the NFC twenty-four. Indeed the NFC ran off a thirteen-year streak against the AFC from the 1985 game to the 1997 game. Since then, the AFC won nine of the last sixteen games. However, at the individual team level there has never been anything beyond back-to-back NFL Champions (Miami 1973–74, Pittsburgh 1975–76 and 1979–80, Denver 1998–99, New England 2004–05 in the AFC; San Francisco 1989–90 and Dallas 1993–94 in the NFC).

This is little solace to the six teams that have yet even to appear in the Super Bowl in the modern NFL from 1970 to date. While we won't cry too much for the relative newcomer Jaguars (1995–2012), it's forty-three years for long-suffering fans of the Lions, Jets, Browns, and Texans (if you count the original Browns and Oilers for the last two). The Chiefs haven't played since the first modern Super Bowl in 1970 (forty-two years ago). Quite simply, it is tough to say there is any such thing as an NFL Champion dynasty. The remaining longest Super Bowl appearance droughts are the Vikings (thirty-four years), Dolphins (twenty-six years), Bengals (twenty-two years), and four more teams between fifteen and twenty years (Washington, Buffalo, San Diego, and San Francisco). So clearly there is concentration in the Super Bowl, but it falls short of any reasonable definition of "dynasty."

The point is that while fans may be great historians of their team and their favorite players, somehow history seems forgotten when turning to issues of competitive balance. MLB fans often complain of the dominance of the New York Yankees, but that dominance is certainly not greater than that of the 1950s Yankees or the 1920s Yankees. Fans may also overstate gains in balance. Since 2000–01, seven different NBA teams have won championships, including "only" four by the Lakers, with observations that balance is better in basketball. But the comparison is to periods of time when there was not just dominance but complete dynasty dominance in the league. Four different teams won in the 1990s, but the Bulls won six, with two three-peats. Four different teams won in the 1980s, but the Lakers won four and the Celtics three. Eight different teams won the title in the 1970s! This was the last decade of competition with the ABA, by the way. Three different teams won it in the 1960s, but the Celtics were eight-time champs and Bill Russell was MVP four times. Six different teams won it in the 1950s, the best was the three-peat by the Minneapolis Lakers. If you just throw in the 1940s, the Minneapolis Lakers dominance increases to five with three for the Celtics.

It may be true that the chances of winning a championship are shrinking for some teams, but this is mainly because there are many more teams than in the past. There can be only one champion per year, and more teams in the league means a smaller percentage of fans see their team win the title.

Given that there are more teams, and thus fewer championships per team, that might describe some of the frustrations with fans regarding competitive balance. There seem to be competing factors at play. In some leagues balance seems to be getting slightly better on some measures, thus increasing the probability that a traditionally bad team will win a title. At the same time there are more teams, which decreases the probability a given team will win the title. Since balance is not changing by much, the second factor seems to be overpowering the first. Consequently, it is getting harder for the Pittsburgh Pirates, Los Angeles Clippers, or Detroit Lions to win the championship. So what some fans perceive as a growing lack of competitive balance is really a lower probability of winning for their favorite team because there are now more teams in the league. While the benefits to owners and fans of expansion are clear (expansion fees to owners, more markets have teams), the cost is also very real, and fewer fans get to see their favorite team win.

So balance or parity depends on many factors, and it depends on what kind of balance people are talking about. If we are talking about having a different team win the championship every year, then the NFL is clearly more balanced than the NBA. If we are talking about having winning percentages relatively equal for a given year, the NBA is more balanced than the NFL. What is striking, is that by nearly any measure, balance does not seem to be increasing over time.

It is also imperative to remember that it is not at all clear that leagues need more balance. Every fall, pundits and sports writers discuss which teams MLB would like to have in the World Series. The ideal World Series match-up is typically not the Pirates and the Royals. Leagues want big market teams to win because that means an increase in revenues. Even though the Yankees have won more World Series than anyone, the league still wants them in the Series. Similarly, the NBA would not be disappointed with another Lakers/Celtics match-up. If a particular match-up leads to higher profits, that is because more fans want to see that match-up. This implies that there are a lot of fans out there that want to see the big name teams year after year. Not only are there more fans in the large markets, but also there are some casual fans that care only if certain teams are in the championship.

Also, it is important to remember that small market teams do succeed sometimes. The Florida Marlins and the San Antonio Spurs have won multiple titles in the last fifteen years, and some leagues have improved in terms of getting different teams to the playoffs year after year.

So if balance is a problem, it is difficult to find in the data, especially any increase in a balance problem in any league. But even if one comes down squarely opposite our view, then what is to be done? Balance is driven by revenue inequality, tempered by finding effective and innovative management approaches in the first place (a la *Moneyball*). There will be imbalance as long as there is different revenue potential. So various ways of overcoming this differential are the point of policy analysis. The preview is already there in the results above—none of these devices appear to have had anything to do with the actual behavior of balance in any of the four major sports in North America. But we can go further.

It is textbook stuff (literally—see Fort, 2011b, ch. 6) for North American pro sports leagues (European analysts have clearly demonstrated that the case is different for world football) that nearly all of the policy devices used in the name of competitive balance (1) theoretically cannot change balance, and (2) actually have not changed balance, by looking at the data. National TV revenue sharing, local revenue sharing in the usual equal-proportional pooling approach, and the usual reverse-order draft will not affect (and have not affected) balance in North American leagues. Just as per the textbook, the so-called luxury tax can have a small impact. The only tool that can actually change balance in any significant way is a hard salary cap, but the caps in the NBA, NFL, and NHL are anything but "hard." On the other hand, all of these devices will lower player pay.

So what do we see in every league? MLB has national TV sharing, local sharing, and the luxury tax. None should be expected to change balance, and there is no evidence that they have changed balance in baseball. The NBA has a salary cap. While a hard cap can change balance, designed exceptions and enforcement are an issue, and apparently the combination of the two has emasculated the NBA cap relative to its theoretical possibilities. The NFL has national TV sharing and a salary cap. Once again, the cap can change balance—but hasn't in the NFL. Finally, the NHL has a salary cap, but with the same results as in the NBA and NFL.

Thus we are left with the observation that the devices chosen in leagues either cannot change balance, or if they can (salary caps), they have been designed and enforced in ways that reduce the theoretical possibilities. But one thing is sure, especially of salary caps but also theoretically for local revenue sharing in MLB and the NFL, player pay is lower under these devices. It is difficult not to be skeptical that this is the intent of all these interventions in the first place and simply note that the chances that anything done by leagues actually improves balance is completely an artifact of other league ambitions.

CONCLUSIONS—WHAT MIGHT REALLY BE BEHIND CALLS FOR MORE BALANCE?

What was interesting about the 2011 Super Bowl? The Green Bay Packers beat the Chicago Bears in the NFC championship game, and the Pittsburgh Steelers beat the New York Jets in the AFC championship game. In this case the two smaller-revenue market teams (Packers and Steelers) won, and both have more Super Bowl history than their larger-revenue market competitors. It is somewhat difficult to know what kind of match-up would have generated the most revenue for the league. One might think that they would love to have two larger-revenue market teams in the Super Bowl and at the same time increase competitive balance. There are a lot of Bears fans as well as Jets fans, and this match-up would have given the first championship to a generation of one of these team's fans.

However, the NFL is more driven by television ratings and shares more revenues than any other league in America, so market size is less important. As a result, it could be the case that the NFL was happy to have two teams with a long Super Bowl history. It is virtually impossible to know what would have been best for the league in the long run, because we do not know how Bears and Jets fans would have reacted in the long run. Nonetheless, that the league might prefer two smaller-revenue market teams with a storied Super Bowl history in the title game is interesting.

As we alluded to earlier, more revenue means more happy fans. And the 2011 Super Bowl aside, more revenue is typically generated when large market teams are playing. It might be easy to blame greedy owners, leagues, or media outlets that might create, or at least hope for, larger-revenue market match-ups. However, if larger-revenue market teams win more often, it is not just team owners and networks that will be happy about this; more fans are better off as well. There is more revenue if the Yankees get to the World Series because there are more fans in New York that want to watch the games or pay for tickets and memorabilia. So while more balance would be better for smaller-revenue market fans, it might not be better for fans as a whole. It can be difficult to know how often leagues want the underdog to win, but complete parity is not optimal for the league or for the fans.

Some sports even thrive on a lack of competitive balance. For example, at one extreme is the Harlem Globetrotters—nobody wants to see them lose. The Globetrotters might be a bad example, and you could argue it is not really sports, but the point is, some fans show up just to see the home team win. In other words, some fans do not care about a lack of uncertainty. On the other side, some fans want to watch an underdog. For example, the NCAA men's basketball tournament thrives on underdogs. The tournament even makes sure we know who the underdog is by seeding every team. Every year they heavily promote that year's Cinderella stories. The term "mid-major" even needed to be invented for these teams. Even before the tournament starts, members of the media harp on the reminders of mid-major success—Butler, George Mason, Gonzaga, and others. In fact, CBS is probably praying for the day that a 16 seed someday beats a 1 seed.

We shouldn't be too surprised that fans don't turn away when there is a heavy favorite. People have been rooting for underdogs at least since David and Goliath. Certainly some fans like rooting for teams they think will win, but Hollywood constantly reminds us that people like to see the underdog win (we think of the classic movie *Hoosiers*). Think of your favorite sports movie, was it about a team or individual that people expected to win? The chances are, it was about a team or person that defied the odds to win, or at least came close to winning. Either that, or it was a documentary. The problem for sports teams is that it is impossible to get heavy underdogs to win very often. If they could get the underdog to win every time, there would be no real underdogs left. Hollywood has the advantage of giving a back-story and then picking who gets to win. Sports leagues do not have that luxury. But the point is, leagues can never have that storybook ending if there is perfect balance in the league.

So a lack of competitive balance can help leagues because of the many different kinds of fans. A lot of fans root geographically. They either root for the local team, or maybe for the team where they grew up. However, other fans root for certain types of teams. For instance, some fans like teams that usually win. The mindset of some fans is that they do not want to root for a loser. Other fans like to root for the underdog. While some fans want to see underdogs, and some fans want to root for heavy favorites, neither of these can happen if the league is perfectly balanced.

For example, Billy Crystal is a Los Angeles Clippers fan. The city of Los Angeles has one of the most storied franchises in the NBA, and then there are the Clippers. Billy Crystal can certainly afford a ticket to a Lakers game but chooses the Clippers instead. He likes to root for an underdog, and he is certainly not alone in this. So is Los Angeles or the NBA better off if there are two average NBA teams in Los Angeles? More likely, they serve the area better if there is one very good team and one not so good team.

Another example is the Chicago Cubs. The Cubs have not won a World Series since 1908, when Teddy Roosevelt was president. While Cubs fans root for their team to win, it might actually change the team's identity if they did win. If the Cubs did win the World Series it would certainly be good for the team, but it would change things. In fact, it might even bring an inordinate amount of revenue to the Cubs if they did win the World Series, since it has been so long. However, you could not have created this situation of potential revenue if they had not been unsuccessful for so long.

Vanderbilt economist John Vrooman has popularized the "Yankee Paradox," whereby a team that becomes too dominant actually suffers from its power. The "paradox" is that it could actually be good for the Yankees if they lost more games. If a team wins so much that there is little or no uncertainty, demand for the league could go down. But empirical evidence suggests that no teams are really at this point. In fact, one could argue that not only the Yankees but also the league would be made better off if they won more. In 1997, *Sports Illustrated* had a cover that asked, "Are the Bulls so good they're bad for the NBA?" Well, that is the question we are asking. Would the NBA have been better off without Michael Jordan. The loss of Michael Jordan would have hurt the talent level of the NBA, which matters, but it probably would have helped balance. However, the NBA seemed to do all right when Michael Jordan was playing. Not only were there many fans that rooted for Michael Jordan, there were also many that rooted against him.

So some level of balance is needed in every league. Economists noted this long ago. However, part of the economists' original point was that a league needed a certain number of financially viable teams. Contrary to what some owners say, financial viability is not quite the concern today that it once was. More relevant to today, fans want to know that their team has some chance of winning, and they do not want to know for sure who is going to win a game. That does not mean it is best if teams are more equal.

There is really no evidence that we are at the point where more balance is critical or even good for the league. People should remember that smaller-revenue market team wins come at the cost of larger-revenue market teams winning. Clearly there needs to be a certain level of uncertainty in sports, otherwise it becomes too much like professional wrestling. But given the rising revenues that leagues are gaining, it becomes hard to argue that balance is a problem.

This myth is destructive because, under fan, press, and congressional insistence, leagues may choose the wrong level of balance (to the extent they can choose balance). The quotation at the beginning of the chapter from Roger Goodell illustrates the issue. Asking if fans want "exciting" games is a bit disingenuous, since less balance may not mean boring games. As we have tried to point out, the most exciting games might be when an underdog beats a heavy favorite.

Regardless, this Goodell quotation comes from the *Wall Street Journal* in 2011, when the NFL owners were beginning the public relations campaign surrounding upcoming negotiations with the players' union. If owners can convince the public that more parity and balance are needed, it helps them negotiate certain policies that just so happen to typically give a lower share of revenues to players. Salary caps, player drafts, revenue sharing, and luxury taxes are typically initiated in the name of competitive balance. This is an intuitive line of reasoning for fans, and pressure might be put on the players to initiate these policies to help competitive balance. However, we should remember that some of these policies have little or no effect on parity, and an increase in balance could actually hurt fans. And we cannot ignore that owners are better off when the price of talent falls!

12 PLAYER DRAFTS AND REVENUE SHARING WILL IMPROVE COMPETITIVE BALANCE

The players' proposal calls for increased revenue sharing, saying small-market teams need relief and it shouldn't be strictly from the players.
—AP report by Brian Mahoney (2010) regarding NBA labor issues

INTRODUCTION

The impacts of policies are often misunderstood. Team owners and sometimes even players' unions argue that leagues need policies such as revenue sharing and/or a reverse-order player draft so that competitive balance will increase. Chapter 11 argued that more parity is not always a good thing, and in this chapter we focus on whether or not the result of these policies actually is more balance. It is intuitively appealing to think that lousy teams will increase their winning percentage by drafting the best players, or if bad teams had a share of the larger-revenue owners' take, then they would spend more money on team payroll. People then believe that a league's success depends on the ability of larger-revenue market owners, smaller-revenue market owners, and players to come together and agree on these necessary policies that create parity and balance.

The problem is that the entire discussion is predicated on a myth. Theoretically, revenue sharing and player drafts cannot change competitive balance. Empirically, they never have done so. It may be the case that owners and players, not just fans, believe that these policies will help balance. Behind the idea that smaller-revenue market teams need more money is the belief that they will then use the money to become more competitive on the field, court, or ice. But there is no reason to have that belief in the first place, and there is no evidence to support it.

So while other league policies such as salary caps, and to a lesser extent luxury taxes, might increase competitive balance slightly, not so for drafts and revenue sharing. Interestingly, however, they all do have one thing in common. Exactly counter to the beliefs stated by players in the epigraph, all of these mechanisms purportedly in place to help with balance will only decrease compensation to players.

For drafts the economic reasoning is a bit complex but overpowering, and so are the empirical results—competitive balance has never increased after the imposition of a draft in a way that can be attributed to the imposition of the draft. For revenue sharing, the logic is much simpler, and the empirical results are completely against the proposition of improved balance. We present the logic and results below.

The destructive power of this myth is clear and indisputable. First, player pay is reduced. This further reduces the incentives to invest in their own level of talent by upcoming players, so the entire talent market is distorted. This can result in a decline in absolute level of play in a given sport. Athletes typically choose at some point in their career to devote themselves to a single sport. If pay in a sport with revenue sharing is artificially lower than the market would dictate according to fan willingness to pay, those players might go to a different sport with higher expected return. Second, owners get off the hook in terms of choosing the best level of balance in the eyes of fans versus the level of balance that simply makes owners the most money. After all, they can argue (and do), they have revenue sharing and drafts in their leagues, so balance must get better. Ignoring the fact that even in a perfectly random world some smaller-revenue teams will do well, owners point to the presence of these bottom dwellers in the playoffs as evidence. But since this really doesn't happen at all, fans end up decidedly unsatisfied since *their* bottom-dweller makes the playoffs only very seldom.

THE DRAFT

The idea that the draft won't change balance in North American leagues is the oldest finding in sports economics. Economist Simon Rottenberg (1956) laid this out when there was only a minor league draft, but the logic holds for all major league reverse-order drafts as well. Yet every year, and among sportswriters that we have personally told better, the myth continues to be foisted on all of us. The draft distributes better players to bad teams and stops higher-revenue owners from buying up all the good talent, according to the myth. Owners have even said the same thing in defense of the draft.

The counterargument goes as follows. At any point in time, a given player has their highest value to some team in the league. In the absence of a draft, and of course subject to random variation in the real world (and a few unbiased mistakes, as we demonstrate in Chapter 8), typically and on average the team that places the highest value on them would simply sign an entering future star. Typically, but not always, these would be pretty good teams located in higher-revenue markets. (Not all great stars go to just the highest-revenue owners, because of diminishing returns and rising marginal costs.) In the presence of a draft, a worse team brings the player into the league. This team is worse because, typically, it is a lower-revenue team by virtue of its fan base willingness to pay. So far, so good.

But then, what is the financial margin confronting the owner of this worse team? They can keep the future star for what he can generate in their market. Or they can move the future star on to their highest valued team. Typically, the margin favors moving the player on. So, in the absence of a draft, the player ends up on the better team, and in the presence of the draft the player ends up in the same place. The only difference is that the player's bargaining strength is reduced upon entry, with the expectation that the player gets paid less upon entry. If it is also the case that there are restrictions on young player movement in the major league, then the worse team also gets part of the value from the better team when the player moves. Note that all of this value would have gone to the player in the absence of the draft in terms of a higher initial contract value.

Take the case of Mickey Mantle. There was no draft in place when Mantle entered baseball. The Yankees signed him on his seventeenth birthday in 1949 to a Class-D farm club. He moved up to the Yankees in 1951 and, after a bit of a shaky start, established himself that year. He played only with the Yankees until 1968, and his career is sports legend. How would it have gone under a draft? The worst teams in MLB in 1949 were the Cubs (0.396 winning percent, thirty-six games back) and the Senators (0.325 winning percent, forty-seven games back). One of these clubs would have drafted Mantle. The Yankees paid Mantle $400 for the remainder of the 1949 season in Class-D, plus a $1,100 signing bonus. Since either the Cubs or Senators could also have signed him, presumably their offers had they been made could only be lower than the Yankees' offer. And under a draft, the offers would have been lower still, since Mantle's next best opportunity (as he often stated himself) was in the Oklahoma mines outside of baseball. And each season, including his first in the majors, either the Cubs or Sens would confront the payment that the Yankees would be willing to make to move Mantle on to the Yankees. Especially in those days, with cash payment for players very common, the margins clearly weighed toward sending Mantle on. Either without the draft or with a draft, Mantle would have been a Yankee. The difference is that Mantle would have made less entering the league in the presence of a draft. In addition, with restrictions on the movement of players at the time, the Cubs' or Sens' owner would have made money that would otherwise have gone to Mantle when he moved on to the Yankees.

The only time the draft can change balance is if the owner of the drafting team has made some mistake in assessing their fans' willingness to pay. Perhaps something about willingness to pay changed, and the owner learns that only by actually putting the better young players on the field and finding it out. In this day and age, with modern demand assessment techniques so easily available, it is inconceivable that owners don't already know their fans' willingness to pay for different quality levels. At its heart, then, the problem with the reverse-order draft is that it does not change a team's market structure or fan base, and thus does not make any difference in the distribution of talent in a league.

While a player draft does change the cost of players, it does not affect their value. With most goods, a change in costs would affect behavior, but in sports there are only so many roster spots, and there are only so many players that teams can draft. For example, suppose a family needed two cars. If one car is given to them it will not affect how many cars they need. Furthermore, suppose one of the cars given to them is a Ferrari. The accepted norms of gift-giving aside, most average-income people would be tempted to sell the Ferrari to someone with a high income and buy a more practical car. That is what happens with players. So when teams are making their talent investment decision at the margin, a player draft will ultimately have no effect on the level of talent for each team if that market is efficient.

Admittedly, modern drafts have evolved over time and are probably a bit less extractive of player value. Some entering players have more power, since the amount of money on the line is so much larger and their agents perhaps have better insight into their highest value than players may have had in days gone by. So the initial entering take by the drafting team may be smaller. But there still remain restrictions on young player movement, so worse clubs still are able to get part of the value of young player movement. And, most important for our point, those players still end up going to the same teams regardless of the presence of a draft. This was Rottenberg's fundamental insight—the distribution of talent across the league is invariant with respect to the presence or absence of an entering draft.

Care must also be exercised when there is more than one policy change under analysis. All leagues except MLB have a salary cap. Caps, by definition, reduce the variation in the ability of owners to buy talent. If a cap and a draft were put in place at the same time, it might appear that the draft had some impact on the distribution of talent. However, that would be a mistaken attribution, revealed as such if the draft were instituted later. In the presence of a cap, Rottenberg's logic still holds; drafts have no impact on the distribution of talent. Let's keep all of this in mind and turn to the data.

Let's also remember our lesson from Chapter 11 and look at end of season, playoff access, and across season balance, so we cover all the types that matter to fans. End of season is clear in even textbook treatments (Fort, 2011). Nothing about the imposition of any draft improved balance except possibly the AL in MLB, circa 1965. But there, we also had the inexplicable treatment of the Yankee roster during ownership by CBS (a mysterious treatment to this very day). So it is doubtful that the draft made the Yankees worse, and their decline can be chalked up to the CBS ownership episode that nobody has been able to explain. Turning to playoff access, all drafts are so old in each league that they were before division play; by definition, we can't look at "playoff access" when there were no playoffs. For example, MLB was at twelve teams without divisions in each league.

So the only thing left is across season balance. There is no evidence that any dynasty was interrupted with the imposition of drafts in any North American major league. The MLB draft around 1965 appears to coincide with the end of the Yankee dynasty, but we go back to the inexplicable CBS episode for that. In the NL, there was no existing dynasty at the time, and the Dodgers and Cards shared the next four titles. The NBA and NFL had drafts from their inception, so nothing about the subsequent dynasties (such as they may have been) can be attributed to its draft. The NHL draft began in 1963, after the Blackhawks ended the long run by the Canadiens. All of the reasonable evidence fails to support that drafts had any impact whatsoever on competitive balance. But, as we said earlier, drafts will reduce player compensation, transferring entering value and value after moves from players to owners.

REVENUE SHARING

The basic problem with revenue sharing, as it pertains to competitive balance, is that the owners of all teams have to share the same percentage of revenues. So suppose that talent is distributed across all teams in a league at a particular time and at that time the only way to increase talent is to trade with the other owners in the same league. Without any revenue sharing, further suppose that the last star player that each owner added to their team is worth around $4 million. Of course, there are fewer stars on smaller-revenue market teams and more stars on larger-revenue market teams, but the best star on the former is worth $4 million, and the last ones hired on the latter are each worth $4 million. This must be true, otherwise there would be a different value of stars at the margin, and the two owners would try to strike a trade.

Now suppose we add revenue sharing to this situation. If teams have to share, say, 25 percent of their revenue, then the $4 million stars on each team are now worth $(1 - 0.25) \times 4 = \$3$ million each to their owners. The critical insight is that while the absolute value of these stars fell, it fell for all owners, so that the relative value across the owners did not change. There still is no reason for either team to want to make any trade, and there won't be any change in the distribution of talent across the league.

We're oversimplifying the issue a bit (again, it is textbook stuff, as we said in Chapter 11, and readers can indulge their curiosity, if any, in the reference there), but basically if all owners have to share their revenue, then it doesn't really change how they see the marginal value of talent in a relative sense. It is true that players will become less valuable with sharing, but that is true across the board. It is also true that smaller-revenue market owners will be thrilled with revenue sharing, since two things happen. First, the price of talent falls, but they are still able to hire the same amount as before. Second, they get a revenue sharing check that is larger than the amount they put into the pot. But it is crucial to remember that there is also lower player pay; the larger-revenue owner gets less than they put in the pot, but they also save money due to reduced player pay! Overall, from the fan perspective, the problem is that weaker smaller-revenue teams stay that way. The value of the logic is that it identifies why. Revenue sharing makes owners better off at the expense of players, but there is no incentive to spend any of the proceeds back on any players, because the relative marginal value of talent remains unchanged.

Revenue sharing in the North American leagues is of two types, equally shared and unequally shared. However, these types of sharing have something important in common—neither of them has any additional enforceable stipulations that shared revenues must be spent to improve team quality! The knowledgeable reader will be quick to point out that the MLB Collective Bargaining Agreement does have such a stipulation currently. However, that's why we include the "enforceable" part of our statement. The requirement that net revenue sharing proceeds be spent on team quality in MLB actually is enforced by the commissioner's office! Since the commissioner serves at the pleasure of the owners, this is clearly a case of the fox guarding the henhouse, and anybody who thinks that the CBA stipulation will work is going to lose some chickens.

Clearly, equally shared revenues (national TV contracts) can't impact balance unless receiving them is contingent on spending them on talent. All owners get their share regardless of how well their team performs, so there is no incentive from this sharing to do anything about team performance. The same goes for revenues that are shared unequally, because only smaller-revenue owners receive them (as in the NBA and NHL). Again, these are lump-sum payments to smaller-revenue owners without any stipulation about how they should be spent. If owners are in equilibrium, with the marginal value of talent equal across all, this payment does nothing to change the marginal value of talent. So owners find no reason to alter their talent purchases.

The remaining form of unequally shared revenues occurs in MLB and NFL pooled revenue sharing. All teams put different amounts into the pool and take equal shares out. The result is that lower-revenue owners take out more than they put in and vice versa for larger-revenue owners. Here is where the power of our equilibrium notion really helps to shed counterintuitive light on the view that this will change balance. While it is true that larger-revenue market owners put more into the pot, all owners put *the same percentage of their revenues* into the pot. As a result, *the marginal value of talent falls equally for all* owners. The counterintuitive insight is that no owner really has any incentive to change his or her choice of talent in this case!

So what really happens with revenue sharing? First, talent is worth less at the margin, so pay will fall. Second, the distribution of talent stays the same. So while competitive balance is not helped, the owners do pay less for talent. This means that larger-revenue market owners do have to give payments to small market owners, but they also pay less for their players. Meanwhile, smaller-revenue market teams get revenue directly and they pay less for their players. Owners are better off, and it is at the expense of players.

No kind of revenue sharing, equal or unequal sharing, can change balance unless there is an additional requirement that revenue sharing proceeds must be spent to improve team quality. But these requirements never appear for equal sharing, and when they do appear for unequal sharing (MLB) the requirement has no teeth. If one turns to the data, the expectation is that the imposition of revenue sharing, or alterations in existing revenue sharing formulas, on mechanisms without additional enforceable spending requirements, cannot change balance.

By the way, even though these policies might give smaller-revenue owners, or poor performing owners, more resources, this is no way implies that they will use this increase in resources to increase their talent level. For most professional sports team owners, having financial resources is not the issue. Most sports team owners have more than enough financial resources to invest more in payroll if they need to, but owners will only increase their investment in the team quality if they forecast an appropriate return on their investment. That is, the expected gains have to outweigh the expected costs. If owners have already figured out the profit-maximizing level of talent, additional payments that are not tied to their talent choice will not change their minds. They will just pocket the money. Indeed, this is the only reasonable expectation, unless spending requirements accompany revenue sharing.

Ultimately, a team's return on an investment in talent depends on the revenue structure confronting the team's owner. If demand for winning is large, as is typically the case in a larger-revenue market, they will win more games barring bad luck or inefficiency in their investment. While there are always some exceptions, many of the larger-revenue market teams that have not been successful over the past decade or two still spent quite a bit on their payroll (New York Knicks, New York Mets, Los Angeles Dodgers). So clearly team management quality, injuries, and just plain luck all play a role in a team's success. Yet how much a team invests financially depends on how many fans are willing to pay to see a successful team. Revenue sharing does not alter fan willingness to pay, and so it cannot alter the distribution of talent.

The conclusion must be put as bluntly as possible, given all of the misunderstanding we see out there concerning revenue sharing. In baseball, for example, it is often put this way. The Yankees share with the Royals, but the Royals then don't put the proceeds into making their team better so that, at least, fan willingness to pay for baseball, in general, might increase with better balance. So the Yankees don't get anything when the Royals just pocket their revenue sharing proceeds. But nothing could be further from this misguided notion. What really happens with revenue sharing is this. The Yankees and the Royals spend less on players in the presence of pooled revenue sharing. They take the proceeds of reduced payroll and put it in the pool for sharing. Apparently, it is agreeable to the league that the Royals take more of this reduced payroll generated pool than the Yankees.

Now, it is conceivable that owners and players may actually believe otherwise. According to MLB's Blue Ribbon Panel Report in 2000, revenue sharing should give the Pirates, and other smaller-revenue market teams, the funds to sign better players and compete. If revenues are more even, team spending and performance should be more even as well. And perhaps players believed that revenue sharing would improve balance, and the rising tide of revenue would float their boats as well as owners' yachts. From this perspective, their initial reduced payment could be viewed as an investment in balance that would then pay off later with general fan payment to more balanced baseball.

It is certainly true that revenue sharing will even out the revenues earned by running a given sport among owners. However, true to our presentation of the theory above, there is no actual evidence that it will increase parity on the field in the two sports that have extensive and well-defined sharing, MLB and the NFL. The data, again paying attention to end of season balance, playoff access, and dynasties, clearly bear this out. For end of season, this is textbook stuff again (Fort, 2011). In both MLB and the NFL, balance typically remained unchanged with pooled sharing. The exception is the AL for MLB. End of season balance worsened in the AL for MLB's first episode of pooled sharing, 1996–2001, and worsened again through the five years after the alteration in sharing in 2002.

Access to the playoffs appears not to really have changed much at all. We already presented the evidence on this for the NFL in Chapter 11. For MLB, the story is much the same. We think of three periods. First, a control period prior to pooled sharing, 1990–95 (a five-year period, since the playoffs were lost to a player strike in 1994). During this period there was only old-style gate sharing. Second, the original pooled sharing episode covered all local revenue including local TV, 1996–2000. Then, 2001–05, the sharing was more extensive and the luxury tax was added to the mix.

The first thing to note is that over the entire fifteen-year period, if playoff access were perfectly equal, each team should have appeared once and few a couple of times. Instead, Atlanta appeared in the NLCS nine times, St. Louis five times, and Pittsburgh three times. Cincinnati, Florida, the Mets, and Houston all appeared twice. A few appeared once, but, more important, Montreal (Washington), Milwaukee (after 1998), and Colorado never made the NLCS. In the ALCS, the Yankees appeared seven times, Boston four times, Toronto, Cleveland, and Seattle three times, and Oakland, Minnesota, the White Sox, Baltimore, and Anaheim two times each. Tampa Bay, Detroit, Kansas City, Texas, and Milwaukee (prior to 1998) never made the ALCS. The World Series, of course, is even worse. Add Pittsburgh and the Cubs, in the NL, and Baltimore and Seattle in the AL to the list of teams that never made it during this fifteen-year period.

But we can bring a sharper lens to this assessment by examining further what happened across the periods we have identified, using our three periods. We take as our metric the proportion of teams that were new to the NLCS, ALCS, and World Series over these periods. For the NLCS, under old-style gate revenue sharing in 1990–95, four different teams played in the NLCS (Cincinnati, Pittsburgh, Atlanta, Philadelphia), and none of the four had made the NLCS in the five years before that. With the advent of pooled sharing, 1996–2000, five different teams played in the NLCS (Atlanta, St. Louis, Florida, San Diego, and the Mets), and four of the five had not made the NLCS in the five years before that. In our final period of more extensive pooled sharing, 2001–05, seven different teams played in the NLCS, but only four of them, again, had not made the NLCS in the five years before that. To us, this isn't much turnover in pooled sharing years, compared with prior periods.

It's a bit different in the AL. While a couple of more different teams play in each period, fewer of them had not done so in the five years before, compared with the NLCS. Only one of the seven different teams playing in the ALCS from 1990 to 1995 did not make the ALCS in the five years before that. In the first pooled sharing period, 1996–2000, only three of the six different teams that made the ALCS had not done so in the five years before. In the last pooled sharing period, 2001–06, only two of the six different teams that made the ALCS had not done so in the five years before.

The results are pretty much the same for the World Series in each league. For the NL, the number of different teams in the World Series across the three periods goes from three (1990–95) to four (1996–2000) to five (2001–06). All three were new in the first period, two were new in the second, and four were new in the final period of altered revenue sharing. For the AL, the number of different teams varied four in the first period to two in the second and on to four in the third period. The number of new teams across the periods went from two to one to three. Again, any claim that these numbers show improved access to the postseason being caused by changes in revenue sharing seems a stretch.

An assessment of dynasties becomes somewhat problematic for our three five-year periods of comparison, but note that Atlanta made the NLCS four times from 1990 to 1995 (again, remember this is a five-year period, because of the strike), and the same number of times with the imposition of pooled sharing, 1996–2000. But for 2001–05 the Braves made the NLCS only once. In the ALCS, the Yankees did not appear at all in the first period prior to pooled revenue sharing, 1990–95, but then appeared four times with the advent of pooled sharing, 1996–2000, and three times in the final period, 2001–05. The Yankees also made the World Series all but once (2004) in their seven chances during the era of modern revenue sharing in MLB. Again, it is difficult to claim this is evidence that revenue sharing impacted dynasties.

CONCLUSIONS—OWNERS WIN, PLAYERS LOSE, AND FANS WONDER WHAT HAPPENED

The most important change from revenue sharing in sports is that player salaries decrease. This helps all owners, not just smaller-revenue market owners. Usually when a company can cut costs, they will jump at the chance, and in sports it is even better than most industries. In most industries a decrease in salaries means less output. For example, if all of the car manufacturers colluded and agreed to reduce output, revenues might go down, but not as much as costs. Therefore it would increase their profits. In sports, costs go down, but revenues are unchanged, so paying players less increases profits even more. For North American sports leagues, if all teams pay less for players, there will still be the same players at first. It is hard to think of an NFL player that would have probably chosen an alternative career path if the decimal point moved one space on their paycheck. But the danger occurs over time. Eventually, where athletes make choices early on in their careers, and relative expected pay is an element in that consideration, they will move toward higher relative pay. Revenue sharing may lead to just such a decision by some athletes. The question in the future may not be where are all the great heavyweight fighters (playing linebacker in the NFL). The question may be where have all the great linebackers gone (back to heavyweight boxing).

Perhaps this will not be as large an issue if the demand for pro sports continues to rise as it has in the past; even lower pay under revenue sharing outstrips other options. However, there are other team investments that leagues need. For example, new stadiums can have a huge impact on revenues. If all revenues are shared, there is a similar disincentive for individual owners to spend on stadiums. And capital, like stadiums, is completely different than labor (players). Taking money out of stadium investment through sharing is no longer reallocating from players to owners. It is only reallocation among owners! Interestingly, leagues have found ways to take care of this problem. Most NFL teams use personal seat licenses to help fund new stadiums, and the revenue from personal seat licenses are not shared with other teams. While revenues from personal seat licenses are exempt from revenue sharing, personal seat licenses can be issued only if teams are building a new stadium. This gives teams an incentive to build new stadiums. MLB simply allows its owners to reduce their share by the amount of their stadium debt.

Some fans may still be skeptical of revenue sharing not helping competitive balance because they don't believe that owners care about profits. We agree completely that a lump sum transfer from revenue sharing will make a difference in competitive balance if teams are "win maximizing." Indeed, the simple prediction would be that the owner with the biggest checkbook will win the most games. Along these lines, salary caps get in the way for the NBA, NFL, and NHL. So Paul Allen, estimated by Forbes to be worth $12.7

billion in 2010, is constrained in trying to win more for both his Trailblazers and his Seahawks.

But what about the case of baseball where there is no cap? Here it is tough to make the case that owners don't care about profits. Franchise prices correspond to the value of revenue potential in distinct geographic markets, as well as on shared TV money. This tells us that demand from fans and revenue generated by teams is more important than owner wealth. This seems to be consistent with maximizing profit instead of maximizing wins. And if owners are maximizing profit, then a lump sum from revenue sharing should have no impact on competitive balance. Besides, the data are strikingly clear on the lack of any consistent impact of drafts and sharing on balance in any league.

Of course, the league could force the teams to use the money on player salaries, but that is easier said than done. This was a critical point for the Blue Ribbon Panel Report in 2000. They understood that teams would be tempted simply to put the money in their pocket. In fact, MLB claims that revenue from revenue sharing should be spent on players. Even if we put the fox and henhouse issue aside, policing this is not as easy as one might think. For one thing, they could replace whatever they are spending on player salaries or investment with the payment from revenue sharing. For example, if a team's payroll is $60 million and the team receives $40 million from shared revenue, are they using the shared revenue on payroll? One could argue that they need to pay players $100 million, but the team could argue that they would pay players only $20 million without revenue sharing. Another reason it is hard to police is that investing in talent is more than player salaries. In MLB, there are an extensive minor league system and other player development costs. Maybe part of the shared revenue would go toward this. However, the last thing the larger-revenue market owners actually want is for the smaller-revenue market owners to increase player salaries. That would mean they are bidding players away from the larger-revenue markets, which they would not want. So not only is this policy surprisingly hard to police, it is not really in the owners' best interest to do so.

A common mistake that some pundits make in analyzing the impacts of some of these policies is comparing balance across leagues. As we saw in the last chapter, different sports can have different levels of balance simply because they are different (roster size, the relative importance of a single game in leagues with shorter seasons), rather than because they have different "competitive balance mechanisms" in place. Suppose we had a league in which the outcome of each game were decided by a coin toss. That would be a very balanced, albeit boring, league, and competitive balance would not change if we implemented a revenue sharing policy or if we had teams that could draft players. On the other hand, Alan Francis won fourteen of sixteen world horseshoe championships between 1995 and 2010, one of the most dominant athletes ever in their sport. It seems unlikely that any kind of revenue sharing policy could make horseshoes as balanced as coin tossing.

This myth is destructive because pressure is put on the players to accept these policies, or as the quotation at the beginning of the chapter indicates, sometimes players think that these policies are in their best interest. However, these policies do very little to help leagues, while they certainly limit players' salaries. This myth can lead to underinvestment by future athletes in the talent required for the sport to maintain its absolute quality of play. And the myth has already created resentment toward both the players and owners. If these policies are not put into place, fans blame players. If these policies are put into place, fans get angry when their favorite team loses and does not pay "enough" for players.

13 OWNERS SHOULD BE MORE VIGILANT IN POLICING PERFORMANCE-ENHANCING DRUGS

INTRODUCTION

The list of users of performance-enhancing drugs (PEDs) is long and covers a surprising number of sports. The users of PEDs in baseball, cycling, and track and field are probably the best known. People such as Jose Canseco, Rafael Palmiero, Floyd Landis, Ben Johnson, and Marion Jones are more famous now because of their PED use. However, other people, such as Arnold Schwarzenegger (body-building) and Chris Benoit (WWE wrestling), have also made headlines with their PED use. Other leagues, like the NFL, have a fairly long history with PED use, and some have even suspected NASCAR drivers of using PEDs. Retired NHL "tough guy" Georges Laraque (2011) claims in his recent autobiography that PED use has also been prevalent in the NHL.

There are a number of arguments against PED use that are probably not new to the reader but set the stage for our myth. The myth is not about the effects of PEDs, but rather that somehow the onus is on team owners to do something about it. One argument has it that fans view some ways of gaining competitive advantage as valid and others as invalid. Training 24/7/365, specialized diet regimens, hyperbaric chambers, and traveling to acclimate are valid. Chemical enhancement is not. The cause and reasoning of this distinction may vary from fan to fan, but according to this argument, leagues that turn away from PED enforcement are messing with the primal force in sport, the fans, and put the economic value of their leagues at risk. In a *New York Times* column, Buzz Bissinger (2005) put it this way for baseball, "[T]he true villains are baseball's owners, greedy and feckless throughout the game's history, and in the case of this latest mess, guilty of cynically jettisoning the game's subtlety and complexity to turn it into a slugfest circus."

A closely related argument lies in the impact of PED use on traditions. For example, it is fairly easy to handle the "dead ball era" when comparing greats over time because the so-called dead ball was exogenous to player investment in skill. All players faced the same dead ball. But PEDs influence sports outcomes through different choices made by different players; some use and some don't. So those interested in tradition cannot hold PED use constant in their comparisons. This is particularly vexing to gatekeepers of the record books, such as members of the Baseball Writers Association of America, that pass judgment on entry into the MLB Hall of Fame. So, in addition to possibly judging actual and suspected users morally, these voters face the additional complexity of judging variation in relative performance. Which is the main reason for denying Mark McGwire entry, something about his performance, or that it may have been invalidated by the use of particular PEDs?

In addition, arguments against PED use cast them as detrimental to the athletes' own long-term health. Because of their general illegality, it is hard to know about the medical impacts of PED use. However, visions of Lyle Alzado, admitted user, dying young and horribly, remain in people's memory whether PEDs were the cause or not. The same goes for the more recent passing of Randy "Macho Man" Savage of pro wrestling fame. This raises two additional specters. That some players *may* put their health at risk (if this is even true) should not mean that all players *must* put their health at risk in order to remain competitive.

Close on the heals of this argument is the ever-present, "Won't anybody think about the children!" Young athletes typically overestimate their athletic future, and they may also underestimate any health effects of emulating PED users in the higher ranks of their sport. Certainly politicians use this as a reason to try to eliminate PEDs from professional sports. In the 2004 State of the Union Address, George W. Bush said that athletes should set a better example to children regarding PEDs. When the U.S. Congress held hearings on PED or steroid use in 2005, Representative Henry Waxman cited an increase in steroid use among children as the main reason.

Economists are of no use in debates over the physiological impacts of PEDs. What your economist authors read suggests to them that massive use will be harmful. But we also read and know from experience that the general public regularly benefits from carefully monitored PED use. Carefully monitored, some PEDs have simply miraculous healing power. Thus we find this argument fascinating in its fixation on monstrous levels of PED abuse. Nearly nobody beyond professional body-builders has ever admitted to this type of abuse. More typically, PEDs are used as long-term enhancements or as rehabilitation aids. We would not deny ourselves the healing and rehabilitation powers of some PEDs that are banned by pro sports leagues.

Some researchers have argued that there is actually no effect from PED use other than maybe a placebo effect. However, any sports fan that has seen before and after pictures of Barry Bonds or Sammy Sosa knows this is probably more than a psychological effect. Current photos, after leaving their sport, show them to now have thinner, more lithe physiques again. Furthermore, Table 13.1 shows the top ten MLB seasons all-time prior to 2011 in terms of at-bats per home run by a player. While Table 13.1 is not definitive proof of PED use, it does seem suspicious that three of the four players on that list have come under fire for PED use. It may or may not be true that things like human growth hormone have no or little effect, but certainly some PEDs help create muscle mass, which helps people become better athletes. As Winfree put it in his work on PEDs and home runs with his coauthor, University of Michigan economist John DiNardo (2010), it seems that it would be impossible to say that steroids have had no effect in sports.

Despite being hamstrung on the physiology issues, economists can be useful here in a variety of ways. First, it is the bread and butter of economics that, scientifically justified or not, people take economic actions, such as buying tickets, based on their perceptions. So regardless of actual impacts, if fans don't like the PED-aided version of a sport, they will buy something else. Thus the economic data on fan choice can prove enlightening. Sec-

TABLE 13.1. *Top Ten Seasons or At-bats per Home Run prior to 2011*

Player	Season	At-Bats per Home Run
Barry Bonds	2001	6.52
Mark McGwire	1998	7.27
Mark McGwire	1999	8.02
Mark McGwire	1996	8.13
Barry Bonds	2004	8.29
Babe Ruth	1920	8.48
Barry Bonds	2003	8.67
Barry Bonds	2002	8.76
Babe Ruth	1927	9.00
Sammy Sosa	2001	9.02

Source: Calculated from data at baseball-reference.com.

ond, right or wrong, the impacts on other players, and on down to young athletes, are a classic case of a negative externality. Economists have been investigating externalities and their remedies for nearly two hundred years, and application to PED use is a natural.

Doing so reveals two things. First, it is difficult to see that fans are actually put off by PED use simply observing their choices. Thus there are mythical possibilities in the "fans hate steroids" argument. This also helps to explain owner behavior when they get together as a league to decide PED policy. Second, the idea that leagues are to blame misses two fundamental points. Value is created by PED use and, as Ronald Coase taught us over fifty years ago, how an externality can be handled is a many-splendored thing—why are owners blamed rather than players (and their unions)?

The tragedies of this myth are many. Some people impose their preferences on others, devoutly to be avoided in free society. The health value of PED use is swept under the rug and denied to injured athletes, when the same is not true for the rest of the citizenry. The economic value of higher absolute levels of play is dismissed offhand as illegitimate. Banning PED use will reduce the value of sports output. Now, banning their use may be the final policy outcome, but if that outcome is based on a logical fallacy, then society pays. Finally, even if there are dangers, the most effective and efficient way of dealing with the problem never sees the light of day. The tyranny of the "Self-Appointed High Inquisitors of PED Use" wins out over the careful consideration of benefits and costs.

THE DATA AND FAN PREFERENCES REGARDING PERFORMANCE ENHANCEMENT

It may seem a glib response to the first argument we state above, but it is difficult to argue that fans hate PED use based on the data of their observed choice. Put another way, how is it that anybody really knows whether fans hate "slugfest circuses" or not? It is not obvious that PED use hurts a league overall, and while there are certainly some costs associated with PED use there are also benefits. Clearly there has been much negative publicity for Major League Baseball (MLB) as a result of PEDs. However, it is probable that MLB increased their revenue, at least temporarily, when players were using PEDs. The same is true for other sports as well.

Football fans like to see really big guys hitting each other hard, and track fans like to see people run really fast. And there has been a clear response in the absolute level of playing talent. For example, the average size of the Super Bowl offensive line increased from 245 pounds (Green Bay Packers, 1967) to 313 pounds (Green Bay Packers, 2010), or 28 percent in forty-three years. The largest offensive lineman in this comparison increased from 249 pounds (Forrest Gregg) to 330 pounds (Chad Clifton), or 33 percent (they were about the same height, six feet five inches). The economics of this increase is almost as massive as the players that create it, upward of $9 billion by popular reports for 2011.

The lesson from these observations is quite important. Fans care about the *absolute level* of quality of a league or sport as well as the *relative level* of quality within the league or sport. PEDs clearly increase the absolute quality of players. If players are using PEDs, it usually does lead to a higher absolute level of play. At the very least, PEDs may lead to extraordinary individual seasons for some players, which fans love to see.

The Barry Bonds's home run chase in 2001 is illustrative (covered as well in Fort, 2011). The context is clearly that suspicion was growing that Bonds was a PED user. What has been swept under the rug is the value that was created by actual fans making choices during his pursuit of the individual season home run record. But the data are readily available, and the value in the eyes of fans easy to see. In 1999, the Giants finished second in the NL West and drew 2,078,365 fans at the gate. In 2000, they won the division and drew 3,315,330 fans. So winning the division was worth 1,236,965 fans and the economic value they brought with them to the ballpark. No doubt there also was TV revenue value to the Giants, but we have no data on that. Now, in 2001, the Giants finished in second place as they did in 1999. But with the Bonds chase attendance was 3,311,958, an increment of 1,233,593; Bonds's chase was worth about as much to Giants fans as finishing first over second in the NL West. We stress that this is at a time when suspicions about his PED use were running rampant. If you use the 2001 fan cost index, this is worth around $50.5 million at the time. Bonds's share was his $10.3 million salary in 2001. And this is just to the owners of the Giants, not to everyone else in the NL when Bonds visited, and this is just for gate, without any other accounting for TV revenue. It is difficult to claim on the basis of this evidence that Giants fans share any hatred of PED use.

In addition, some work done by one of your authors suggests an interesting thing about the rise of PED use in MLB (Fort and Lee, 2013). American League per game attendance increased steadily from 1965 to 1985. However, in 1986 and 1987, there is a dramatic shift upward in attendance that does not correspond to anything structural in baseball. For example, over this same time period, attendance simply increased steadily in the NL without any shift. One of the differences between the two leagues is that the late 1980s was characterized by the new age of hitter power (as opposed to statistically measured "power hitting"), exemplified by the "Bash Brothers" of the Oakland A's (Jose Canseco and Mark McGwire). Of course, this also marks the beginning of a period retroactively cast under the shadow of PED use. The shift up in attendance is consistent with AL fans identifying with more exciting hitting power. Further, surely the dramatic shift upward for AL attendance was not lost on team owners. Indeed, increased attendance could help explain MLB's reluctance to intervene strenuously on behalf of clean play at that time, and that same logic could prevail today. The league owners may just be weighing the preferences of some fans clean play against the observed fact of a large AL attendance jump.

If the absolute level of talent increases from PED use, this will have a positive financial effect on the league. The magnitude of this effect could be in question, but certainly fans would rather see a high absolute level of play. For example, Major League Soccer suffers from the fact that they do not put the highest-level soccer in front of fans. Many soccer fans in the United States are fans of other soccer leagues. So if Major League Soccer could increase its overall quality level, revenues would increase. Furthermore, fans know when the quality of the athletes improves. When athletes start doing things that no one has done before, fans get excited. In track and field, winning a gold medal in the Olympics is one thing, breaking a world record at the Olympics is another. In baseball, when home run records are broken it becomes a very big deal; many credited Mark McGwire and Sammy Sosa with saving baseball after the 1994–95 work stoppage (see David Leonhardt's 2005 New York Times article for a different slant). Most people would contend that at least a few records were broken in baseball and track and field with the help of PEDs. It becomes very difficult to put a dollar value on the total benefit of PED use to leagues, but surely leagues want athletes to be as good as they can be.

If PED use does increase revenues for leagues, the money came from fans that are willing to spend more over time, including the PED use baggage. Anything that increases demand for a league does so because fans are willing to pay more for it. Perhaps some (many?) fans abhor PED use, but the offset is the additional interest that even these same fans show in the increased absolute level of player quality. Some fans don't even mind if players are using PEDs, they simply want to see better players. Some see little difference between PEDs and other legal drugs that have similar but usually mitigated effects. Sometimes the line between what should be allowed and what is not allowed is not clear. Regardless, to have a serious discussion, the benefits of PEDs cannot be dismissed.

THE EXTERNALITY PROBLEM

Just because an increase in player quality can help the league financially does not mean everyone will benefit financially. Revenues are split between the owners and players. Over time the players have been getting a larger share, but nonetheless each side takes their cut. Therefore the owners themselves will gain some revenue. On the player side, it is a bit more complicated. On average, player salaries should go up with league prosperity. But certainly players benefiting from PEDs will be the ones to really take advantage of this. Theoretically, players not using PEDs could also benefit if the overall league increase in revenue outweighed the fact that non–PED using players were now relatively worse compared with the other players in the league. But this seems very unlikely. Almost certainly non–PED using players are worse off if others are using PEDs.

And herein lies the other economic issue—if PED use is detrimental to athlete health, then pressure on those that would rather not use PEDs is a cost that users create but not bear, themselves. This is a classic case of negative externality. That the externality extends to young athletes should be clear enough. Note that anybody can argue that those players that would rather not use don't have to. They can just find another job. But the difference between their higher value, in the absence of anybody using any PEDs, and the value of their alternative job is a very real loss to them and to society.

In the usual way that leads people to despise us, University of Chicago economist (and Nobel Prize winner) Ronald Coase taught us long ago that there are a variety of ways to achieve social ends in the case of externalities. For example, to reduce pollution, you can punish the polluter when they do so, pay the polluter to reduce pollution, tax consumers for their purchase of pollution-producing goods, or pay consumers for buying alternative goods. All will have the same effect of reducing pollution under certain conditions. Things that might lead to choosing one solution over another would include other costs of carrying it out. For example, if paying polluters not to pollute caused more firms to claim that they wanted to pollute, then there would be a problem of whom to pay. Or maybe society simply would prefer not to pay people to do what it judges as "the right thing to do" in the first place. The fact that we choose one of these options over the other may be a reflection that one type of device is cheaper to impose, or it may just be that our values lead us to one over the other. Paying polluters to stop it is a bit like paying thieves not to rob us; it rankles a bit.

For PEDs and sports, we make the following observations. Although we do believe the evidence and arguments are far from convincing, let's suppose the goal is to reduce PED use because it is an externality issue as described. What is the variety of ways to accomplish the goal, a la Coase? We can punish the user. We can pay the user not to use. We can tax owners that knowingly pay PED users their PED-induced premium. We can pay owners to hire nonusers over users. And the devices all require enforcement administration. Let's focus on owners policing players and player unions doing their self-professed job of watching out for the best interests of their players.

Player unions fought against rigorous testing of PEDs when owners brought this topic up, at least in MLB. Union leadership cited invasion of personal privacy. Well and good, players versus owners, but this is clearly crazy if the comparison is player versus player, an arena ignored by the unions at the time. Unions are voluntary organizations that can impose requirements on their members, and this is hardly a constitutional issue. From the perspective of Coase's work, the question is just which enforcer is more likely to succeed and at what cost. There is a good case to be made that the players policing themselves would be the more effective and lower cost approach. As noted above, there is an economic value to owners that offsets any gains they may earn from stopping PED use. Instead, put a bounty on cheaters and let their teammate bounty hunters collect the reward. While reducing long-term health effects to users (remember, this is the presumed problem to begin with), this approach would also reduce the incentive to use in the first place, thereby protecting those players that would rather not use PEDs.

A la Coase's original line of thinking, rather than paying bounties, owners could use the same money to incentivize drug testing. In other words, they could pay a reward to players that test clean. The size of this payment should roughly approximate what the players would otherwise make if they used PEDs. Removing the differential should benefit all players—those that don't want to use PEDs don't have to and pay no penalty for choosing not to, and those that previously used face a disincentive to continue to do so.

Clearly the owners could have fought harder to prevent PED use and were pronounced "greedy and feckless" for their claimed puny efforts. It is interesting to us that players' unions, again self-professed protectors of labor, were not also labeled greedy and feckless. One could certainly argue that team owners have a moral obligation to curtail PED use, but that could be said of anyone. Moving away from morality to actual harm, players are the ones potentially negatively impacted by PED use. It would seem that since players bear the cost of PED use, we would expect the players to want regulation more than owners.

While any benefits from PEDs are shared between owners and players, all costs are borne by the players (and some emulating young people). This is why it is fascinating the way owners and players have handled PEDs through the collective bargaining agreements. In MLB the owners did push for stricter policing of PEDs, although they may have fought for this half-heartedly. Surprisingly, the players' union fought against policing of PEDs. Obviously players that used PEDs did not want to be caught, but what about the players that were not using PEDs? It seems surprising that the players' union did not stand up for these players. Owners received most of the bad press, but wasn't the players' union also culpable?

The story of Ken Caminiti seems illustrative. Caminiti had a fifteen-year MLB career, the highlight of which was a Most Valuable Player award in 1996 when he was playing for the San Diego Padres. Before his death in 2004 he admitted to using steroids that season, as well as some other seasons. Kevin Towers, the former general manager of the Padres, admitted to suspecting Caminiti's steroid use, and he felt guilty for not speaking up. According to an AP release by the *New York Times* (2005), the reason Towers kept quiet is that his third baseman was having a terrific year. The point of this chapter is neither to curse nor to exonerate general managers, owners, or other executives. Knowing about illegal behavior and not speaking up while profiting from it is certainly serious, and the Penn State case reveals that it can be both tragic and ruinous.

However, the owners did try, albeit possibly not strongly enough, to reduce PED use. In a 1991 memo to all major league clubs signed by Commissioner Fay Vincent, players using steroids "are subject to discipline by the Commissioner and risk permanent expulsion from the game" (Vincent, 1991, p. 1). However, this threat was mitigated by the fact that there was no testing. In 2002, the collective bargaining agreement did allow for testing on a trial basis for the 2003 season. It was the player's union that fought against this. Because of high rates of positive tests, PED testing increased for the 2004 season. After pressure from the public, testing has become more prevalent, and punishments have become more severe. But again, the question is, why wasn't the players association ahead of the owners in this situation, since they bear the costs? In other words, why would one expect Kevin Towers to "out" Caminiti when collectively the players where fighting for not testing him (or at least players that played after Caminiti)?

The behavior of MLB's player's union might be explained by the mechanism that was clearly preferred, punishment for PED use. With the possible exception of fan repercussions, the owners do not face any punishment from the PED era. At least some of the PED using players have been punished, however. The problem is that it would be difficult to construct a system where the owners were punished. For example, there is no law dictating that Kevin Towers should be punished for having done nothing after suspecting Caminiti's PED use. Thus there are no grounds for prosecution (as there are for those failing to report the abuse by Jerry Sandusky at Penn State). And if the owners should be held accountable, what about the fans or other players that also had suspicions? Given that the players were essentially the only ones punished, this may help to explain the animosity toward the owner. Nonetheless, the policy debate has always been to decide what type of testing and punishment to give PED users. Furthermore, more stringent policies were and are in the best interest of the players, more so than the owners.

How different this all would have been under an entirely different enforcement regime. If the majority will of the union membership were against PED use, then player-police would have handled the problem quite nicely. A bounty system would even have led to more vigorous reporting by teammates. Again, doing well by doing good would have been the outcome, rather than hegemony and weak enforcement. Indeed, on the field, pitchers with a preference against PED use would be able to send the message loud and clear to users.

We should note that other leagues have been more diligent in their PED policies than MLB. The NFL's steroid policy has generally been much stricter than MLB's. This almost seems counterintuitive, given that baseball fans like to compare statistics of present players with players of the past. One might suspect, and it seems to be the case, that there is less outrage from PED use from football fans. So it is somewhat surprising that the NFL has generally had a stricter policy. On the other hand, it may be the love of statistics that also gave MLB a bigger gain from PED use. For example, home run records have always been important events in American sports history. Regarding the NBA, it does not appear that they have had a serious problem with PEDs, but it is difficult to know. However, the history of the NHL and PED policies seems to be more like MLB. For example, the NHL does not test players for PEDs during the off-season or during the playoffs. It is difficult to know what causes these differences between leagues, but certainly some leagues have tried to eliminate PEDs more than others.

CONCLUSIONS—PEDS ACTUALLY
ARE EVERYWHERE (AN ADDERALL ANALOGY)

We conclude with an analogy. In academics, some researchers (and students) have begun using Adderall or other drugs that help concentration. One of the benefits of these types of drugs is higher research productivity. Again some might question the magnitude, but society will benefit if research productivity is higher. The ones that bear the cost are researchers. Researchers that use these drugs might have side effects such as higher blood pressure, aggression, changes in vision, or other things. Researchers that do not use these types of drugs will be less productive in a relative sense. So who, if anyone, should ban and/or police the use of these drugs for researchers? One might hope that university administrators would sense that it is in their best interest to regulate such things, but the researchers themselves should not balk at such regulations. They should be the ones to embrace such regulations.

This myth that PED enforcement should come from owners is destructive because if PED use is harmful to society, and higher levels of PED use by professional athletes does cause more widespread use, then it is most likely to be eliminated by those who benefit from their elimination. Owners and players' unions appear unwilling, and fans have not shown any inclination at all to shun leagues where this type of use is documented or, at least, admitted by some players. It also distracts attention from other issues harmful to player health (training regimes, equipment, field conditions).

In addition, some people impose their preferences on others, an imposition most Americans also abhor. The health value of PED use is swept under the rug. In the longer term, learning the actual effects of PEDs is hindered. It could end up that injured athletes are being denied rehabilitation when the same is not true for the rest of the citizenry. The economic value of higher absolute levels of play is dismissed offhand as illegitimate, but banning PED use will reduce the value of sports output. Now, banning their use may be the final policy outcome, but if that outcome is based on a logical fallacy, society pays.

14 EVERYBODY LOSES WHEN LABOR-MANAGEMENT RELATIONS GO SOUTH

INTRODUCTION

A common theme dominates the press during any work stoppage—nobody wins during a lockout (by owners) or a strike (by players). Players lose current salary payments while they battle over collective bargaining agreement (CBA) minutiae. Owners cannot collect the value of ownership in the absence of play, and run the risk of lower fan attention to their sport (at the gate and on TV) once play resumes. All of the supporting casts, from parking attendants to concessionaires, twiddle their thumbs waiting for the stars of the show, owners and players, to get their act together. Finally, fans lose the object of their affection (or affliction, depending on your view of fandom). Only one thing makes fans angrier than the high prices they must pay to enjoy their teams, and that is not getting to enjoy any of it at all.

We note simply in passing that too much is made of the losses to the supporting cast. In general, money that is not spent by fans on their favorite pro teams is just spent elsewhere. One parking lot's loss is another's gain at some other entertainment event. Concessionaires, by and large working for that minimum wage, just move to some other job. And money that would have been spent at restaurants and bars around the home facility of the pro team just go to other entertainment and restaurants someplace else close by. We spend no more time on this and refer the reader to the vast literature on this topic. We also take the completely uncontroversial as given—by and large, fans lose out during a lockout or strike. Instead of these distractions, we focus on the main event between owners and players.

It is possible for both sides to lose, and we cover this below. But this is simply an outcome that is due to bargaining mistakes or poor choice of negotiators and really shouldn't happen very often. Typically, when both sides sincerely do not want a lockout or strike, one will not happen. But in other cases, where a lockout or strike occurs, it is clearly the misunderstanding of strategic manipulation that leads to the general myth that "everybody," players and owners alike, loses during a strike or lockout.

This myth comes from the intuitive idea that nobody could possibly want to stop play that generates billions of dollars annually for sports team owners and, consequently, multi–million dollar salaries to athletes. Interrupting this flow of revenue just seems plumb crazy. We agree that it is true that *both sides* cannot "win" from a work stoppage. However, it is pretty simple to show that one side clearly can win, and win big. And this can be true even if an entire season is lost, lock-stock-and-barrel, as occurred in 2004–05 in hockey.

This is a destructive myth because it leads fans to hold a grudge against the "perps" of such an "irrational" crime against fans. This could typically benefit owners in their dealings with players—players either strike on their own or owners portray the issues in ways complimentary to themselves. Fans carry out this grudge in the form of short-lived attendance holdouts the next year, but owners have already built this into their decision. Now, fans might still be angry about being denied some of their favorite consumption, but at least they should be angry for the right reasons!

WHY DO LOCKOUTS AND STRIKES HAPPEN?

Before we get too far about winners and losers in collective bargaining agreements, we should start with the basics of collective bargaining in sports. While some of the bargaining is about growing the overall financial pie, most of collective bargaining is about slicing up the financial pie. After all, if there were an easy way to increase league revenues as a whole, it would not take collective bargaining to get it done. Typically league policies such as player drafts, revenue sharing, luxury taxes, and salary caps are the crux of collective bargaining agreements. As we already pointed out in Chapter 12, these policies usually do not have a huge impact on competitive balance, and even if they did it is not clear if they would help league revenues, as we showed in Chapter 11. However, these policies can have a big impact on who gets the revenue. All of the aforementioned policies will end up decreasing player salaries in one way or another. Player drafts take away the ability of players to negotiate with other teams, which decreases pay. Revenue sharing creates less of an incentive for teams to win, which means the value of players is less. Luxury taxes usually tax large payrolls, increasing the cost of large salaries. Salary caps simply limit pay. While some of these policies could pit large market owners against small market owners, the biggest rift is typically between owners and players.

Ignoring the details of the bargaining, it essentially boils down to what percentage of revenues is going to go to players and what percentage is going to go to owners. Certainly not all of the revenue is going to go to the players. After all, teams do have other costs besides player salaries. Certainly the players will get some percentage of revenues, since they have to be paid. However, there is a huge difference between what players are paid and what they would need to be paid to ensure that most of them would still play in the league. And this illustrates the problem. With one extreme being a reserve clause where players are paid very little, and the other extreme being free agency for all players where players receive huge salaries, there is a vast difference between outcomes. Also, given the increases in revenue over the past few decades, there is a huge amount of money on the table to be split up between owners and players. This means that "winning" in collective bargaining can be very lucrative.

The sports industry has an interesting history, suggesting that the beneficiaries of interruptions to play have changed over time. Nearly all of the work stoppages prior to the mid-1990s were strikes, initiated by the players. The interruptions in MLB in 1972, 1981, and 1994–95; the NFL in 1982 and 1987, were all strikes. Although it varied by league, the percentage of revenue given to the players was small. Economist Gerald Scully (1974) estimated that in the early 1970s MLB players received roughly 10 to 20 percent of what they generated for teams. This means that they had everything to gain by striking. Certainly, every players' strike has its collateral damage to some players. Expos fans were disappointed in 1994 because their team was finally off to a fantastic start, but the players' hopes of being winners also were dashed. Also, some players could have their careers cut short by a strike. But it is easy to see that striking was financially worth it to the players on average; the short-term loss for players was worth the long-term gain.

On the other hand, recent interruptions to play were instigated by owners. The interruptions in the NHL in 1994–95 and 2004–05; the NBA in 1998 and just recently in 2011 were lockouts initiated by the owners. There were earlier lockouts in sports, but they were not as long as the more recent lockouts and caused no interruption in play. The reason lockouts instead of strikes started happening is that the percentage of revenues going to players increased. By the mid-1990s, most players were receiving a vast majority of revenues that they generated. Fort (2011) documents the following in his textbook. From 1991 to 1996 the percentage of revenue going to players went from 45 percent to 54 percent in MLB, 39 percent to 47 percent in the NBA, 47 percent to 67 percent in the NFL, and 33 percent to 51 percent in the NHL. Therefore, more recently the owners have had more to gain. While the early strikes focused on things such as getting free agency for the players, more recently lockouts have focused on instituting salary caps and making them more binding.

In some competitive markets there is not much money to haggle over, since the market sets salaries. Given the market power in sports, there are huge amounts to be gained or lost during collective bargaining. Because each league is essentially a monopoly, and by the definition of collective bargaining the players are negotiating as one unit, there are a wide range of possible outcomes. That is why it is hard to compare the sports industry with other industries in this regard. In most industries, employees have a reasonable chance of finding work for another firm if they want. In a lot of industries firms can relatively easily replace employees. That is a completely different situation from sports leagues.

According to Paul Gomme and Peter Rupert (2004), economic advisors to the Cleveland Fed., labor has received an average of 71.7 percent of revenues across industries since 1970. In industries that derive most of their revenue from labor, this percentage is higher. In industries that are more capital intensive, this percentage will be lower. In most professional sports leagues, the amount of revenues that go to the players typically fluctuates between one-third and two-thirds, although that number seems have been close to two-thirds recently. While the percentage of revenue that goes to players is not that far off the national average, one might think that athletes would receive an even higher share of revenue compared with the average, since fans pay money to watch the players. However, we should not dismiss the importance of the stadium, and maybe more important, the market structure in the sports industry is completely unique.

Another important aspect of collective bargaining, or any type of bargaining really, is alternatives. For example, suppose that NHL owners feel they could make almost as much money by having concerts in their venue rather than hockey games. In this situation, the NHL owners are much more willing to entertain the idea of a lockout than if they have no other entertainment to put in their arenas. Undoubtedly, a full understanding of the next best alternatives for players led to the quick end of the NBA lockout that began the 2011–12 season; by the end of November 2011, players had missed two paychecks and their next best options were being revealed as not very valuable to many players.

There are other more subtle effects as well. Winfree (2009) showed that during the 2004–05 NHL, lockout attendance at NBA games did increase a bit in cities that had NHL teams. What makes this interesting is that NHL owners owned some of the NBA teams. So this softened the financial blow of not receiving revenue during the 2004–05 lockout. On the other side of the bargaining table, suppose NBA players feel they could all become movie stars and do almost as well as when they're playing basketball. After all, Shaquille O'Neal made movies. OK, bad example (and bad movies). Looking back at the NHL lockout, many of the players tried to find other leagues to play in. So the short-term loss for those players depended on the difference between the NHL and the new league they were playing in. One of the contributing factors as to why the owners did well in negotiations during the lockout could be that their alternatives were better. After all, there is quite a difference between playing in the NHL and a minor league or even a European league. The owners may have been more effective at using their arenas during the lockout. It is possible that the lockout was all about NHL owners losing too much money with their hockey teams, but examining the alternatives for owners and players does tell an interesting story.

Work stoppages can also lead to fan resentment, which can hurt the league in the long run. During each work stoppage, there seems to be a certain percentage of fans that claim their fanaticism toward the league is over. However, after looking at the data, this doesn't seem to hold true. Surely there are some fans that never went to or watched games from that league after a work stoppage, but any effect is undetectable by looking at the data. There seemed to be a widely held belief that MLB was hurt badly by the 1994–95 strike. However, as Portland State University economist Martin Schmidt and his coauthor, Southern Utah University economist David Berri (2004), originally showed, it is not at all obvious from MLB's attendance data that there ever was any attendance decline after this strike (or any other strike prior to that). University of Maryland (Baltimore County) economists Dennis Coates and Thane Harrison (2005) used a more detailed data set and found that the impacts were even smaller. Leagues typically pick up right where they left off with regard to attendance. So while it is certainly true that fans are put off by work stoppages, it does not appear that it has a significant impact on fan demand.

Each side should consider all of these elements when deciding whether or not to have a lockout or strike. Specifically, each side should think about the potential gains, the probability of getting those potential gains, the short-term revenue loss from a lockout (or salary loss from a strike), what they would do as an alternative if play stops, and finally any fan repercussions. Essentially the probability of winning the work stoppage and the gains from winning the work stoppage should be weighed against the net short-term losses and any fan resentment.

Now, let's run quickly through three main settings for negotiation. Each has to do with the amount of information available to each side and the "expected value" of stopping play (that is, the value in an uncertain situation as we detail below). Suppose both sides know everything about the other. Owners know player pay and the next best options facing players. Players know the revenue generated in a season, and the next best options for owners. Both sides know fan costs, if any. It is well known from bargaining theory (and backed up by nearly all of the data on management-labor negotiations) that the most likely outcome in this setting is, most of all, that a bargain will be reached as early as possible. Whatever the split that eventually is agreed upon, the only rational outcome is to preserve the entire pie for that split. A lockout or strike would just reduce the size of the pie.

The second thing that is known (and backed up by the data on negotiated outcomes) is that the next best option for each side must be covered and then the rest is split 50–50. For example, suppose a $4 billion season is on the table. (Let's go ahead and forget about fan irritation costs.) Owners can make $1.5 billion with their next best option and players can make $2 billion. After covering both options, there is another $500 million left, split 50–50 is another $250 million for each side. The outcome is $1.75 billion for the owners and $2.25 billion for the players, approximately a 44–56 owner-player split. Since both sides know all of this, the most they can make is this split without any interruption to play. Note that another way to describe this situation is that the expected value of a lockout is zero or worse for the owners, and the expected value of a strike is zero or worse for players.

This is the world of sports league negotiations writ large. There have been many bargaining points in the four pro sports leagues and nearly no actual interruptions in play. Player associations have been around about forty-five years. On average, CBAs last about three years (although more recent agreements go much longer). That's about fifteen bargaining chances per league, or sixty in total. There have been only seven strikes and lockouts combined that actually interrupted play. The success rate on average is 88 percent. Not too shabby, but not all-encompassing either.

So what if the world is fraught with uncertainty instead? For example, each side knows that the other side *has next best options*, but must estimate *the value* of those options. In addition, players must estimate the actual value of the season that owners surely know better. How is our "full information" outcome altered by this need to estimate some values? The basic answer should be that nothing changes, because it is in the best interests of both sides just to tell the other side the truth. If they did, and they had impeccable reputations, each side would believe the other and we would be right back to the previous outcome—namely, 44–56 split without any interruption to play. Once again, the expected value of any interruption in play is zero or worse for both owners and players. But . . .

If the other side can only generate imperfect estimates of the values involved, and each side knows this, then there can be interrupted play even if the expected value of any interruption in play is zero or worse for both owners and players! Each will try to convince the other that the data are such that their own share should be larger. But at the same time, each side knows this is true and will naturally adjust any claim made by the other to this effect. The result can be an interruption in play even if both sides would be better off without one just because correct information is difficult to come by. This type of information asymmetry characterizes many negotiations besides those between management and labor. There is an entire branch of economics dedicated to solving contract problems in the face of asymmetric information.

So, we have one case where play can be interrupted. Even if both sides would be better off without any such interruption, information asymmetry may lead to estimates in conflict between the two sides. There can be an unintentional lockout or strike. This type can be resolved in an instant, by the way, with the introduction of some form of mediation where an independent third party just goes through all of the relevant data and simply states the truth of the matter to both sides. But before the mediator is introduced, there may be some interruption in play.

Which brings us to our final setting. It can simply be the case that one side finds the expected value of interrupted play to be significantly positive. If one side thinks that with a work stoppage they gain a higher percentage of revenue in the future, then a work stoppage can benefit them in the long run. Indeed, there is just enough data to flesh in this basic logic and show why the NBA lockout at the beginning of the 1998–99 season and the NHL lockout of the entire 2004–05 season made perfectly rational sense from the perspective of team owners (these are textbook examples, literally, from Fort, 2011). This is true in the latter case even though it cost an entire season, including the playoff determination of the NHL champion that year.

NBA Lockout 1998–99

In this case, the owners exercised a clause in the CBA that forced a new negotiation if the player share of revenues reached 57 percent. Negotiations opened but ended in disaster, and the NBA owners announced that there would be no 1998–99 season without a new agreement with a tighter salary cap. The players didn't budge, and the owners were as good as their word. The evidence on the profitability of this lockout, rather than the possibility that it was driven by asymmetric information alone, is pretty easy to follow.

Let's think about the revenues lost from a lockout. The NBA generated $1.7 billion at the time. The 57 percent going to players would amount to $969 million, leaving $731 million for owners. About 30 percent, or $510 million, would typically go to other expenses, leaving the owners 13 percent, or $221 million. So if the lockout lasted the entire season, the owners were risking about $221 million. The owners would also count the later costs of fan irritation if any.

What did the owners stand to gain? Shooting for a 50–50 split, the owners would gain $119 million *per year*. The subsequent CBA held for eight years, a total of $952 million. At 5 percent, the discounted present value is $769 million. Data on the next best option for owners were unavailable, but one can imagine that filling arena dates was possible. So the owners had to consider whether it was worth it to risk $221 million plus fan irritation costs in hopes of gaining $769 million, softened by the net of their next best alternative. Abstracting from fan irritation and the owners' next best alternative, if the owners felt it was certain that the players would fold in the face of the lockout, they could pocket $769 − 221 = $548 million, or $18.3 million each. Fan irritation would have to exceed the owners' next best option by this amount to drive the gain to zero, which seems extremely unlikely—to cancel $548 million would mean that irritation, in excess of the owners' next best alternative, would have to be worth the league profit of 2.5 full NBA seasons under the old business model!

Of course, winning is nearly never a sure thing, so the NBA owners had to assess their chances of winning. Then the lockout turned into a gamble, and the well-known logic of decision-making under uncertainty came into play. The expected value is less than the sure thing value, since one of the possibilities is that the owners could get less only if the players do not fold. However, as long as the odds of players folding were "big enough," the expected value would still be positive and the owners would go for it. Since the owners did lock the players out, we can conclude that was the case. It didn't have to be asymmetric information to force the lockout. It could have simply been a matter of a large enough prize.

In these situations, you can get a little more insight by finding the probability that makes the expected value go to zero, known as the break-even probability. If NBA owners thought that their chance of winning the lockout was greater than the break-even probability, the expected value would at least be positive, and perhaps their gamble was worth a try. Without boring the reader with a bit of arithmetic, if we assume that the owners' next best alternative and fan irritation costs were a wash, the data on owner gains and losses above give a break-even probability of 29 percent; if owners thought that the chance the players would fold was higher than 29 percent, then the expected value of the lockout was positive. Now we don't know how the owners felt facing such a risk, but the odds were pretty clearly in their favor.

While the sports economics literature noted earlier suggests that later costs of fan irritation are actually quite small, it is easy to demonstrate that even if otherwise the odds were still long in the owners' favor. For example, fan irritation costs exceed the owners' next best alternatives by $163.5 million to drive the break-even probability to 0.5; the owners would face a coin toss concerning any net gain from the lockout. But this would require that angry fans would stay away from the NBA for three-fourths of an entire season *after the lockout ended*; $163.5 million is 75 percent of league profits for a season. There is no evidence indicating this could ever happen. Indeed, the following is much more likely. If owners believed that their next best alternative would exceed any losses to fan irritation, then the break-even probability is even lower than 29 percent. Again, it is tough to envision any scenario in which the odds weren't stacked against the players.

In any event, the owners did lock the players out. We are left to suspect that NBA owners felt that at least a couple of hundred million dollars could be won from players with an effective lockout. Further, since there was a lockout, and since most would agree that the owners did win the lockout, it would be reasonable to assume that owners perceived the chance of winning to be reasonably good heading into the lockout.

NHL Lockout 2004–05

The data on the NHL lockout of 2004–05 are even more compelling than for the 1998–99 NBA lockout. In his report covering through to the 2002–03 season, former chairman of the Securities and Exchange Commission, Arthur Levitt, Jr., shows NHL revenues at $1.996 billion at the time. Throughout the lockout, the owners claimed that players were receiving 75 percent of revenues, or about $1.494 billion. Other costs of operations were $775 million, or 39 percent of revenues. And there's the rub for the owners—costs were 14 percent larger than revenues combined across the NHL, about $272.6 million. However, a lockout was not inevitable just on the basis of this combined accounting. Levitt also reported that eleven owners earned profits, the largest at $14.6 million. But it is pretty clear that the gains even to those earning profits would prove lockout arguments convincing even for these eleven teams.

Eventually, the new CBA put the share to players at 54 percent, which comes to $1.078 billion. So the end result was 54 percent to players and still 39 percent to other operations, leaving the owners about 7 percent, or $140 million. But the gain is the entire amount of the difference between what they used to pay players, $1.492 billion, and what they ended up paying players, $1.078 billion, or about $416 million. The duration of the new CBA was six years, a simple total of $2.496 billion that becomes $2.111 billion if discounted at 5 percent.

Turning to the lost value of an entire season, the nineteen teams that lost money reported an average loss of $18.0 million. This is their *gain* to stopping play for an entire season, so $342 million across all nineteen of these owners. The eleven teams that made money reported an average profit of $6.4 million, their loss if an entire season were lost to a lockout, so $70 million for these eleven owners. Clearly the teams losing money could pay the teams making money to forgo the season. In this case, losing an entire season would erase the $273 million combined loss reported by Levitt. Again, we have no knowledge of fan irritation costs or the value of the owners' next best alternatives..

Using the same ideas from our NBA example, the lockout was a no-brainer for the NHL owners. We err on the low side and suppose that the $273 million loss would have ended after a lockout anyway. Again, as in the NBA example, we also assume first that fan irritation costs and the next best alternatives for owners were a wash. If the owners knew for sure that the players would fold, they stood to gain the $273 million loss and the $2.1 billion in revenues transferred from players over the life of the CBA, or about $2.4 billion. That's $80 million for each owner. Again, the payoff would be lower as the probability that the players might fold declines, but $2.4 billion covers a lot ground on this dimension. For example, it is impossible even to get a positive break-even probability unless fan irritation costs exceed the owners' next best alternatives! And to confront the owners with a 50–50 chance, it would have to be the case that fan irritation costs exceeded the owners' next best alternative by $1.328 *billion*. Put another way, fans would have to stay away for many seasons in a row before the break-even probability even got to 50–50, and the owners would know that is absurd. The NHL owners had a greater than 50–50 chance, anyway, since the players did fold in a historic way. Owners had a pretty good idea from the outset that they stood to gain the $2 billion or so they eventually did gain from their lockout.

The lesson here is that play can be interrupted in a way that both sides wish hadn't happened. But in that special case, the introduction of an impartial third-party mediator will clear things up in a big hurry. And both sides will be glad it happened, since only asymmetric information was in the way of an agreement in the first place. But other interruptions in play can result simply because stopping play is profitable. In this case, nothing could be further from the truth than the oft-announced myth that everybody loses when labor-management relations go south.

CONCLUSIONS—MOSTLY CAVEATS

There are a few caveats with our basic analysis. For one thing, most of the players in the player's union do not care about player salaries in ten years. While the owners should care about player costs far into the future, most players have a fairly short time horizon. The shorter the horizon for players, the more certainty they need for expected benefits.

Another caveat is that owners and players receive some pleasure from playing. Fans are not the only ones that are disappointed by the loss of games. As Joe Jacoby, former offensive tackle for the Washington Redskins, once said, "I'd run over my own mother to win the Super Bowl." Matt Millen agreed and said, "To win, I'd run over Joe's mom too." So owners and players might be willing to play if the expected benefit is small. The drive to play is one of the psychological factors affecting negotiations.

There also are chances for human error. For example, sometimes there is a bit of "brinksmanship" that goes on in negotiations, requiring steady nerves. As things get closer and closer to the brink, the chance for mistakes to have a big impact also increases. Nobody knows what James Dean's rival said as the brinksmanship game of chicken they played in *Rebel without a Cause* came to its tragic end. But as he sailed off the cliff in his car, he surely knew that he had made a mistake.

While the percentage of revenue that players receive has certainly increased over time, this is not true of all players. Outside of first round draft picks, new players to the league typically face tight CBA restrictions on pay. They also are not eligible for free agency immediately. These restrictions on new players might satisfy some fans' sense of fairness. However, economists have a different explanation. Any change in these restrictions only helps future players and not current players. Since players' unions are made up of current players, they are more likely to negotiate in their own best interest. The same happens at the other end—that is, regarding current union bargaining for former players. Past players, greats and the rest alike, who built the fan base currently generating the billions for pro sports leagues face an uphill battle in gaining any share.

For the most part, just as we found out as kids sharing popsicles, negotiations most often lead to a clear, quick settlement before any of the treasure is lost. It is true that asymmetric information can lay the best-laid plans of owners and players asunder. They might all genuinely wish to reach agreement but not be able to overcome the difficulty of obtaining the information that leads to that end. In such cases, everybody would, indeed, be worse off if any interruption in play occurs.

However, in a critically important subset of the cases in which play is interrupted, it is because one side or the other has gone through a careful calculus that clearly dictates they are better off with a lockout or strike. If the expected value of a lockout or strike is positive, fully incorporating information about what is at risk and what is to be gained, plus information on next best alternatives and the possibility of fan irritation down the line, then expect a strike or lockout. Owners expect to be better off when they win their lockout. Players expect to be better off when they win their strike.

And anybody can see that the idea that nobody wins during a lockout or strike is a myth simply weighing the successes of players that strike against owners and owners who lockout players. It is generally agreed that MLB players have never lost a strike, most notably 1981 and 1994–95. The verdict on NFL strikes in 1982 and 1987 is a bit more mixed, but it is also the case that their willingness toward activism set the stage for major gains through collective bargaining in the mid-1990s and for labor-management harmony since then. Recently, nobody doubts that the owners won significantly in the NHL in 1994–95 and again in 2004–05, or that NBA owners won in both 1998 and 2011.

This is a destructive myth that deserves busting because it leads fans to believe that interruptions to play are an "irrational" crime against them. This allows owners and players to foist the actual blame off on their opponent in each case. Fans then hold grudges against the perpetrators of the interruption that are misplaced. Fans are confused enough by the business machinery of pro sports and are often asked to contribute significant tax monies to these sports, as well as their allegiance. Fans deserve to be angry when they are denied some of their favorite consumption, but they also deserve to be angry for the right reasons!

15 MAJOR LEAGUE BASEBALL SHOULD EMULATE THE NATIONAL FOOTBALL LEAGUE

MLB, the NBA and the NHL should all emulate the NFL: the ONLY sport where a contest between Indianapolis and Boston (or Arizona and Denver for that matter) can generate significant national interest.
 —Mike C, posted at *Bats*, Tyler Kepner's *New York Times* blog, October 11, 2007

INTRODUCTION

It's a common perception that the National Football League has sur- passed Major League Baseball in the eyes of fans over the last three or four decades. It is surely true that the NFL currently generates greater revenues (although we will have more to say on that shortly). Poll results also typi- cally show that football, especially the NFL variety, is the nation's game. Now, just why it is that the NFL obtained its lofty status and manages to hold on to it remains a mystery to these same observers. Maybe the NFL has better marketing, suggesting that MLB leadership emulate the NFL ap- proach. Maybe American sports fans have simply drifted more toward a faster paced, violent sport, suggesting that MLB needs to speed up their game. Maybe most important, MLB needs to level the playing field for smaller-revenue owners relative to their larger-revenue competition. What- ever the reason, if it is going to stay relevant, attract young fans, and grow its fan base, then (so the conclusion typically goes) MLB should look more like the NFL.

Since marketing is marketing and there is no reason to suspect that the MLB version is somehow dumber or less apt than the NFL version, and since baseball is baseball (the essence is that there is no clock!), one prescription always seems to come to the fore—if MLB wants to give the NFL a run for its money, it needs to do something about competitive balance. But we have already covered the basics of competitive balance and the prospects for meaningful intervention by leagues in Chapter 12. The NFL is the most balanced sport on the playing field. But the prospects for any other league to achieve the same type of balance as the NFL are slim to none. It is true that the NFL used to be the model of revenue sharing, but MLB has adopted a very similar sharing process in both breadth and scope without impact on balance. MLB also has the additional luxury tax, which has had no effect. The defining difference whittles down to the NFL's salary cap, but no impact of that league's cap on balance can be found, and caps in both the NBA and the NHL follow suit.

We follow through on this myth, for myth it surely is, that somehow MLB will be better off if it emulates the NFL. First, let's spend a little time with the idea that the NFL has *become* the most successful of North American pro sports leagues. Note that this suggests that MLB is somehow falling behind football. In fact, it's not clear that the NFL has *surpassed* MLB rather than just holding its advantage over time. Attendance figures and fan popularity may always have been higher in the NFL, so that there has been no change over time. It could simply be the case that the current popularity of MLB and the long-standing affinity between Americans and their brand of football has gone understated in this discussion.

HISTORICAL POPULARITY CONTEST

We begin with the longest standing poll results on the relative popularity of baseball and football. Figure 15.1 is a reproduction from Jones's (2008) summary of the Gallup Poll on sports popularity, begun in 1936. The poll results show that prior to 1972 a higher percentage of those polled gave the nod to baseball. After that, based on percentage responses, fans almost exactly reversed their previous preference margin for baseball over to football by the early 1980s! Clearly, something happened . . . *beginning in the 1950s*. Many point to the magic of "The Greatest Game Ever Played" as the watershed. The Baltimore Colts won the 1958 NFL Championship in

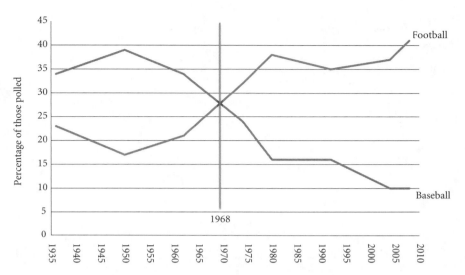

FIG. 15.1. "What is your favorite sport to watch?" Gallup Poll Results, 1936–2008. Jones (2008).

overtime, 23–17 over the New York Giants, live nationally on NBC. However, the reversal of MLB's popularity fortunes began long before that, in the late 1940s, according to Figure 15.1. Baseball may be the national pastime, but according to the Gallup Poll people's preferences for football over baseball began in the late 1940s, the popularity of football over baseball is now nearly thirty years running, and the level of that preference has remained stable since, say, 1982. The NFL may be gaining against MLB over the last decade, but Figure 15.1 shows that cannot be attributed to any further decline in the popularity of MLB. It also is not a clear call, since the historically high popularity of the NFL in the figure actually is a blip, and only more data can settle the issue.

It's also the case that the NFL has long been more mentioned in books than MLB (Muglia 2010). Google allows us to see how often football, baseball, NFL, and MLB have been mentioned in books over a long period of time. Figure 15.2 shows that football has been mentioned more than baseball since as far back as we can tell. It is true that football might mean something different in 1800 than it does today, and even today it's probably fair to

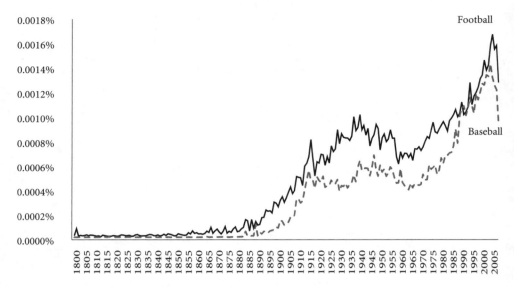

FIG. 15.2. Relative Word Frequency in Books from 1800 to 2008 of "football" and "baseball." Google Ngram. Google and the Google logo are registered trademarks of Google Inc., used with permission.

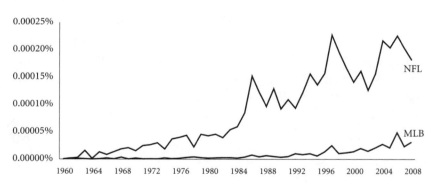

FIG. 15.3. Relative Word Frequency in Books from 1960 to 2008 of "NFL" and "MLB." Google Ngram. Google and the Google logo are registered trademarks of Google Inc., used with permission.

say that some of these mentions are not about American football, but baseball has never been more a reading topic than football. Figure 15.3 shows the difference between the NFL and MLB. Mentions of the NFL have been greater than MLB since 1960. And while it might look like the NFL is putting distance on MLB, if anything the ratio between the NFL and MLB is actually decreasing.

All of this also is consistent with our understanding of history. In 1888, John Montgomery Ward wrote the pamphlet "Baseball: How to Become a Baseball Player." Ward was a celebrated pitcher, shortstop, manager, and then an important player in the earliest days of the baseball business. In his pamphlet, Ward shares the strategy of each position on the field, offers batting and base running tips, and his thoughts on the early history of baseball. He declared (p. 21) that baseball was "a fruit of the inventive genius of the American boy" and in no way the product of that "silly little British game" of rounders. He adds (p. 26) that baseball was becoming our national pastime as early as 1860. According to Ward, even as far back as 1861, in the midst of the Civil War, around fifteen thousand fans were reported to have watched a game between a New York team and a Brooklyn team. The Public Broadcasting System's "Freedom: A History of US" (2010) reports that only hundreds went to watch the first battle of Bull Run. Of course, the cost of picnicking at Bull Run may have been higher than at the baseball game.

Clearly a passion for baseball continued into the twentieth century. George "Babe" Ruth and the Yankees' "Murderer's Row" played to unprecedented attendance in the 1920s. The older of your authors can remember when all of his baby-boomer friends wanted to be baseball players, and we all spent hours in seemingly endless summer days chasing that dream. American youth in the 1950s and 1960s either loved or hated the Yankees. Hank Aaron, Sandy Koufax, and Bob Gibson were household names. The sports that can rival contemporary baseball, such as football and basketball (sorry hockey fans, you are devout but relatively smaller in number), don't have baseball's history. No sport has been at the constant forefront of American sports like baseball, early on dubbed the national pastime.

But, historically, football is a close second on this dimension. College football has a long tradition of popularity. Red "The Galloping Ghost" Grange and Notre Dame's "Four Horsemen"—Harry Stuhldreher, Jim Crowley, Don Miller, and Elmer Layden—are its earliest icons. Professional football added George "Papa Bear" Halas, Norm "The Flying Dutchman" Van Brocklin, and Elroy "Crazy Legs" Hirsch to the list.

In particular, the NFL began play in 1920 as the American Professional Football Association, adopting its current name in 1922 (this is some twenty years after peace was struck between the older National and American leagues in baseball in 1903, the creation of what we now refer to as MLB). The Pro Football Archives (2010) document early NFL attendance and a variety of sources do the same for MLB. NFL attendance was originally small relative to MLB attendance, but NFL teams popped up all over the Midwest, and many were quite popular. In 1922, the Chicago Bears drew 3,000 or more for all home games and 14,000 when the cross-town rival Cardinals visited. The largest attendance at a league home game that year was 28,000 against the Kansas City Cowboys. MLB's 1922 attendance averaged 7,913 in the AL and 6,399 in the NL. According to William Cook's biography of Jim Thorpe, an NFL exhibition game between the Bears and Giants that featured Red Grange drew 73,000 fans in 1925. In 1926, the rival American Football League's New York Yankees never drew fewer than 11,560 for a league game and topped out at 35,000 against the Rock Island Independents. MLB's 1926 attendance averaged 7,975 in the AL and 7,913 in the NL. In 1934, in the midst of the Depression, the Chicago Bears played in front of 79,432 at Soldier Field against a college all-star team. That year all Bears home games drew 10,000 or more, with a high of 34,412 against the Detroit Lions. MLB's New York Yankees drew fewer than 13,000 fans per game in 1934 (the St. Louis Browns drew about 1,600 fans per game). But let's not forget that baseball teams play more games, so over the regular season the Yankees did draw almost four times as many fans as the Giants that year.

Over the last seventy-five years, the crowds at the football Giants games have about doubled, but the crowds at Yankees game have about tripled. In recent years, the Yankees typically draw about six times as many fans as the

Giants. Even today the total stadium revenue generated by the typical MLB team dwarfs the stadium revenue generated by the typical NFL team. And it is this evolution over time, comparing the two that gets to the heart of the discussion, especially since polls and total attendance (and its related revenues) are only part of the story about popularity.

HISTORICAL ECONOMIC COMPARISONS

Economic performance offers added insights that simple preference statements cannot. In a poll, a vote is a vote. In the marketplace, relative spending on MLB and the NFL reveals intensity of preference. First of all, various popular reports estimate 2010 revenues of $6.8 billion for MLB and $7.8 billion for the NFL, almost a 15 percent difference. So recent totals do match up with the perceptions presented previously. However, the data tell quite a different story about whether MLB is *falling behind* the NFL over time.

Figure 15.4 shows the ratio over time of total MLB attendance to total NFL attendance. The solid line represents the ratio of known regular season MLB yearly attendance divided by known regular season NFL yearly attendance. However, complete, continuous attendance data across all teams are not available for the NFL until 1966. The dashed line assumes that teams without data have the same average attendance as other NFL teams. While both leagues enjoyed increased attendance after World War II, MLB fared considerably better than the NFL! But around 1950 the ratio heads steadily toward 3, where it stayed for the duration of the 1970s. Stepping back to take a look at the big picture, post–World War II aside, there was a decrease in this ratio from the mid-1930s to around the mid-1970s. Work stoppages in MLB and the NFL cause some spikes in 1981, 1982, 1987, 1994, and 1995. However, it seems as though MLB has been holding its own against the NFL in terms of total attendance since the 1970s; the ratio hovers around four. In recent years NFL attendance has been around 17 million, while MLB attendance was 73 million.

While looking at totals is informative, it is also useful to examine attendance on a per game basis. After all, much changed for both leagues from

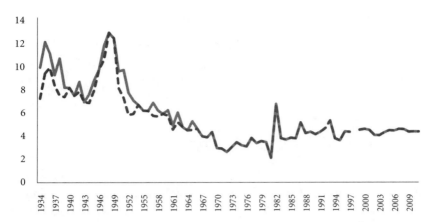

FIG. 15.4. Ratio of MLB/NFL Total Attendance. Created from data at Fort (2012) and Pro Football Archives (2012).

FIG. 15.5. Ratio of MLB/NFL per Game Attendance. Created from data at Fort (2012) and Pro Football Archives (2012).

1934 to 2011. Both leagues have expanded, and population has increased dramatically. In addition, relative to MLB, changes in the length of the schedule have been much more frequent and larger in percentage terms in the NFL. The NL went from 154 games to 162 in 1961, and the AL did the same in 1962; in 1934 there were sixteen teams and now there are thirty. In 1934 there were eight NFL teams and now there are thirty-two; schedule length was highly variable in the 1930s and 1940s, eventually settling on twelve games until 1961, when it went to fourteen, and then again to sixteen in 1977. Figure 15.5 shows the ratio of *per game attendance* for MLB to per game attendance for the NFL. In 1934, the average attendance at MLB games was 5,652 and for the NFL it was 15,976 (a ratio of about 0.35). Again, the heyday was the postwar period for MLB. The comparison at totals would have missed the steady increase in relative per game attendance for MLB from the early 1970s to today. In 2011, the average attendance of an MLB game was 30,227, compared with 66,892 for the NFL. Put another way, MLB has actually had a higher rate of growth in per game attendance than the NFL since 1972.

An examination of television revenues proves especially insightful in a comparison of the two leagues. After all, currently the NFL makes most of its revenue from TV contracts; it is difficult to generate stadium revenue comparable to that of MLB with only eight home games. It is true that the NFL has been very successful at generating huge broadcasting rights contracts. But just like attendance, this has been true for quite a while. Figure 15.6 shows the magnitude of national television contracts adjusted to 2012 dollars (complete, recent MLB data are not available). Again, over the period where we have data, the NFL (blue line) has always dominated MLB (green line) in the national rights market. In inflation-adjusted values, in 1964 the NFL generated more than three times the revenue of MLB from national broadcasting rights ($8.5 million per team vs. $2.6 million per team). In addition, the NFL has increased their national contracts faster than MLB. Currently, the NFL generates roughly five times the revenue of MLB from national broadcasting rights ($126 million per team vs. roughly $20 to $30 million per team). In short, these revenues have increased dramatically for

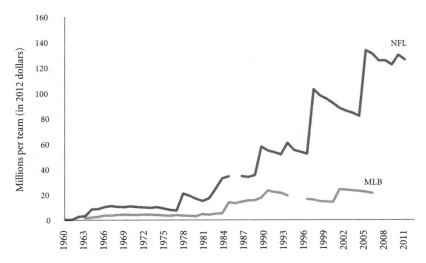

F IG . 15.6. Revenue from National Contracts (Dollars Per Team). Authors'
collections of various articles on national contract values.

both MLB and the NFL over the last few decades, with the NFL gaining in a
"ratcheted" way, especially in its last two contracts.

But this analysis of *national* contracts misses the obvious—MLB teams
have significant *local* TV/radio contracts, while the NFL sells all of its rights
in national contracts. Local contracts for MLB teams vary greatly. However,
over the last forty or fifty years, some MLB teams have seen high growth
rates pertaining to their local media revenues. For example, it has been reported that the Yankees generate nearly $200 million a year through the
YES network. Unfortunately, there are only scant data on the value of local
TV rights across MLB, but there are some. In 2001, MLB commissioner
Bud Selig released an annual operations statement by team. The point was
to present a consolidated operations statement as a precursor to collective
bargaining. The consolidated "Local TV, Radio, and Cable" category totaled
about $571 million, or $739 million adjusted to 2012 dollars. The national
contract totaled $720 million, or $932 million in 2012 dollars. On a per MLB
team basis, that's $55.7 million for each of the thirty MLB owners. Refer-
ring to Figure 15.6, $55.7 million significantly reduces the 2001 NFL national
contract advantage of about $65 million.

As our final basis for comparison, intensity of spending can also be revealed in the way that franchise values change over time. Revenues heavily influence what one might pay for a sports team, and revenues are just collected spending. However, there are a couple of shortcomings with this type of analysis. First, it is possible that franchise values do not translate directly to relative popularity. For example, if the MLB players association is stronger than the NFL players association, then the players will get a higher share of total revenue in MLB. If this means that profit margins are lower in MLB, then team values will be relatively smaller not because of lower popularity but because the NFL is more successful at capping player pay. This tells us something about how to run a successful league from the owners' perspective, but it would distort perceptions of the overall popularity of the NFL relative to MLB. Second, as plagues most economic assessments of sports, there are data shortcomings. For example, your author Fort (2006) documents the shortcomings in the annual *Forbes* estimates of franchise value relative to the total value of ownership. Fortunately, there also are popular reports of actual sale values to facilitate such a comparison.

Warts and all, Table 15.1 shows the *Forbes* values over the last decade adjusted for inflation to 2012 dollars. First, notice the truly impressive rates of growth across the board. Remember, these are adjusted for inflation and typically the riskless rate (approximating the real growth rate in the economy at large) is between 2.5 and 3 percent, and it's even less over this time period. The rate of return on MLB and NFL teams over the last decade has beaten that rate handily. Second, NFL teams are and always have been simply worth more than MLB teams. According to *Forbes*, in 2011 the average NFL team was worth just over $1 billion, ranging from $725 million for the Jacksonville Jaguars to $1.85 billion for the Dallas Cowboys. In 2011, MLB's lowly Pittsburgh Pirates were valued at "only" $304 million, and the average MLB team was worth $523 million, about half of the average NFL team. However, the most valuable MLB team, the New York Yankees, is worth $1.7 billion, less than 10 percent less than the Cowboys.

Finally, and the most important observation from the perspective of whether or not MLB has been losing ground against the NFL, only at the median does the *growth* in NFL team value exceed that of MLB teams. At

TABLE 15.1. *Forbes Team Value Descriptive Statistics, 2000–10 (2012 Dollars)*

Year	MLB			NFL		
	Min	Med	Max	Min	Med	Max
2000	$119.14	$280.55	$733.70	$408.38	$526.16	$992.18
2001	$119.35	$316.53	$823.66	$438.40	$548.65	$1,032.45
2002	$137.35	$340.38	$958.81	$477.31	$661.10	$1,078.37
2003	$140.69	$316.22	$1,056.82	$628.67	$757.44	$1,185.07
2004	$175.95	$337.98	$1,009.54	$669.78	$866.96	$1,339.57
2005	$206.18	$368.42	$1,113.00	$770.94	$952.53	$1,480.89
2006	$238.29	$403.04	$1,169.80	$820.94	$1,011.32	$1,622.53
2007	$270.51	$414.65	$1,330.57	$867.07	$1,029.00	$1,663.22
2008	$273.12	$442.27	$1,393.44	$895.21	$1,087.79	$1,719.91
2009	$295.51	$430.03	$1,600.45	$850.33	$1,087.79	$1,760.50
2010	$302.31	$425.22	$1,673.68	$758.38	$1,049.71	$1,888.12
2011	$312.89	$445.67	$1,749.73	$746.21	$1,022.56	$1,904.12
2012	$321.00	$489.00	$1,850.00			
Growth	9.43%	5.18%	8.77%	6.21%	6.87%	6.74%

Source: Calculations and inflation adjustments by the authors from data appearing annually in *Forbes* Team Valuations.

Notes: Growth is real annual growth rate, 2000–11 for the NFL and 2000–12 for MLB.

both the minimum and maximum values, the growth rates in MLB have swamped those in the NFL. The lowest valued MLB teams have grown in value by 50 percent more than the lowest NFL teams; the highest-valued MLB teams by 30 percent more! Put another way, in 2000, the minimum MLB team value was 30 percent of its NFL counterpart, but by 2011 it had risen to 40 percent. The maximum team value started at 70 percent but grew to 90 percent. MLB has made significant strides against the NFL over the last decade in "growing" the value of its owners' assets.

By way of comparison, reported actual sale values buttress all of the observations above, from the poll results to the *Forbes* valuations (a collection of team sale prices is available at Rodney Fort's Sports Business Data Pages, 2012). Early examples of MLB team sale price dominance over NFL prices abound. The first NFL team sale price to top the $100,000 mark was the Lions in 1940 at $225,000. A year later, 65 percent of the NL's Boston Braves sold for $750,000, implying a full price of just over $1 million, or five times the Lions' price! By the 1970s, the tide had turned. The cleanest example is

in expansion team prices that are almost entirely revelations of expected fu-
ture value. Lloyd W. Nordstrom of Seattle and Hugh Culverhouse of Tampa
each paid $16 million for NFL expansion teams in 1974 (the Seahawks and
Buccaneers, respectively). Two years later, a syndicate led by entertainer
Danny Kaye paid a $6.25 million expansion fee for the Seattle Mariners,
and the Labatt's Brewery syndicate paid a $7 million expansion fee for the
Toronto Blue Jays. At least in terms of expected future value, clearly the
NFL dominated in terms of expansion fees at about the same time that the
"favorite sport" gap, NFL over MLB, reached its wide point in Figure 15.1.

OTHER JUSTIFICATIONS FOR
ACTING LIKE THE NFL

There are other arguments raised to support the idea that football has
surpassed baseball. For example, one of the fundamental issues is "growing"
the fan base—Americans love to watch the games they played. To many,
baseball is in trouble in this regard because it seems to them that participation in the sport by young people is declining. This simply is not true.
The National Association of High School Federations surveys participation,
and a brief summary of some past findings is shown in Table 15.2. Clearly,
participation has increased over the most recently depicted decade, so actually more young people are playing baseball. But the increase is smaller in
percentage terms than the overall increase in participation. Quite interestingly, this is also true of football (both the increase in football and baseball
are lower than the increase for all sports in percentage terms)! Of course,
any comparison like this simply begs additional questions. How much of
the increase in participation *should* each sport get? Are some young players

TABLE 15.2. *High School Participation, Male*

Sport	1997–98	2007–08	% Change
Football	971,335	1,108,286	14.1%
Baseball	449,897	478,029	6.3%
All Sports	3,763,120	4,372,115	16.2%

Source: Calculated across various reports by the National Association of
High School Federations.

TABLE 15.3. *World Series and Super Bowl Ratings and Shares, by Decade (through 2009)*

Decade	Ave. Rating	% Change	Ave. Share	% Change
World Series				
1970s	27.5		53.2	
1980s	25.5	−7.1%	42.9	−19.4%
1990s	18.4	−27.7%	31.1	−27.5%
2000s	12.1	−34.7%	20.2	−35.1%
Super Bowl				
1970s	43.1		72.7	
1980s	46.1	6.8%	67.2	−7.6%
1990s	42.7	−7.3%	64.2	−4.5%
2000s	41.7	−2.5%	62.6	−2.5%

Source: Calculated by the authors from data originally reported at SportsBusinessNews.com, October 30, 2010.

changing over from baseball to football? Or is it the case that boys simply have more different sports to choose from, so that there simply are more options for kids today? In any event, interest in baseball by young people is clearly not declining.

Another common argument is that World Series ratings are down compared with a few decades ago. Indeed, Table 15.3 shows that viewer interest in World Series has fallen through the last four decades, measured either by ratings (percent of total television households) or shares (percent of sets in use tuned to the program). Again quite interestingly, the same is true of the Super Bowl! Declines are larger for the World Series in percentage terms, but perhaps the more general insight is that both baseball and football could be worried about declining fan attention to television broadcasts of their postseason gems. The results in Table 15.3 further suggest that the real answer to these declines isn't about football gaining over baseball so much as the fact that more options to sports viewing on television have appeared over time for both of these sports. Many fans follow baseball and football in new ways, on the Internet and broadband. In making comparisons of league popularity, it would be important to know how MLB stands relative to the NFL on these other viewing options.

Other calls to make leagues more like the NFL concern the business model—comprehensive revenue sharing, especially through an exclusively national TV contract, plus a salary cap. But these arguments are specious, since they already buy into the myths exposed in Chapter 11 and Chapter 12—revenue sharing and salary caps actually haven't had much impact on balance, if any at all in any league including the NFL. Furthermore, it really isn't even the case that fans see any difference between the different approaches in MLB (local TV and national TV rights) and the NFL (national TV rights only). Broadcasts are regionalized in every sense in both leagues. Aside from the occasional NFL blackout, fans in any city can rest assured that they will see their NFL team every week and their MLB team every night. There clearly is a difference for the marketing choice and the strategic business strategy used by the NFL against media providers. Which will be higher, the revenue from selling the single package of regional broadcasts, or selling each set of regional broadcasts? But from the fan perspective, there is no difference at all!

CONCLUSIONS—SAME AS IT EVER WAS (SO WHY CHASTISE BASEBALL?)

As we move toward concluding thoughts, our point here is not to tarnish the NFL's reputation as a successful league. The survey here suggests that it is clearly the most popular league, and it surely has been by total revenue the most successful league. Our point is that even if the NFL has been more successful than MLB on some dimensions, first, Americans have always enjoyed football, and second, MLB is also successful on many measures. Why is it worth pointing out that America has not turned into NFL crazed maniacs overnight? The answer is that the myth that such has occurred simply allows observers, primarily in the media, to exercise their biases about which league is better. And when they do so without any appeal to the facts of the matter, busy people who rely on their reports and opinions are also led down the garden path on the issue.

There is nothing wrong with preferring one league to another. In this sense those ignoring the facts of the matter on popularity are in the same class as comedy legend George Carlin, who (when he was alive) favored baseball over football. Our favorite excerpts from his comedy routine on this subject (Baseball Almanac, 2010) has a transcript:

> Baseball is a nineteenth-century pastoral game. Football is a twentieth-century technological struggle . . . . Baseball begins in the spring, the season of new life. Football begins in the fall, when everything's dying . . . . Football has hitting, clipping, spearing, piling on, personal fouls, late hitting and unnecessary roughness. Baseball has the sacrifice . . . . Baseball has no time limit: we don't know when it's gonna end—might have *extra* innings. Football is rigidly timed, and it will end even if we've got to go to sudden death . . . . In baseball the object is to go home! And to be safe! I hope I'll be safe at home!

Mr. Carlin was also insightful about another aspect of sports in the same routine, "Baseball and football are the two most popular spectator sports in this country. And as such, it seems they ought to be able to tell us something about ourselves and our values." To this we can only say, "Amen, brother."

The problems caused by the myth that baseball should be more like football are both subtle and malevolent. The myth creates a setting where people simply proclaim their preferences over obvious data or, worse yet, enter the political process under seemingly justifiable arguments that owners in one league are too dumb even to see what owners in other leagues are doing and amend their leagues to their own financial self-interest. By those preferences, anybody can see that every league, especially unwilling-to-change baseball, should become more like the NFL. When they don't, then there must be something wrong and a mythical, specious momentum to "do something about it" is born. While the original source is disputed (various Internet sources identify John Kenneth Galbraith, others deny this), George Carlin also had the great good sense to repeat a warning about what can invariably happen in such a situation, "Never underestimate the power of stupid people in large groups."

And the humor just keeps on coming. The following sequel to "baseball ought to be more like football" might be entertaining if it weren't so misguided. Matt Egan (2009) argues that even Wall Street should be more like the NFL. Ezra Klein (2010) also argues that the media could learn from the NFL; he claims that previous GM chairman Rick Wagoner wouldn't have lasted long had he been guiding the Detroit Lions—his point being that NFL owners notoriously do not suffer losers. (Wagoner became president and chief executive officer in June 2000 and was elected chairman of GM in 2003. Under his leadership, GM suffered more than $85 billion in losses, but he didn't step down until the U.S. Congress demanded it as a requirement for the GM bailout in 2009.)

This perpetuation of the myth of NFL superiority (now over the business world) actually reveals a further lack of basic understanding of the NFL, and Egan couldn't have chosen a worse example than the Lions! Wagoner led GM (2003–09) for exactly the same number of years, and at approximately the same time in history, that Matt Millen led the Detroit Lions (2001–07). The outcome was probably even worse for the Lions than for GM. Under Millen's seven seasons as the Lions' CEO, the team went 31–81 with at least nine losses each season. Only the Chicago Cardinals (1939–45) and the Tampa Bay Buccaneers (1983–89) had worse seven-year strings than Detroit's .277 winning percentage under Millen. During the early part of Millen's tenure (2001–03) the team failed to win a road game, but Lions ownership stuck with him for four more years! At least one Wall Street observer had the talent to observe what Egan did not. Allen Barra (2008) writing in the *Wall Street Journal* noted that NFL executives admitted in private that Millen "has made more bad draft decisions than anyone else in two centuries." This is hardly a stunning recommendation for either GM or MLB to follow.

CONCLUSIONS

We wrote this book because the economists in us began to see that many pre-conceived and deeply emotional notions in sports are simply not true. And upon further consideration, we began to see that these "misunderstandings" actually hinder the games we love.
—The Introduction

Nicely put, if we do say so ourselves. Whereas a traditional concluding chapter would offer further research areas or simply summarize the myths busted, that is not the intent of this section. Instead, we just want to contribute some orderly thinking to intuitive belief in order to reveal a few final truths and identify some culprits. You see, there is some coherence across the myths on a couple of dimensions. Overall, the myths, as a collection, work just as we claimed in the Introduction: They are based on arguments that appeal to intuition; some people benefit from the perpetuation of the myths and others pay as a result; and they occur in settings where analysis isn't done, holds no sway, or is shunned completely. Much to our dismay, the other commonality across the myths in this book is that they all continue to prevail (and probably will continue to do so despite our best efforts to the contrary).

One reason this is so is that people seem satisfied enough to act on simple correlation. Title IX is put in place, and men's teams get cut at a few colleges. The culprit is obvious—namely, Title IX, rather than the discretion allowed to athletic directors pointed out in the first few chapters. Player pay increases at dramatic rates and so do ticket prices (or cable subscriptions), and fan wrath turns to players rather than their own voracious spending on sports. Sometimes this desire to act on correlation itself falls on inconsistency. After all, how can the football and men's basketball teams pay for the rest of the athletic department and, at the same time, the athletic department is viewed as a drain on the rest of the university? Our apologies to Ralph Waldo Emerson, but it appears that foolish *inconsistency* is sometimes the hobgoblin of minds bent on taking correlation at face value.

When people forget to think first about the objectives of sports decision-makers, it is easy to fall prey to simple correlation. We have tried always to make the objectives of the primary decision-makers clear in every instance—owners, university administrators, athletic directors, and athletes do not necessarily pursue the same things that fans and boosters hold most dear. Of course, owners would like to win, but that is not the same thing as saying that owners will do *everything they can* to win. And it is the latter that fans naively expect. While university administrators would like their teams to win, they will not do everything they can to win either. While pundits and critics argue that they do so, the chapters in this book make it clear that they do not. While the pro athlete's desires are probably closest to the fans, their consideration of economic welfare can lead to withholding services. And in dealing with the tension between scholarship and athletic performance in the college case, athletes seem destined to let everybody down by devoting too much or too little to the latter over the former.

Another reason these myths tend to linger is that the casual observer does not get paid to think about the economic structure of college and professional sports like we do. After all, people enjoy sports, but they do not enjoy spending an inordinate amount of time thinking economically about causality, organizations, and incentives. On top of that, it is human nature to become frustrated when products we enjoy become more expensive and/ or quality goes down. If ticket prices go up for your favorite team, or they start losing while owners and players are getting rich (or worst of all, both!), it is easy to eschew orderly thinking in favor of roasting scapegoats. Exacerbating the problem is the fact that some sports reporters often do not know any better, and always write what sells even if they do. The typical result is to fan the flames, demonizing people or policies that are widely believed to be the problem.

We hasten to add that sports are not unique in this sense. If you have recently read an article in your area of expertise, there is a good chance that you were disappointed about how the issues were represented to the lay public. It's just that the sports industry is a very public one, with many casual, but emotionally invested, observers involved. Economists have been dealing with this type of case nearly forever. When we see owners, university administrators, athletic directors, the media, sports policy makers do something, the lesson taught in this book is to determine why it is in their best interests, rather than just to accept what comes out of their mouths as justification. The result is productive. The benefits accruing to the myth-pushers always come at a cost to everyone else and often in a wasteful way. While myths are likely here to stay, public opinion is built one person at a time. So we invite you: Spread your new knowledge. Impress your friends over the coming seasons by busting the myths in this book for them and creating more discerning eyes. Economists like us will continue to hunt for new disconnects, and we'll keep sports under the microscope. But, in the meantime, busting the myths in this book is a good start, and we fans will all be better for it.

INTRODUCTION

Chapter 1

Fulks, D. L. 2011. *2004–2010 Revenues and Expense of Division I Intercollegiate Athletic Programs Report*. August. NCAA, Indianapolis, IN.

IndyStar.com. 2012. "NCAA Financial Reports Database." Last accessed August 30, 2012. http://www2.indystar.com/NCAA_financial_reports.

Leeds, M. A., Suris, Y., and Durkin, J. 2004. "College Football and Title IX." In John Fizel and Rodney Fort (eds.) *Economics of College Sports*. Westport, CT: Praeger, pp. 137–52.

Office of Post-Secondary Education. 2012. "The Equity in Athletics Data Analysis Cutting Tool." Last accessed August 30, 2012. http://ope.ed.gov/athletics.

Scranton Times-Tribune.com. 2012. Editorial, "NCAA Should Halt Talk of 'Death Penalty.'" July 17. Last accessed August 30, 2012. http://thetimes-tribune.com/opinion/ncaa-should-halt-talk-of-death-penalty-1.1344251.

Sheehan, R. G. 2000. "Academics, Athletics, and Finances." In William S. Kern (ed.) *The Economics of Sports*. Kalamazoo, MI: W. E. Upjohn Institute for Employment Research, pp. 75–91.

USAToday.com. 2012. "USA Today Sports' College Athletics Finances." Last accessed August 30, 2012. http://www.usatoday.com/sports/college/story/2012–05–14/ncaa-college-athletics-finances-database/54955804/1.

Women's Sports Foundation. 2002. "Title IX Q & A." Last accessed August 30, 2012. http://lobby.la.psu.edu/_107th/135_Title%20IX/Organizational_Statements/Womens_Sports_Fdn/Womens_Sports_Fdn_Title_IX_Q_&_A_041902.htm.

Chapter 2

Clotfelter, C. T. 2011. *Big-Time Sports in American Universities*. Cambridge: Cambridge University Press.

Edwards, H. 1984. "The Collegiate Athletic Arms Race: Origins and Implications of the 'Rule 48' Controversy." *Journal of Sport and Social Issues* 8: 4–22.

ESPN.com News Services. 2009a. "Too Costly, Football Done at Northeastern." November 30. Last accessed August 30, 2012. http://sports.espn.go.com/boston/ncf/news/story?id=4681701.

———. 2009b. "Hofstra Drops Football after 69 Seasons." December 3. Last accessed August 30, 2012. http://sports.espn.go.com/ncf/news/story?id=4709412.

Frank, R. H. 2004. "Challenging the Myth: A Review of the Links among College Athletic Success, Student Quality, and Donations." Knight Foundation Commission on Intercollegiate Athletics, May. Last accessed August 30, 2012. http://www.knightcommission.org/fiscal-integrity/fiscal-integrity-research-a-polls.

Fulks, D. L. 2011. *2004–2010 Revenues and Expense of Division I Intercollegiate Athletic Programs Report*. August. NCAA, Indianapolis, IN.

Goff, B. 2004. "Effects of University Athletics on the University: A Review and Extension of Empirical Assessment." In J. Fizel and R. Fort (eds.) *Economics of College Sports*. Westport, CT: Praeger, pp. 65–86.

Gordon, R. A., and Howell, J. E. 1959. *Higher Education for Business*. New York: Columbia University Press.

Humphreys, B. R. 2006. "The Relationship between Big-Time College Football and State Appropriations to Higher Education." *International Journal of Sport Finance* 1: 151–61.

Humphreys, B. R., and Mondello, M. 2007. "Intercollegiate Athletic Success and Donations at NCAA Division I Institutions." *Journal of Sport Management* 21: 265–80.

Khurana, R. 2007. *From Higher Aims to Hired Hands: The Social Transformation of American Business Schools and the Unfulfilled Promise of Management as a Profession*. Princeton: Princeton University Press.

Knight Commission on Intercollegiate Athletics. 2009. "Presidential Survey on the Cost and Financing of Intercollegiate Athletics." July. Last accessed August 30, 2012. http://www.knightcommission.org/fiscal-integrity/fiscal-integrity-research-a-polls.

———. 2010. "College Sports 101: A Primer on Money, Athletics, and Higher Education in the 21st Century." Chapter 2: "Expenses." Last accessed August 30, 2012. http://www.knightcommission.org/fiscal-integrity/fiscal-integrity-research-a-polls.

Litan, R. E., Orszag, J. M., and Orszag, P. R. 2003. "The Empirical Effects of Collegiate Athletics: An Interim Report." August. National Collegiate Athletic Association. Last accessed August 30, 2012. http://www.sc.edu/faculty/PDF/baseline.pdf.

Luebchow, L. 2010. "College Sports Reform: Opening up the Budget Books." *Higher Ed Watch*, New America Foundation. Last accessed August 30, 2012. http://higheredwatch.newamerica.net/node/19292.

Orszag, J., and Israel, M. 2009. "The Empirical Effects of Collegiate Athletics: An Update Based on 2004–2007 Data." February. National Collegiate Athletic Association. Last accessed August 30, 2012. http://fs.ncaa.org/Docs/DI_MC_BOD/DI_BOD/2009/April/04,%20_Empirical_Effects.pdf.

Orszag, J. M., and Orszag, P. R. 2005a. "The Physical Capital Stock Used in Collegiate Athletics." April. National Collegiate Athletic Association. Last accessed August 30, 2012. http://www.ncaapublications.com/p-3964-athletic-spending-physical-capital-stock-used-in-collegiate-athletics.aspx.

———. 2005b. "The Empirical Effects of Collegiate Athletics: An Update." April. National Collegiate Athletic Association.

Pierson, F. C. 1959. *The Education of American Businessmen: A Study of University-College Programs in Business Administration.* New York: McGraw-Hill.

Smith, D. R. 2008. "Big-Time College Basketball and the Advertising Effect: Does Success Really Matter?" *Journal of Sports Economics* 9: 387–406.

Stafford, L. 2010. "College Sports 'Arms Race' Not Sustainable, Say University Presidents." *Atlanta Journal Constitution.* Last accessed August 30, 2012. http://www.ajc.com/news/sports/college-sports-arms-race-not-sustainable-say-unive/nQbgL/.

Tucker, I. B. 2004. "A Reexamination of the Effect of Big-Time Football and Basketball Success on Graduation Rates and Alumni Giving Rates." *Economics of Education Review* 23: 655–661.

———. 2005. "Big-Time Pigskin Success." *Journal of Sports Economics* 6: 222–29.

Tucker, I. B., and Amato, L. T. 2006. "A Reinvestigation of the Relationship between Big-Time Basketball Success and Average SAT Scores." *Journal of Sports Economics* 7: 428–40.

Women's Sports Foundation. 2008. "Dropping Men's Sports—The Division I Football/Basketball Arms Race Is the Culprit in the Cutting of Men's Olympic Sports: The Foundation Position." Last accessed August 30, 2012. http://www.womenssportsfoundation.org/en/home/advocate/title-ix-and-issues/title-ix-positions/football_basketball_arms_race.

Chapter 3

Associated Press. 2010. "NCAA Report: Economy Cuts into Sports." Sports. espn.go.com, August, 23. Last accessed August 30, 2012. http://sports.espn. go.com/ncf/news/story?id=5490686.

Bastiat, F. 1850. *Ce qu'on voit et ce qu'on ne voit pas.* (What Is Seen and What Is Not Seen). http://www.econlib.org/library/Bastiat/basEss1.html.

Crabbe, N. 2011. "UF Athletic Association Raising Ticket Prices, Bolstering University Budget." *Gainesville Sun*, June 15. Last accessed August 30, 2012. http://www.gainesville.com/article/20110615/ARTICLES/110619734/1109/ sports?p=1&tc=pg.

Fulks, D. L. 2011. *2004–2010 Revenues and Expense of Division I Intercollegiate Athletic Programs Report.* August. NCAA, Indianapolis, IN.

Noll, R. G. 1999. "The Business of College Sports and the High Costs of Winning." *Milken Institute Review.* September, pp. 24–37.

Sander, L. 2011. "22 Elite College Sports Programs Turned a Profit in 2010, but Gaps Remain, NCAA Reports Says." *Chronicle of Higher Education*, June 15, 2011. Last accessed July 23, 2012. http://chronicle.com/article/22-Elite-Col- lege-Sports/127921/.

Sperber, M. 1990. *College Sports Inc.* New York: Henry Holt and Company.

Weiberg, S., and Whiteside, K. 2007. "Why Bigger Is Better at Ohio State." USA- Today.com, January 23. Last accessed August 30, 2012. http://www.usatoday. com/sports/college/2007–01–04-ohiostate-finances-cover_x.htm.

Chapter 4

Bowl Championship Series. 2011. "Bowl Championship Series 2011–2012 Media Guide." Last accessed August 30, 2012 (the 2012–13 version is available at the BCS web page, www.bcsfootball.org, under "Media"). http://espn.go.com/i/ ncf/bcs/2011BCSGuide2.pdf.

Brown, R. W. 1992. "Incentives and Revenue Sharing in College Football: Spreading the Wealth or Giving Away the Game?" *Managerial and Decision Economics* 15(5): 471–86.

Hoover, J. E. 2011. "Spreading the Wealth: As Big 12 Withers, Other Conferences Thrive with Equal Revenue Distribution." tulsaworld.com, November 2. Last accessed August 30, 2012. http://www.tulsaworld.com/sportsextra/article. aspx?articleid=20111002_92_B1_Equalr807124.

Smith, M. 2010. "The BCS' Big Split." Street & Smith's SportsBusiness Journal, January 25. Last accessed August 30, 2012. http://www.sportsbusinessdaily. com/Journal/Issues/2010/01/20100125/This-Weeks-News/The-BCS-Big-Split.aspx.

Chapter 5

Aaronson, M. 2010. "Pay for Play: Why Colleges Should, Probably Can't and Most Likely Won't Pay Student-Athletes." *Michigan Daily*, October 13. Last accessed August 30, 2012. http://www.michigandaily.com/content/pay-play-feature.

Brown, R. W., and Jewell, R. T. 2004. "Measuring Marginal Revenue Product in College Athletics: Updated Estimates." In John Fizel and Rodney Fort (eds.) *The Economics of College Sports*. Westport, CT: Praeger Publishers.

Brown, R. W., and Jewell, R. T. 2006. "The Marginal Revenue Product of a Women's College Basketball Player." *Industrial Relations* 45: 96–101.

Nocera, J. 2011. "Let's Start Paying College Athletes." *New York Times*, December 30. Last accessed July 26, 2012. http://www.nytimes.com/2012/01/01/maga-zine/lets-start-paying-college-athletes.html?pagewanted=all.

Remy, D. 2012. "Why the *New York Times*' Nocera is Wrong." NCAA.org, January 6. Last accessed July 26, 2012. http://www.ncaa.org/wps/wcm/connect/public/NCAA/Resources/Latest+News/2012/January/Why+the+New+York+Times+Nocera+is+wrong.

Rottenberg, S. 1956. "The Baseball Players' Labor Market." *Journal of Political Economy* 64: 242–58.

Sherman, M. 2012. "How Early Is Too Early? Recruiting Progressing to Offering, Accepting Commits from Junior High Kids." ESPN.com, July 26. Last accessed July 27, 2012. http://espn.go.com/college-sports/recruiting/football/story/_/id/8201126/junior-high-athletes-being-offered-football-recruiting-starts-earlier-earlier.

Winfree, J. A., and Molitor, C. J. 2007. "The Value of College: Drafted High School Baseball Players." *Journal of Sports Economics* 8: 378–93.

Chapter 6

Brady, E. 2007. "James Madison's Hard Cuts Spur Title IX Debate." USAToday, April 19. Last accessed August 30, 2012. http://www.usatoday.com/sports/col-lege/other/2007–04–19-title-ix-jmu-cover_N.htm.

Giannotto, M. 2012. "Maryland Cuts Seven Sports on 'Sad Day' in College Park." *Washington Post*, July 2. Last accessed August 30, 2012. http://www.washingtonpost.com/sports/maryland-cuts-seven-sports-on-sad-day-in-college-park/2012/07/02/gJQAqJFBJW_story.html.

Lee, J. 2001. "Fiscal Crunch Squeezes out 2 Kansas Sports." *Sports Business Journal*, March 12. Last accessed August 30, 2012. http://m.sportsbusinessdaily.com/Journal/Issues/2001/03/20010312/This-Weeks-Issue/Fiscal-Crunch-Squeezes-Out-2-Kansas-Sports.aspx.

Thomas, K. 2011a. "Colleges Cut Men's Programs to Satisfy Title IX." *New York Times*, May 1. Last accessed August 30, 2012. http://www.nytimes.com/2011/05/02/sports/02gender.html.

———. 2011b. "College Teams, Relying on Deception, Undermine Gender Equity." *New York Times*, April 25. Last accessed August 30, 2012. http://www.nytimes.com/2011/04/26/sports/26titleix.html?pagewanted=all.

Watson, G. 2009. "Porgrams in Precarious Position." *ESPN*, July 14. Last accessed August 30, 2012. http://sports.espn.go.com/ncaa/news/story?id=4313320.

Znidar, M. 2007. "Running on Empty: Ohio University's Decision to Ax Track and Field Leaves Athletes Hurt, Disillusioned." *Columbus Dispatch*, November 9. Last accessed August 30, 2012. http://www.dispatch.com/content/stories/sports/2007/05/03/ou_track.ART_ART_05–03–07_C1_JV6IUI9.html.

Chapter 7

Fort, R., and Quirk, J. 1995. "Cross-Subsidization, Incentives, and Outcomes in Professional Team Sports Leagues." *Journal of Economic Literature* 33: 1265–99.

Mountain West Conference. 2010. "Mountain West Conference Handbook, 2010–11." Last accessed August 30, 2012. http://www.themwc.com/about/mw-handbook.html.

Wetzel, D., Peter, J., and Passan, J. 2010. *Death to the BCS: The Definitive Case against the Bowl Championship Series*. New York: Gotham.

Chapter 8

Fort, R. 2012. "Rodney Fort's Sports Business Data," at Rod's Sports Economics. Last accessed August 30, 2012. https://sites.google.com/site/rodswebpages/codes.

Lewis, M. 2003. *Moneyball: The Art of Winning an Unfair Game.* New York: W. W. Norton and Company.

Lowenfish, L. 2007. *Branch Rickey: Baseball's Ferocious Gentleman.* Lincoln: University of Nebraska Press.

Rosen, S. 1981. "The Economics of Superstars." *American Economic Review* 71: 845–58.

Sauer, R. D., and Hakes, J. K. 2006. "An Economic Evaluation of the 'Moneyball' Hypothesis." *Journal of Economic Perspectives* 20: 173–85.

Scully, G. W. 1994. *The Market Structure of Sports.* Chicago: University of Chicago Press.

Wagenheim, K. 1974. *Babe Ruth: His Life and Legend.* New York: Henry Holt and Company.

Chapter 9

Center, B. 2011. "Padres Dispute Claim Team Led MLB in Income." San Diego Union Tribune, sduniontribune.com, March 23. Last accessed August 30, 2012. http://www.sduniontribune.com/news/2011/mar/23/padres-president-disputes-forbes-claim-padres-turn.

Damodaran, A. 2012. "PE Ratio by Sector," at Damodaran Online. Last accessed August 30, 2012. http://pages.stern.nyu.edu/~adamodar/New_Home_Page/datafile/pedata.html.

Fort, R. 2006. "The Value of Major League Baseball Ownership." *International Journal of Sport Finance* 1: 3–8.

———. 2012. "Rodney Fort's Sports Business Data," at Rod's Sports Economics. Last accessed August 30, 2012. https://sites.google.com/site/rodswebpages/codes.

Humphreys, B. R., and Mondello, M. 2008. "Determinants of Franchise Values in North American Professional Sports Leagues: Evidence from a Hedonic Price Model." *International Journal of Sport Finance* 3: 98–105.

Quirk, J., and Fort, R. D. 1992. *Pay Dirt: The Business of Pro Team Sports.* Princeton: Princeton University Press.

Sandomir, R. 2007. "Yankees' YES Network Stake Not for Sale." *New York Times*, nytimes.com, August 3. Last accessed August 30, 2012. http://www.nytimes.com/2007/08/03/sports/baseball/03yes.html?_r=1.

Scheck, J. 2008. "Questions for Ted Leonsis: Washington Capitals Owner on Why Hockey Will Never Have as Many Fans as NFL, MLB." *Wall Street Jour-*

nal, online.wsj.com, April 10. Last accessed August 30, 2012. http://online.wsj.com/article/SB120777206831802569.html.

Van Riper, T. 2009. "The Most Valuable Teams in Sports: More Clubs than Ever Are Worth a Billion. Is It a Bubble Ready to Pop?" Forbes.com, January 13. Last accessed August 30, 2012. http://www.forbes.com/2009/01/13/nfl-cowboys-yankees-biz-media-cx_tvr_0113values.html.

Weil, D. 2010. "The Jockstrap Bubble Bursts, and Now Sports-Team Owners Are Paying the Price," at bnet.com, May 11. Last accessed August 30, 2012. http://www.bnet.com/blog/business-news/the-jockstrap-bubble-bursts-and-now-sports-team-owners-are-paying-the-price/1407.

Zimbalist, A. 1992. *Baseball and Billions: A Probing Look inside the Big Business of Our National Pastime*. New York: Basic Books.

Zimbalist, A. 1998. "Just Another Fish Story." *New York Times*, October 18, www.nyt.com.

Chapter 10

Fort, R. 2011. *Sports Economics 3rd Edition*. Upper Saddle River, NJ: Prentice Hall.

Heath, T. 1997. "Pollin: Salaries Cause Increases in Ticket Prices." *Washington Post*, November 27, B7. washingtonpost.com. Last accessed August 30, 2012. http://www.washingtonpost.com/wp-srv/sports/longterm/general/mciarticles/launch/pollin.htm.

Jehl, D. 1995. "BASEBALL; Clinton Warns Major Leagues to Settle Strike." *New York Times*, www.nytimes.com, January 27. Last accessed August 30, 2012. http://www.nytimes.com/1995/01/27/sports/baseball-clinton-warns-major-leagues-to-settle-strike.html.

Jones, J. M. 2002. "Baseball Fans Favor Owners If There Is a Strike: Majority of Fans Think There Will Be a Strike." Gallup, www.gallup.com, August 28. Last accessed August 30, 2012. http://www.gallup.com/poll/6700/baseball-fans-favor-owners-there-strike.aspx.

Chapter 11

Bianchi, M. 2011. "If NBA Players Are Bolting, Then Why Shouldn't Fans?" *Orlando Sentinel*, February 25. orlandosentinel.com. Last accessed August 30, 2012. http://articles.orlandosentinel.com/2011-02-25/sports/os-bianchi-saturday-circus-0226-20110225_1_ucf-basketball-hard-salary-cap-markets.

Fort, R. 2011a. "Competitive Balance in the National Football League." In K. Quinn (ed.) *Economics of the National Football League: The State of the Art.* New York: Springer, pp. 207–24.

———. 2011b. *Sports Economics 3rd Edition.* Upper Saddle River, NJ: Prentice Hall.

Fort, R., and Lee, Y. H. 2007. "Structural Change, Competitive Balance, and the Rest of the Major Leagues." *Economic Inquiry* 45: 519–32.

Fort, R., and Quirk, J. 2010. "Optimal Competitive Balance in Single-Game Ticket Sports Leagues." *Journal of Sports Economics* 11: 587–601.

———. 2011. "Optimal Competitive Balance in a Season Ticket League." *Economic Inquiry* 49: 464–73.

Goodell, R. 2011. "Football's Future If the Players Win." *Wall Street Journal,* April 26. Last accessed August 30, 2012. http://online.wsj.com/article/SB10001424052748704132204576285090526726626.html?mod=WSJ_hps_RIGHT-TopCarousel_1.

Lee, Y. H., and Fort, R. 2005. "Structural Change in MLB Competitive Balance: The Depression, Team Location, and Integration." *Economic Inquiry* 43: 158–69.

Levin, R. C., Mitchell, G. J., Volcker, P. A., and Will, G. F. 2000. "The Report of the Independent Members of the Commissioner's Blue Ribbon Panel on Baseball Economics." July. Last accessed August 30, 2012. http://www.mlb.com/mlb/downloads/blue_ribbon.pdf.

Lowenfish, L. 2007. *Branch Rickey: Baseball's Ferocious Gentleman.* Lincoln: University of Nebraska Press.

Pedulla, T. 2003. "NFL Dynasties Go 'Way of the Dinosaurs.'" USAToday.com, January 23. Last accessed August 30, 2012. http://www.usatoday.com/sports/football/super/2003-01-23-1acover-dynasties_x.htm.

U.S. Senate. 1958. "Hearings before the Subcommittee on Antitrust and Monopoly, Committee on the Judiciary, 85th Congress," 2nd Session, July.

Chapter 12

Mahoney, B. 2010. "Person Familiar with Talks: Union Tells NBA Players It Won't Accept Hard Cap." Associated Press, December 8. Last accessed August 30, 2012. http://www.startribune.com/templates/Print_This_Story?sid=111536089.

Rottenberg, S. 1956. "The Baseball Players' Labor Market." *Journal of Political Economy* 64: 242–58.

Chapter 13

Bissinger, B. 2005. "Home Runs Wanted. No Questions Asked." *New York Times*, www.nytimes.com, May 5. Last accessed August 30, 2012. http://query.nytimes.com/gst/fullpage.html?res=9E00E4DD1730F936A35756C0A9639C8B63&sec=health&spon=&pagewanted=all.

DiNardo, J. E., and Winfree, J. A. 2010. "The Law of Genius and Home Runs Refuted." *Economic Inquiry* 48: 51–64.

Fort, R. 2011. *Sports Economics 3rd Edition*. Upper Saddle River, NJ. Prentice Hall.

Fort, R., and Lee, Y. H. 2013. "Major League Baseball Attendance Time Series: League Policy Lessons." In P. Rodriguez, S. Kesenne, and J. Garcia (eds.) *Econometric Practices in Sports*. Oviedo, Spain: Oviedo University Press.

Laraque, G. 2011. *Georges Laraque: The Story of the NHL's Unlikeliest Tough Guy*. Toronto: Penguin (Viking) Canada.

Leonhardt, D. 2005. "Myth of Men Who Saved Baseball." *New York Times*, March 30. www.nytimes.com. Last accessed August 30, 2012. http://www.nytimes.com/2005/03/29/sports/29iht-fans.html.

New York Times. 2005. "BASEBALL: ROUNDUP; Padres' Towers Says He Knew Caminiti Was Using Steroids." www.nytimes.com, March 1. Last accessed August 30, 2012. http://query.nytimes.com/gst/fullpage.html?sec=health&res=9F04E4DD123DF932A35750C0A9639C8B63.

Vincent, F. 1991. Memo, To: All Major League Clubs, Re: Baseball's Drug Policy and Prevention Program. June 7. Last accessed August 30, 2012. http://bizofbaseball.com/docs/1991Memo_Baseballs_Drug_Policy_And_Prevention_Program.pdf.

Chapter 14

Coates, D., and Harrison, T. 2005. "Baseball Strikes and the Demand for Attendance." *Journal of Sports Economics* 6: 282–302.

Fort, R. 2011. *Sports Economics 3rd Edition*. Upper Saddle River, NJ: Prentice Hall.

Gomme, P., and Rupert, P. 2004. "Measuring Labor's Share of Income." Cleveland Federal Reserve Policy Paper Number 7, November. www.clevelandfed.org. Last accessed August 30, 2012. https://www.clevelandfed.org/Research/PolicyDis/No7Nov04.pdf.

Schmidt, M. B., and Berri, D. J. 2004. "The Impact of Labor Strikes on Consumer Demand: An Application to Professional Sports." *American Economic Review* 94: 344–57.

Scully, G. W. 1974. "Pay and Performance in Major League Baseball." *American Economic Review* 65: 915–30.

Winfree, J. A. 2009. "Owners Incentives during the 2004–05 National Hockey League Lockout." *Applied Economics* 41: 3275–85.

Chapter 15

Barra, A. 2008. "The Sleeping Lion." *Wall Street Journal*, April 26, p. W7, at online.wsj.com. Last accessed August 30, 2012. http://online.wsj.com/article/SB120915476422645617.html.

Baseball Almanac. 2010. "George Carlin in 'Baseball and Football.'" Last accessed August 30, 2012. http://www.baseball-almanac.com/humor7.shtml.

Cook, W. A. 2011. *Jim Thorpe: A Biography*. Jefferson, NC: McFarland and Company Publishers.

Egan, M. 2009. "Why Wall Street Should Be More Like the NFL." *FOX Business* online. Last accessed August 30, 2012. http://www.michaelpage.com/content/197-why-wall-street-should-be-more-like-the-nfl.html.

Fort, R. 2006. "The Value of Major League Baseball Ownership. *International Journal of Sport Finance* 1: 3–8.

———. 2012. Rodney Fort's Sports Business Data Pages. Last accessed August 30, 2012. https://umich.box.com/s/41707f0b2619c0107b8b.

Jones, J. M. 2008. "Football Remains Runaway Leader as Favorite Sport." www.gallup.com, December 29. Last accessed August 30, 2012. http://www.gallup.com/poll/113503/football-remains-runaway-leader-favorite-sport.aspx.

Klein, E. 2010. "What the Media Could Learn from the NFL." *Washington Post*, January 11, at voices.washingtonpost.com. Last accessed August 30, 2012. http://voices.washingtonpost.com/ezra-klein/2010/01/what_the_media_could_learn_fro.html.

Muglia, A. 2010. "Football as America's New Pastime: Stories as the Gridiron Stole the Crown." *Sports, Inc.* 3: 21–23.

Pro Football Archives. 2010. Data from 1922, 1926, 1934, and 1937. Last accessed August 30, 2012. www.profootballarchives.com.

Public Broadcasting System. 2010. "Freedom: A History of US." Page Title: Webisode 6: "A War to End All Wars." Last accessed August 30, 2012. http://www.pbs.org/wnet/historyofus/web06/segment1b.html.

Ward, J. M. 1888. "Baseball: How to Become a Player: With the Origin, History and Explanation of the Game." Project Gutenberg EBook, last updated May 28, 2012. Last accessed August 30, 2012. http://www.gutenberg.org/files/19975/19975-h/19975-h.htm.

INDEX